# FEDERAL REGULATION
## OF THE RADIO AND TELEVISION
## BROADCAST INDUSTRY
## IN THE UNITED STATES
### 1927-1959

## With Special Reference to the Establishment
## and Operation of Workable Administrative Standards

This is a volume in the
Arno Press collection

# DISSERTATIONS IN BROADCASTING

*Advisory Editor*
Christopher H. Sterling

*See last pages of this volume
for a complete list of titles.*

# FEDERAL REGULATION
## OF THE RADIO AND TELEVISION
## BROADCAST INDUSTRY
## IN THE UNITED STATES
## 1927-1959

### With Special Reference to the Establishment
### and Operation of Workable Administrative Standards

Robert Sears McMahon

## ARNO PRESS
**A New York Times Company**
New York • 1979

**Publisher's Note: This book has been reproduced from the best available copy.**

Editorial Supervision: Andrea Hicks

---

First publication 1979 by Arno Press Inc.

**DISSERTATIONS IN BROADCASTING**
ISBN for complete set: 0-405-11754-X
See last pages of this volume for titles.

Manufactured in the United States of America

---

**Library of Congress Cataloging in Publication Data**

McMahon, Robert Sears.
    Federal regulation of the radio and television
broadcast industry in the United States, 1927-1959.

    (Dissertations in broadcasting)
    Reprint of the author's thesis, Ohio State
University, 1959.
    Bibliography:  p.
    1.  Radio--Law and legislation--United States--
History.   2.   Television--Law and legislation--
United States--History.  3.  Broadcasting--Law and
legislation--United States--History.  4.  United
States.  Federal Communications Commission--History.
KF2805.M3  1979       343'.73'0994       78-21727
ISBN 0-405-11766-3

FEDERAL REGULATION OF THE RADIO AND TELEVISION
BROADCAST INDUSTRY IN THE UNITED STATES
1927 - 1959
WITH SPECIAL REFERENCE TO THE ESTABLISHMENT AND
OPERATION OF WORKABLE ADMINISTRATIVE STANDARDS


DISSERTATION

Presented in Partial Fulfillment of the Requirements
for the Degree of Doctor of Philosophy in the
Graduate School of the Ohio State University


By

ROBERT SEARS McMAHON, B. A., A. M.


* * * * *


The Ohio State University
1959

# TABLE OF CONTENTS

CHAPTER                                                          PAGE

I.   INTRODUCTION. . . . . . . . . . . . . . . . . . .     1

    The Purposes of This Study. . . . . . . . . . .     4

    A Review of the Literature Dealing with

    the Subject . . . . . . . . . . . . . . . . .     8

    The Scope and Development of the

    Present Study . . . . . . . . . . . . . . . .     14

II.  THE REGULATION OF BROADCASTING PRIOR TO 1934. . .     17

    Early Broadcast Regulation. . . . . . . . . . .     17

    The Post World War I Situation in Broad-

    casting - Rapid Growth with Consequent

    Complications. . . . . . . . . . . . . . . .     18

    The Breakdown of Regulation as the Result

    of Adverse Court Decisions. . . . . . . . . .     19

    The Issues Before the Congress Relative to

    the Passage of a New Broadcast Law. . . . . .     22

    Other Points of Debate in Connection with

    the Passage of the Radio Act of 1927 -- Its

    Passage and Approval by the President . . .     34

    A Brief Analysis of the Radio Act of 1927 . . .     37

    The Federal Radio Commission, 1927-1934 . . . .     41

III. THE EVENTS LEADING UP TO THE ABOLITION OF THE

    FEDERAL RADIO COMMISSION AND THE ESTABLISHMENT

    OF THE FEDERAL COMMUNICATIONS COMMISSION. . .     62

CHAPTER                                                          PAGE

    First Attempts at Passage of a Compre-

    hensive Bill - H. R. 7716. . . . . . . . . . . 62

    The President Requests Congress to Enact

    Comprehensive Broadcast and Communica-

    tions Legislation. . . . . . . . . . . . . . . 69

    S. 2190. . . . . . . . . . . . . . . . . . . . 72

    The Wagner-Hatfield Amendment. . . . . . . . . 80

    The Senate Report on S. 3285 . . . . . . . . . 82

    The House Report to Accompany S. 3285, and

    Final Passage of the Bill. . . . . . . . . . . 87

IV.  AN ANALYSIS OF THE FEDERAL COMMUNICATIONS ACT. . . 93

    Purpose. . . . . . . . . . . . . . . . . . . . 93

    General Provisions . . . . . . . . . . . . . . 94

    Common Carriers. . . . . . . . . . . . . . . . 96

    Provisions Relating to Radio . . . . . . . . . 97

    Procedural and Administrative Provisions . . . 107

    Penal Provisions and Forfeitures . . . . . . . 111

    Miscellaneous Provisions . . . . . . . . . . . 111

    Conclusions Based on an Analysis of the

    Federal Communications Act . . . . . . . . . . 113

V.  TEN YEARS OF OPERATION OF THE FEDERAL

    COMMUNICATIONS ACT, 1935-45. . . . . . . . . . . 117

    The Fair and Equitable Distribution of

    Broadcast Frequencies by the Commission.

    S. 2243. . . . . . . . . . . . . . . . . . . . 118

CHAPTER                                                          PAGE

          Freedom of Speech and the Broadcaster Censor-
          ship -- Ex Post Facto and Otherwise, and
          Regulation Affecting Program Content. . . .    121
          The Monopoly Issue. . . . . . . . . . . . . .  128
          The So-called "Cox Investigation" . . . . . .  133
VI.  ATTEMPTS ON THE PART OF CONGRESS
     TO REORGANIZE THE COMMISSION. . . . . . . . . .     143
          The White-Wolverton Bill, S. 1333 . . . . . . 146
          An Analysis of the More Important Provisions
          Contained in S. 1333, as It Was Originally
          Proposed to the Congress. . . . . . . . . .    147
          The Testimony on the Bill . . . . . . . . . .  152
          Revision of the White-Wolverton Bill (S. 1333)
          in Senate Committee, Its Final Failure to
          Come to a Vote in Either Senate or House. .    162
          An Assessment of the White-Wolverton Bill . . . 167
VII.  THE "McFARLAND" BILL. . . . . . . . . . . . . .    170
          The Senate Report and the Hoover Study. . . . .170
          The McFarland Bill, S. 1973 . . . . . . . . . . 176
          The Sadowski Bill, H. R. 6949 . . . . . . . . . 186
          The Revival of the McFarland Bill (S. 658). . . 198
          Passage of the McFarland Bill (S. 658)
          Following Joint Senate-House Conference
          Committee Hearings. . . . . . . . . . . . .     209

CHAPTER                                                          PAGE

VIII.  AN ANALYSIS OF CERTAIN McFARLAND AMENDMENTS

       THEIR INFLUENCE ON THE ADMINISTRATIVE

       FORMULATION OF POLICY IN THE COMMISSION. . .  218

       An Analysis of Certain McFarland

       Amendments . . . . . . . . . . . . . . . . .  218

       The Influence of the Aforementioned

       McFarland Amendments on the Administrative

       Formulation of Policies in the

       Commission . . . . . . . . . . . . . . . .  228

IX.    THE COMMISSION AS A LICENSING BODY . . . . . . .  243

       Licensing Standards as Applied in Compara-

       tive Television Cases. . . . . . . . . . . .  246

       Licensing Standards as Applied in TV

       Station Transfers. . . . . . . . . . . . . .  267

       The Background of the Transfer Situation . .  269

       Factors Previously Considered by FCC in

       Transfers. . . . . . . . . . . . . . . . . .  270

       Current Factors Considered by FCC in

       Transfers. . . . . . . . . . . . . . . . . .  274

       Licensing Standards as Applied in "Payoff"

       and Merger Agreements. . . . . . . . . . . .  280

       Summary and Conclusions Based on an Examina-

       tion of FCC Standards as Applied in

       Comparative TV Cases, TV Station Transfers,

       and "Payoff" and Merger Agreements . . .  283

CHAPTER                                                 PAGE

X.   CONCLUSIONS AND RECOMMENDATIONS. . . . . . . . . . 286

APPENDIX I . . . . . . . . . . . . . . . . . . . . . . 309

APPENDIX II. . . . . . . . . . . . . . . . . . . . . . 326

BIBLIOGRAPHY . . . . . . . . . . . . . . . . . . . . . 340

# CHAPTER I

## INTRODUCTION

Since the word "broadcasting" first became a common household word in the early 1920's, its importance as a medium of mass communication has grown to such an extent as to equal that of any other form of mass communication.[1] Its tremendously rapid growth has been phenomenal. Although there is much debate as to its effectiveness in comparison with other media in regard to its abilities to inform, entertain, or persuade, there is every indication of its increasingly widespread use by the public.[2] There are also numerous instances which attest to its success in taking an almost completely unknown product and in a short space of time making

---

[1] As defined in Section 3 of Public Law No. 416, 73rd Congress (the Communications Act of 1934) -- "broadcasting means the dissemination of radio communications intended to be received by the public." Although the word "television" does not appear in the Communications Act, there has never been any question that the word broadcasting includes television as well as radio. For the sake of convenience in this discussion, we may define broadcasting in the same manner as do Giraud Chester and Garnet R. Garrison in Television and Radio (New York: Appleton-Century-Crofts, Inc., 1950), p. 4. Thus "Broadcasting (is) the transmission through space, by means of radio frequencies, of signals capable of being received either aurally or visually or both aurally and visually by the general public."

[2] The Broadcasting Yearbook of 1958 quotes from figures, charts, and tables furnished by the A. C. Nielsen Co., (a nationwide firm which supplies quantitative information regarding the size and composition of radio and television audiences), and points out that "Radio set ownership extended to virtually 97% of all U. S. homes and television saturation was 85% in mid-summer 1958." (p. B-131)

it one with a nation-wide market.[3] The results of recent sur-
veys indicate that the amount of time the American public
spends listening to radio or watching television, equals or
even surpasses time spent in the enjoyment of all other
leisure time activities.[4] According to information contained
in the Nielsen Television Index for Nov.-Dec., 1957, the time
the average TV family spends watching television each day was
estimated in excess of six hours per day average throughout
the week. In-home radio listening was estimated as averaging
somewhat less than one hour per day throughout the week. It
therefore becomes an obvious fact that radio and television
play a vital role in the social and economic patterns of
American life.

Although they are similar to other basic forms of mass
communication in many ways, radio and television broadcasting
differ from these other media in one important respect...only
a limited number of broadcast stations can operate effectively without resulting in technical impairment to the entire
engineering system by which broadcasting is carried. While
it is certainly true that the number of newspapers, magazines,
and film companies that an economic system can support is
limited by the economic realities, the number of broadcast

---

[3]As for instance the case histories of such products
as Hadacol, Lestoil, and the Richard Hudnut line of hair pre-
parations and shampoos, which initially advertised on the
broadcast media alone.

[4]Broadcasting-Telecasting Yearbook of 1958,
pp. B-132-133.

stations is further limited by the number of available broadcast channels. Rather than have these available channels
taken over in a haphazard and wholly self-serving fashion by
interested parties wishing to operate in the broadcast field,
both industry and government early in the history of the
medium came to the conclusion that some form of regulation
was necessary, especially in connection with the licensing of
and the assignment of frequencies to broadcast stations.
Thus the license-regulating process became an integral part
of the business of broadcasting.

The philosophy behind the licensing procedure since
its inception has been that the "air waves" belong to the
people. The regulatory body created for the purpose of
assigning broadcast frequencies to operators can only assign
them for limited periods of time after which the licensee may
make application for license renewal. It is clearly stated
in the Act that during this time the operator acquires no
property rights to the channel which he occupies.[5] Since
1934 the regulatory body charged with the duty of licensing
broadcast operators has been the Federal Communications Commission; from 1927 until that time such powers had rested with
the Federal Radio Commission; prior to this the task of licensing stations had been the task of the Secretary of Commerce.
All three of these licensing bodies obtained the powers and
authority under which they operated from the U. S. Congress.

---

[5]Section 301 of the Communications Act, Public Law
No. 416, 73rd Congress (1934).

It follows therefore that the activities of the Congress in respect to broadcast regulation are of utmost importance to all who would have a clear understanding of the duties and obligations of the independent commission created to implement its licensing laws. It is equally true that an understanding of the intent of Congress in the passage of its broadcast legislation is a vital requirement to any person interested in assessing the degree of success the Commission has enjoyed in the carrying out of such congressional intent.

In order to best establish this intent, it is necessary that an analysis of the statutory basis of regulatory law affecting broadcasting be made. Such an examination of the manner in which Congress over the years has attempted to provide solutions for the problems emerging out of the tremendously rapid technical and economic development of broadcasting will further serve to illustrate the major difficulties arising out of broadcast regulation. As a result of this analysis, the writer expects to show that from the outset of formal, systematized broadcast regulation Congress bestowed broad powers upon the regulatory body, employing the phrase "public interest, convenience, and necessity" as the yardstick against which the Commission's policy decisions might be measured.

## 1. The Purposes of This Study

The phrase "public interest, convenience and necessity" which first came into use in connection with the broadcast licensing function with the passage of the Radio Act of 1927 was carried over into the Communications Act of 1934. At the time of passage of the Communications Act, Congress continued to employ this imprecise language. It drew attention to its own lack of expert knowledge in the still relatively new field of broadcasting as its reason for doing so, giving this as the reason for passage of its so-called "skeleton legislation," which still left to the newly formed Commission as much room for maneuver as the old had formerly possessed.

The reasons for the employment of such broad language are of major importance to the student of the evolution and status of broadcast regulation. It may be that a possible explanation for the philosophy which provided the Commission with such broad powers is that Congress expected the Commission would take advantage of these to develop, on its own, adequate and reliable standards upon which it could base its licensing decisions. This assumption might provide an explanation for the fact that the Communications Act, even as amended, does not provide definitive criteria to guide the Commission in the selection of the applicant "best qualified" among the several who may be competing for a particular channel or facility.

Thus the major purposes of this study are

a) To determine whether or not it was the intent of Congress that the Commission expand its broad "public interest" mandate into firm and dependable policies. Such an assumption certainly could serve as a possible explanation for its use of the broad "public interest" phrase.

b) To determine whether in fact the FCC has expanded its broad mandate into "firm and dependable" policies. Should it become clear from an examination of the legislative history of the Communications Act that Congress intended that the Federal Communications Commission expand the "mandate" in the 1934 Act into "firm and dependable policies" in the granting of licenses, license renewals, and license transfers, the question will be raised as to whether these policies do in fact exist. The object will then be to investigate the Commission's policies and actions in its licensing procedures in the light of what Congress presumably has intended in order to determine whether or not the Commission has come up with firm and dependable policies that do in truth carry out the intent of Congress.

For this purpose the writer, while he was a staff member of the Subcommittee on Legislative Oversight of the House of Representatives in 1958, made a study and examination of some sixty competitive television license grants (where the Commission had to consider the qualifications of competing applicants) made to broadcasters since the lifting of the channel freeze in 1952.[6] He further examined the

---

[6]The so-called television allocations "freeze" was put into effect in 1948 by the Commission because the demand for available VHF channels had so far exceeded the supply at that time, and the Commission was looking for a means to expand the number of available frequencies for television broadcasting. Although it was originally expected that the duration of the "freeze" would be for no longer than a period of six months, its actual duration was four years, since it was not lifted until 1952. At that time, the UHF bands were made available for television broadcasters, and applications for both UHF and VHF channels were again received. Station licenses which have been granted and have gone on the air since that time have

methods and circumstances under which some 80 Very High
Frequency television station transfers were permitted.  The
study was limited in all cases to television licensing because in recent years this form of broadcasting has so far
eclipsed all others in its socioeconomic impact upon the nation.

    c) To determine whether failure by the FCC to establish
firm and dependable policies can be attributed to a lack of
sufficient "guidance" from Congress.

    Should the writer be able to successfully demonstrate
the failure of the Commission to establish firm and dependable policies relative to its licensing procedures during
its twenty-five years of xistence, he will then investigate
the effects of this failure upon the public confidence in
the integrity of its quasi-judicial activities.  If such
confidence has in fact been impaired, and if it is demon-
strably true that the Commission itself has proved historical-
ly unable to formulate dependable standards and policies on
its own, it may be that, to some extent at least, this failure
is the result of a lack of sufficient guidance by Congress,
and that Congress itself should undertake to provide the Commission with more definitive guides -- upon which it can base
its decisions in its licensing cases -- than those which are
now contained in the language of what constitutes the so-
called public interest.

------------------------------

generally been called "post freeze stations" to differentiate
them from the "pre freeze stations" which did most of the
actual pioneering in the early days of telecast development.

d) If such a need for clarification can be demonstrated, the author will, as a final measure, suggest certain
specific areas where this further guidance would be most
appropriate.

## 2. A Review of the Literature Dealing with the Subject

Among the various studies of the administrative formulation of policy in the Commission made during the twenty-
five years of its existence, few have attempted to analyze
and appraise the Commission decisions in its competitive licensing hearings, where it has been called upon to consider
the qualifications of competing applicants. Yet this is an
excellent means of ascertaining the degree of consistency the
Commission has reached when it has been faced with the task
"in the public interest" of deciding which one of several
applicants is best qualified to operate a broadcast station.
But, when one stops to consider why analyses have been so
rare until recent years, one becomes immediately aware of
the fact that such

> comparative hearings were not commonplace until the radio
> spectrum became crowded and radio stations constituted a
> profitable investment. The above situation developed just
> before World War II and from 1939 to 1942 the Commission
> considered a number of cases involving competing appli-
> cants.

It was not until about that time that the Commission

-----

[7]Paul Clifton Fowler, "The Formulation of Policy for
Commercial Broadcasting by the Federal Communications Commis-
sion" (unpublished PH.D. dissertation, Indiana University,
Department of Government), 1956, p. 398.

was faced with the problem of establishing dependable criteria that would enable it to decide among applicants for the same channel. Up to that time, most of its more important policy decisions had been made in its relicensing cases.

Among the studies of the Commission emerging after World War II, which did not make any separate and distinct analysis of Commission decisions in comparative cases, the so-called "Hoover Report on FCC" is one of the most interesting and valuable inquiries into Commission organization and procedure that has ever been made.[8] In general, the study found what it termed to be "serious weaknesses" in the performance of the Commission, "certain deficiencies" in its planning and policy making, and "repeated departures" from stated FCC policies. The report concludes the Commission has been generally lacking in a regulatory philosophy.

The "Hoover Report" pointed out that, instead of employing its discretion to "seek regulatory objectives," the Commission had devolved into a body that was little more than an advocate of the interests of the broadcast industry, which in general performed only those tasks that the industry wanted it to accomplish. This result is predicted in Mr. Marver H. Bernstein's study of the seven major independent agencies, where Mr. Bernstein concludes that organized group

---

[8]See the "Report of the Commission on Organization of the Executive Branch of the Government, Committee on Independent Regulatory Commissions, Staff Report on FCC," prepared for the Committee by William W. Tolub, September 15, 1948. (Released March 7, 1949; mimeographed copies of this report are on file in the National Archives.)

pressures can heavily effect regulatory programs and present
the problem of an independent agency's becoming nothing more
than a tool in the hands of those it was created to regulate.[9]

Professor Charles S. Hyneman is of much the same opinion in that he argues that Congress should specify the
standards of public policy.[10] This is the thesis of his book,
in which he urges the necessity of assuring public control
over administration by subjecting it to the elected officials
of the government.[11] Professor Hyneman thus contends that
Congress, rather than the President, should assume "continuing direction and control of administration."[12] He even seems
to suggest that this review be on an almost day to day basis.

Paul Clifton Fowler agrees with Professor Hyneman
insofar as he believes that the regulatory effectiveness of
the Commission would be improved if the Commission were to
formulate its policy subject to definite review by Congress
and possible enactment into legislation.[13] At the same time,
however, he concedes that the rather sporadic congressional
review of Commission policy up to the present time has been
almost entirely negative in nature.[14]

Until the recent hearings of the Legislative Oversight

---

[9]Regulating Business by Independent Commission (Boston:
University Press, 1955), p. 128.

[10]Bureaucracy in a Democracy (New York: Harper Bros.,
1950), p. 137.

[11]Ibid., p. 56.     [12]Ibid., p. 167

[13]Fowler, op. cit., p. 405.     [14]Ibid., p. 411.

Committee, best indications of how the criteria which the Commission employs in making its decisions were being manipulated emerged from an examination of a few recent comparative cases. Two articles appearing in periodicals in September, 1957, are of interest in this connection. Both articles were published at a time when investigations into the nature of FCC decisions in certain of its comparative cases were beginning, and served to point up the serious nature of the charges that had been laid at the Commission's door.

Robert Bendiner's composition, appearing in a September, 1957, issue of The Reporter[15] drew attention to a number of recent Commission decisions in initial licensing as well as transfer cases where the writer alleged certain "inconsistencies" existed in the manner in which the Commission had made its awards.[16] The use of "political pressure" was said to be a common occurrence greatly influencing the outcome of these cases. Mr. Bendiner suggests, as a solution to the problem of outside pressures upon the Commission, that its members be invested with judicial status, and that its administrative work be divorced from that of its adjudication.

"The Scandal in TV Licensing" appeared that same month in Harper's magazine and was authored by Professor Louis L.

---

[15]"The FCC, Who Will Regulate the Regulators?" The Reporter, September 19, 1957.

[16]Among them were McClatchy, the Madison Capital Times, Boston Channel 5, Miami Channel 10, and Indianapolis Channel 13 cases, as well as the Westinghouse WPTZ sale.

Jaffe, Byrne Professor of Administrative Law at Harvard Law
School.[17]  Professor Jaffe in much the same vein charged
that "seven men in Washington are giving away broadcasting
channels worth millions of dollars -- apparently with no
clear guide except their personal whims and political pressure." Professor Jaffe concluded that Congress has been
weak in providing policy guides and that strong administration has equally failed to fill the void. He suggested that
Congress by statute contribute to the establishment of a
tradition which would make the show of influence as unthink-
able in an administrative proceeding as in that of a court.

The most detailed analysis of post-freeze comparative
television cases decided by the FCC in any recent publication
is that made by Professor Bernard Schwartz, former Chief
Counsel of the House Subcommittee on Legislative Oversight.[18]
Although fully half of its contents are devoted to a detailed
apologia of the events and circumstances by which Professor
Schwartz lost his position as Chief Counsel for the committee,
its later chapters do examine the more important cases themselves and the manner of their outcome. After an examination
of the legislative evolution, present status, and more
questionable recent adjudicatory decisions of the six major
independent agencies, Professor Schwartz proposes the following

---

[17]"The Scandal in TV Licensing," Harper's magazine
(September, 1957).

[18]The Professor and the Commissions (New York: Alfred
A. Knopf, 1959).

across-the-board remedies as solutions to the present day
difficulties of the commissions.

The first suggestion is that Congress impose a code
of ethical standards for the commissions to adhere to, with
criminal penalties provided for violators of the code.

Next, Professor Schwartz recommends that the independence of the "independent agencies" be restored to them, in
order that their members may "enjoy an independence comparable
to that of...judges."[19]

What is even more important, however, in Professor
Schwartz's opinion, is the elimination of presidential control over chairmen. He recommends that this be accomplished
by continuing to allow the President to appoint them to office,
but that his power of removal be withdrawn since he believes
that present day presidential control stems "from the President's complete discretionary removal authority."[20]

In conclusion, even with these recommendations being
realized, Professor Schwartz doubts whether complete independence can be restored to these agencies. Thus, as an ultimate
solution to the dilemma, he recommends the oft-proposed plan
to establish an "Administrative Court" which would completely
separate administrative from judicial functions in the independent regulatory commissions.[21]

---

[19]Schwartz, op. cit., p. 267.    [20]Ibid.

[21]Ibid., p. 275. Administrative Court bills have been
a frequent subject of debate before the Congress since the
first of them was proposed by Senator Norris of Nebraska in
1933. (S. 1835, a bill to establish a United States Court of

## 3. The Scope and Development of the Present Study

In order to throw further light on the question of
the efficacy of the commission procedure, the writer has
attempted a study of the operations of the FCC, based largely
on what it has had to work with in the way of legislation,
advice, and affirmation of its policies by Congress.  The
study first attempts to determine what the mandate of Congress
was in respect to broadcast regulation.  Once that has been
established, the writer will attempt to discover whether the
FCC has erected standards to follow that mandate.  On the
basis of what many of the critics referred to in the preceding pages have said, it would seem that a reasonable hypothesis is that (a) Congress had certain intentions and expectations about what the Commission might be expected to accomplish when it originally passed the Communications Act, and
(b) the FCC has not been able on its own to the present time
fulfill these intentions and expectations.  In addition, (c)
it would seem to be useful knowledge to try and ascertain
certain of the factors that may have worked to prevent such a

---

Administrative Justice, 73rd Congress, 1st session, 1933.)
Other bills introduced since that time are S. 3787 and H. R.
12297, 74th Congress, 2nd session, 1936, S. 3676, 75th Congress, 3rd session, 1938, H. R. 234, 76th Congress, 1st session,
1939, and S. 916, H. R. 4235, 76th Congress, 1st session, 1939.
Beginning in 1939, proposals for the establishment of an administrative court began to go somewhat out-of-style as the
first of a series of so-called administrative law bills was
introduced.  Finally, in 1946, when the Administrative Procedure Act was passed, the question for a time became moot, and
the subject of the establishment of an administrative court
was less frequently expressed.

goal from being realized by the Commission, and to what extent, if any, Congress itself may have failed to provide the Commission with additional guidance when it was needed; (d) if such is the case, and Congress in turn has failed to give proper guidance and support to the Commission when this was needed, it might be of further use to suggest, on the basis of the study, certain specific areas in which the additional guidance by Congress should be provided.

Naturally, in testing the validity of the above hypothesis, it will be necessary to trace the development of broadcast legislation in the Congress, as well as the development of Congressional relations with the Commission. Much of the dissertation deals with these aspects of the study.

Chapter II analyzes the early legislative history and development of the regulation of interstate communication. Chapter III makes note of the events leading up to the abolition of the Federal Radio Commission and the establishment of the Federal Communications Commission. Chapter IV analyzes the Federal Communications Act of 1934 and calls attention to the various significant court decisions which interpret certain of its provisions. Chapter V delineates and explains what was behind the various attempts at legislative amendment to the Communications Act between the year of its original passage and the advent of the Second World War. Chapters VI and VII follow the trends in Congress which led to the passage of the McFarland Amendments of 1952, and Chapter VIII makes a detailed analysis of these amendments.

An effort is then made to examine the operations of the Commission to ascertain whether it has been able to establish firm, dependable policies as an outgrowth of its broad legislative mandate. This examination is made primarily in Chapter IX, in which significant comparative television cases decided since the lifting of the television freeze are considered. Finally, in Chapter X an attempt will be made to draw conclusions from the preceding chapters, and to suggest what steps might be taken to contribute to the more effective functioning of the Commission.

# CHAPTER II

## THE REGULATION OF BROADCASTING PRIOR TO 1934

### 1. Early Broadcast Regulation

The earliest regulation of radio transmission had
little to do with broadcasting as such.[1] Its main purpose
centered around the protection of life at sea. A radio law
passed in 1910 required installation of wireless equipment
on all passenger vessels carrying 50 or more men including
passengers and crew.[2] Power to administer the law was given
to the Secretary of Commerce and Labor while the task of enforcement was assigned to the Bureau of Navigation which had
charge of the enrollment and licensing of vessels. In 1912
a new law was passed by which full administration of the
statute was placed in the hands of the Secretary of Commerce
and Labor.[3] All regulations were embodied in the Act itself,

---

[1]As defined in Section 3 of the Communications Act of
1934 (Public Law No. 416) for the purposes of the Act...
"broadcasting" means "the dissemination of radio communications
intended to be received by the public" -- contrast this with
the terms "radio communication" or "communication by radio"
which means "the transmission by radio of writing, signs,
signals, pictures and sounds of all kinds" -- either on a point
to point or broadcast basis. According to the Act, a station
may be licensed either as a broadcast station (i.e., a station equipped to engage in broadcasting as herein defined) or
it can be licensed for radio communication from point to point --
thus it can perform one of the two functions, but never both
of them.

[2]S. 7021, a bill to require apparatus and operators for
radio communication on ocean steamers (36 Stat. L., 629,
effective July 1, 1911).

[3]Public Law No. 264, 62d Cong., 37 Stat. L., 302.

17

and no power to make additional regulations was conferred on the Secretary. The act provided for nothing more than the licensing of stations and local operators and set aside certain radio frequencies between the limits of which it was permissible for stations to broadcast. Since radio broadcasting was employed primarily for the point to point transmission of messages prior to World War I, this meager legislation was entirely adequate for the purpose of licensing the few stations in existence at the time. Licenses were granted upon request, and except for ships at sea, nothing more was required of the licensee than that he remain within the frequency limits set aside for the particular type of station (commercial or private) to which the license was issued.

## 2. The Post World War I Situation in Broadcasting
### Rapid Growth with Consequent Complications

After World War I, however, the formal broadcasting of programs intended for reception by the general public began, and with it also came new problems connected with the licensing and operation of stations.[4] Because of the tremendous proliferation of radio stations in the early 1920's and the

---

[4]Up to that time radio's chief advantages had seemed to lie in the area of point to point communication with consequent little attention being given to its enormous potential as a source of broadcast information and entertainment. Now that manufacturers were beginning to realize that radio broadcasts were attracting millions of potential purchasers of radio receivers, radio broadcasting itself became important. Earliest stations sold no time and were quite frequently maintained and operated by manufacturers and suppliers of radio equipment.

resultant overcrowding of the narrow limits of broadcast bands, the industry began to show alarm and to request further regulation from the government. Accordingly, in February, 1922, the Secretary of Commerce called the first of a series of industry conferences designed to bring about a solution of the problem.[5] At the conference legislative recommendations were made calling for complete government control of broadcasting and the assignment of a particular frequency to each broadcast station. Neither of these bills passed.[6]

By 1923 the situation had grown considerably worse. The number of broadcast stations in the United States jumped from 60 to 588 within a single year. As Mr. Hoover stated:

> Public broadcasting has practically been limited to two wave lengths, and I need not dilate to you on the amount of interference there is and the jeopardy in which the whole development of the act stands.[7]

### 3. The Breakdown of Regulation as the Result of Adverse Court Decisions

The mere proliferation of radio stations and consequent interference was not the only problem the Secretary of

---

[5]The radio conferences were attended by representatives of the radio industry, members of both the House of Representatives and the Senate, and personnel from various governmental agencies interested in communications. They formulated the basic principles of legislation which were ultimately incorporated in the Radio Act of 1927. From 1922 to 1925, four radio conferences were held.

[6]S. 3694 and H. R. 11964, 67th Cong., 2d sess., "to amend an Act to Regulate Radio Communication."

[7]New York Times, March 21, 1923.

Commerce had to contend with, however, for he had run into difficulty in his administration of the Act. As early as 1912 an opinion of the Attorney General stated that the Secretary of Commerce and Labor could exercise no discretion in the issuance of licenses.[8] Yet, in the summer of 1921, assuming that he was acting under the authority of that Act, Secretary Hoover designated two wave lengths for broadcasting (750 and 833 kc) and licensed all stations to operate on whichever one of these they pleased.[9]

Almost immediately, however, the demand in New York City exceeded the supply, and when the license of the Intercity Radio Company expired in November, 1921, the Secretary declined to grant a new one, on the grounds that he could not assign an applicant a wave length that would interfere with stations nearby. Intercity Radio contested this decision in the Court of Appeals of the District of Columbia, in February, 1923, where it was ruled that the Secretary's action in licensing cases was purely ministerial and that he could not refuse to issue a license whenever it was requested by an applicant. The court agreed, however, that the assignment of a wave length was entirely under the Secretary's control.[10]

On the strength of this ruling, an order was issued dividing stations into three classes according to their

---

[8] See Ops. Atty. Gen. (1912) 579.

[9] Radio Service Bulletin, Sept. 1, 1922, p. 10.

[10] Hoover v. Intercity Radio, 286 Fed. 1003 (1923).

assigned wave length and power. The United States was divided into five zones, with separate wave lengths designated
for certain localities in each zone. This ruling also was
the subject of court appeal by a disappointed licensee and
resulted in a ruling by the United States Court for the
Northern District of Illinois which held that in the Zenith
case there was "no express grant of power in the Act (of
1912) to the Secretary of Commerce to establish regulations."
"The Secretary of Commerce," it continued, "is required to
issue the license subject to the regulations in the Act" and
"the Congress has withheld from him the power to prescribe
additional regulations."[11]

The effect of this decision was immediate and dis-
astrous to all attempts of the Secretary of Commerce to regulate broadcasting. Since the Radio Act of 1912 provided
that broadcast wave lengths should be within certain limits,
after the Zenith decision a station could use any wave length
it chose as long as it was within the limits specified by the
Act. Furthermore, since the Court of Appeals of the District
of Columbia had previously held that the Secretary could not
refuse to issue a license, but that he did have discretion in
the assignment of a wave length, there was an apparent conflict between the two decisions and the Attorney General was
asked to rule. The Attorney General on June 4, and the Acting

---

[11]United States v. Zenith Radio Corporation, 12 Fed.
(2d) 616, 617 (1926).

Attorney General on June 8, ruled as follows:[12]

a) A license is required to operate a radio station.

b) The Secretary is required to issue such a license upon request.

c) Radio communication is a proper subject for Federal regulation under the commerce clause of the Constitution.

d) The Secretary of Commerce has no power to specify wave lengths, assign hours of operation (except for the first 15 minutes of each hour as specified in the Radio Act of 1912, to be reserved if necessary, in designated localities for Government stations), and he likewise had no authority to limit power or issue licenses of limited duration.[13]

In the final paragraph of his opinion, the Attorney General expressed the opinion that

> It is apparent from the answers contained in this opinion that the present legislation is inadequate to cover the art of broadcasting, which has been almost entirely developed since the passage of the 1912 act. If the present situation requires control, I can only suggest that it be sought in new legislation, carefully adapted to meet the needs of both the present and the future.[14]

### 4. The Issues Before Congress Relative to the Passage of a New Broadcast Law; in Particular, that of Monopoly

By this time it was obvious that broadcasting was

---

[12]Ops. Atty. Gen. 126-32.

[13]Because of the rapid development of broadcasting and consequent overcrowded bands the Secretary had been issuing licenses for only 90 days.

[14]Ops. Atty. Gen. 132.

rapidly becoming a most important means of communication and
source of pleasure to the American public, and that it could
not be allowed to continue to grow haphazardly and without
control.  Because the alternative to regulation was so obviously that of broadcast chaos, the radio industry itself
demanded that the Federal Government take a hand in the
situation.  Almost no one at this time was concerned with
questions pertaining to the qualifications of a prospective
broadcast licensee (other than that he be a citizen of the
United States).  Nor was any interest as yet manifested in the
manner of service he was to furnish, or the method of programming to be followed.  Those who were affected by the problem
were most interested in the establishment of a governmental
body to act as a kind of traffic policeman whose task would
be to eliminate, as much as was possible, the interference
between various broadcast transmitters.  There was, however,
one area, touching upon an applicant's fitness to be a licensee, in which Congress was already beginning to show some concern, and this was the area of broadcast monopolies.  As
Lewellyn White points out: "Fear of monopoly manifested itself in congressional councils in the earliest days of broadcasting, and has never wholly been absent from them since."[15]
This fear was based primarily in the area of broadcast manu-
acturers and had to do with patents.  Until the Supreme Court's
ecision in the famous Button Makers' Case, courts had usually

_____

[15]The American Radio (University of Chicago Press,
947), p. 154.

placed major emphasis in decisions regarding patents on the
public interest aspects rather than the exclusive rights of
the patentee evolving out of the patent on his invention.
Following this decision, however (which came at about the
same time Marconi first took out his patents on his radio invention), patents tended to become exclusive over extended
periods of time. This phenomena particularly complicated
the development of the radio industry, where literally hundreds of patents involving very small refinements of radio
tubes and apparatus were needed in order to manufacture a
radio set.

Until the outbreak of World War I, practically all radio equipment in use in this country had been manufactured by
or leased from British Marconi, Ltd., which by United States
treaty agreement held all important radio patents. Even ships
of the United States Fleet were forced for a time to lease
equipment from the British firm. Among the sweeping powers
that were given President Wilson, however, was one which
authorized him,

> ...in time of war, to supervise or take possession and
> assume control of any telegraph, telephone, marine cable
> or radio system or systems...and to operate the same in
> any manner as may be needful or desirable for the duration
> of the war, and to provide just compensation therefor.[16]

With the advent of war, therefore, all such broadcast
equipment and manufacturing outlets were seized, and under a
subsequent governmental program of scientific development,

---

[16]Public Res. No. 38, approved by the 65th Cong. on
July 16, 1918.

great technical strides (among them the development of the
Alexanderson alternator which made possible the sending of
radio messages over great distances) resulted in so many new
inventions that the radio monopoly held by British Marconi
was broken up at the war's end.  Thus,

> by the end of World War I, General Electric had
> acquired the patents on the Alexanderson Alternator;
> American Telephone & Telegraph had bought all the DeFor-
> est rights, including his audion tube; and Westinghouse
> had developed important new transmission equipment, all
> vitally important to the future of the wireless, yet
> none complete without the others and without devices
> controlled by American Marconi.  The infant industry
> faced a wasteful patent war, in which the British might
> come off winners.  To meet this threat, Navy Secretary
> Daniels proposed Government ownership.  The Army, the
> Navy "brass" and majority in Congress opposed such a
> step, but they agreed that the patents should be secured
> to the United States.  Owen D. Young, chairman of the
> board of General Electric, had a solution:  Let the three
> American firms directly involved pool their resources and
> buy out American Marconi.  Pursuant to Young's suggestion,
> on October 17, 1919, the Radio Corporation of America
> (RCA) was formed.[17]

The new corporation was begun for "patriotic reasons"
in order to take over as an American firm the radio monopoly
that had been the exclusive property of British Marconi and
its American subsidiary until the outbreak of war.  RCA was
formed as the sales outlet for the participating competing
American organizations that signed the cross-licensing pact
which came into being at this time.  These organizations were
General Electric, American Telephone & Telegraph and its subsidiary, Western Electric, and by 1921, Westinghouse and the
United Fruit Co.  RCA thereby became a company in which the

[17]White, op. cit., pp. 11-12.  Also see Gleason L.
Archer, Big Business and Radio (New York: The American Histor-
cal Co., Inc., 1939), 503 pages.

chief corporations of the "radio group" held stock for money advanced, for patent rights surrendered to RCA, or for other considerations. In addition, General Electric and Westinghouse made RCA their exclusive outlet to handle the sale of radio sets.

## The Growth of RCA

Westinghouse and General Electric began to manufacture "Radiola Sets," the earliest of which were nothing more than crystal apparatus, in 1920-21. The great radio boom burst on the nation in 1922. Radio sales quickly became big business, with the total industry share of $60,000,000 in 1922 skyrocketing to $358,000,000 by 1924. RCA's share of the gross figure was $11,000,000 and $50,000,000 respectively. It would have been much higher if the "radio group" had realized the potential of the business earlier and had been fully prepared to take full advantage of their patent monopoly. Coordination between production and sales in the separate organizations was much slower than it would have been in a single organization. Since the demand for radio sets was great, this resulted in a consequent loss of business to other companies which frequently infringed upon RCA's patents without concerning themselves about possible consequences. Models coming to RCA were not standardized, and technological improvements and changes in design were slow to come about. All of this contributed to the development of competition from such companies as Atwater Kent, Crosley, Grebe, Grigsby-Grunow, Fried-Eisemann,

Fada, Philco, Zenith, and several others.

By 1923, however, RCA was ready to begin its first patent infringement suit -- drawn against the A. H. Grebe Company. Because of RCA's size and power, strong public reaction in favor of the Grebe Company resulted in the filing of a complaint on January 28, 1924, by the Federal Trade Commission against the Radio Corporation. The complaint charged "monopoly in radio apparatus and communication, both domestic and transoceanic..." and also charged the group with "efforts to perpetuate the present control beyond the life of the existing patents...."[18]

## Congressional Reaction to RCA's Suit

Congress also was aroused as a result of the public furor over RCA's suit against the Grebe Company, and two bills were introduced in 1923 which contained anti-monopoly provisions designed to disqualify as a broadcast licensee any corporation which sought either by direct or indirect means to monopolize radio communications.[19] With regard to the events leading up to the introduction of H. R. 13773 and H. R. 13777, and their influence on later legislation, particularly with respect to sections 13 and 15 of the Radio Act of 1927, H. P. Warner states:

On January 11, 1923, Mr. White (later Senator), of Maine,

---

[18]United States of America before the Federal Trade Commission, Docket No. 1115.

[19]H. R. 13773 and H. R. 13777, 67th Cong., 4th sess., 1923.

introduced H. R. 13773 to amend the Radio Act of 1912.
This bill authorized the Secretary of Commerce to refuse
a station license, where, in the judgment of the Secretary, the applicant was "monopolizing or seeking to monopolize radio communication, directly or indirectly,
through the control of the manufacture or sale of radio
apparatus, or by any other means."[20] This bill was favorably reported by the House Committee on Merchant Marine
and Fisheries and passed the House without amendment on
January 31, 1923. Apparently because of the fear of a
radio monopoly expressed by the committee report, the
Congress then adopted a resolution calling upon the Federal Trade Commission to investigate and report to the
House various facts relating to radio patents, contracts,
leases, etc., together with such other facts as might aid
the House of Representatives in determining whether "the
antitrust statutes of the United States have been or now
are being violated by any person, company or corporation
subject to the jurisdiction of the United States."[21]
Pursuant to this resolution, the Federal Trade Commission
investigated the radio industry and reported to the House
on December 11, 1923.[22] This report was the subject of
much discussion in both Houses of Congress and is of vital
significance in the development of the antitrust provisions
of the Radio Act of 1927.[23]

---

[20]H. Rept. No. 1416 by the Committee on Merchant Marine,
Radio and Fisheries, which accompanied H. R. 13733 (1923),
stated: "Apprehension has been expressed and there is evidence
sufficient to raise the question in reasonable minds, that
certain companies and interests have been endeavoring to
establish a monopoly in wireless communication through control
of the manufacture and sale of radio instruments, through contractual arrangements giving exclusive privileges in the transmission and exchange of messages or through other means. Your
committee believes that the subject should be carefully investigated and appropriate action taken at an early date."

[21]H. Res. 548, 67th Cong., 4th sess. (1923), introduced by Mr. White of Maine.

[22]Federal Trade Commission Rept. No. 1686. As a result
of this investigation the Commission filed a complaint, docket
No. 1115, on January 25, 1924, against the companies listed in
note 21. The complaint was dismissed on December 19, 1928.

[23]H. P. Warner, Radio and Television Law, p. 483. On
p. 769 Mr. Warner states: "Both the radio industry and Mr.
Hoover were of the opinion that the determination and enforcement of antitrust laws by an executive officer was too great
a power to be lodged in an individual; secondly, the Department of Commerce lacked the personnel, machinery, and techniques
for administering the antitrust laws to radio." (Mr. Warner

On December 15, 1925, Representative White (R. of
Maine) introduced a bill, H. R. 5589, for the regulation of
radio communication and for other purposes, which was referred
to the Committee on Merchant Marine and Fisheries. H. R. 5589
contained a provision which authorized the Secretary of Commerce to refuse a license to anyone who had been convicted
in court for violation of the antitrust laws. The bill established a National Radio Commission of nine members, and the
Secretary was authorized to refer to the Commission any application for frequency, power, "or any other matter, the
determination of which is vested in him under the terms of
the act." The decision of the Secretary was to be final,
subject to the right of appeal. The appellate provisions for
review authorized the court to alter or revise the decision
appealed from and enter a just judgment. Secretary Hoover
urged at the hearings that the Commission be given more authority and that "any question of dispute as to who shall enjoy
the radio privilege may be referred to that body, not through
the volition of the Secretary of Commerce but by either applicant or disputant to the question."[24] As a result of the de-
liberation on H. R. 5589, after consideration by the committee,
H. R. 9108 was reported out.

H. R. 9108 created five zones of approximately equal
population in the United States. It proposed a radio

---

is one of the outstanding writers on radio law.)

[24]Hearings before the Committee on Merchant Marine and
Fisheries on H. R. 5589, 69th Cong., 1st sess., p. 12 (1926).

commission of five members, one from each of the five zones.
Any person aggrieved by a decision of the Secretary could
appeal to the Commission, which would hear the case de novo.
The decision of the Commission was also appealable.

Congressman Edwin L. Davis (D. of Tennessee) submitted
a minority report on the bill in which he criticized its antitrust provisions for not adequately suppressing monopoly. He
urged the establishment of a full-time independent Commission
to administer radio, and complained that private censorship
was being exercised by individual or corporate licensees. He
described the provisions for appeal to the courts as "shadowy,"
and claimed that the right of appeal should be extended to
any person (i.e. "party in interest") feeling aggrieved.[25]
In regard to the Davis objections, H. P. Warner writes:

> It is significant that some of the minority views
> of Mr. Davis were incorporated into the Radio Act of
> 1927, particularly the appellate provisions for
> review.[26]

H. R. 9108, as reported by the committee to the House,
contained the following provision:

> Sec. 4. It shall be unlawful for any person, firm,
> company, or corporation, in any manner or by any means
> (a) to send or carry...(b) to bring, or to cause to be
> brought, into the United States...any radio vacuum tubes
> or other radio apparatus...the purpose and/or effect of
> which is to fix the price at which the purchaser may re-
> sell the same or to prohibit or restrict the parties by
> whom or the purposes for which said tubes and apparatus
> or the parts thereof may be used.

---

[25]H. Rept. 404, 69th Cong., 1st sess., H. R. 9108.

[26]Warner, op. cit., p. 773.

This section was naturally aimed at those companies that had
entered into the cross-licensing agreement at the time of the
formation of the Radio Corporation of America, or RCA.

H. R. 9108 was debated in the House and subsequently
tabled, but again introduced by Representative White on
March 3, 1926, as H. R. 9971, and, on March 5, it was favorably reported out by the committee. The new version entirely
eliminated the section dealing with the monopoly control of
apparatus.[27]

Representative Davis, in an extended debate on the
floor of the House on March 12, 1926, vigorously attacked the
bill (H. R. 9971) on the grounds that it contained provisions
which would encourage the monopoly situation in the radio industry. He maintained the bill would make it possible for
manufacturers of radio equipment to reap excessive profits
and stated:

> Its teeth have been pulled. It's the weakest bill on
> radio ever introduced. The Radio Corporation of America
> is the biggest monopoly in radio, having a capital stock
> of $25 million. This stock is owned by other members of
> the monopoly, allocated to their respective fields. About
> 2,500 patents have been pooled.[28]

A second amendment in the White bill was also subjected
to extensive analysis and criticism by Mr. Davis. The
amended section reads as follows:

---

[27]Sec. 4 was deleted by the House committee because it
claimed the subject matter "related to patent rights and interstate commerce, over which two subjects the Committee on Merchant Marine and Fisheries has no jurisdiction." H. Rept.
No. 464, 69th Cong., 1st sess., p. 2.

[28]New York Times, Saturday, March 13, 1926.

The Secretary of Commerce is hereby directed to refuse a station license and/or the permit hereinafter required for the construction of a station to any person,
firm, company, or corporation, or any subsidiary thereof,
which has been found guilty by any Federal court of unlawfully monopolizing or attempting to unlawfully monopolize after this act takes effect radio communication,
directly or indirectly, through the control of the manufacture or sale of radios or radio apparatus, through exclusive traffic arrangements, or by any other means.[29]

Mr. Davis wanted to change this language to read:

The Secretary of Commerce is hereby directed to refuse
a station license to any person, company, or corporation
which, in his judgment, is unlawfully monopolizing or
seeking to unlawfully monopolize radio communication,
directly or indirectly, through control of the manufacture or sale of radio apparatus through exclusive traffic
arrangements, or by any other means.[30]

On March 13, Representative Davis again took the

floor to criticize the revised measure. He stated:

This bill is weaker than the first bill which the
committee reported out during this session of Congress,
so far as embracing any check on monopolies is concerned....

In the bill reported and passed through the House in
the 67th Congress and in the bill reported in the last
Congress, each time unanimously reported by the committee,
this section then authorized indirectly to the Secretary
of Commerce to refuse a broadcasting license to any applicant provided the Secretary of Commerce himself was of
the opinionthe applicant was monopolizing or attempting
to monopolize any field of the radio business. It has
now been so changed that he is not authorized to do that
until the applicant shall have been convicted or as the
language reads: "shall have been found guilty of a violation of the antitrust laws." Why you even refuse to
strike out the word "guilty" so as to permit him to refuse a license upon an adjudication of such facts in a
civil proceeding.

And as this bill was first introduced in the present
Congress, it did not have the words "after this Act takes
effect" but the committee amended the bill by inserting

---

[29]Congressional Record, 69th Cong., 1st sess., p. 5501.

[30]Ibid., p. 5502.

those words. Why? Because there is now pending a
complaint of the Federal Trade Commission charging that
certain companies are in a monopoly and are violating the
antitrust laws of the United States....(This allows)
these companies, even if found guilty, to come in and receive license anyway. The present act makes liable only
those guilty of the anti-monopoly practices accruing after
the passage of the act.[31]

Mr. Davis then introduced an amendment calling for the filing

of all such contracts by applicants for licenses which might

disclose the relationship of the applicant to other companies

or corporations. This amendment was rejected by a vote of

92 to 105.[32]   Similar amendments were again offered by

Mr. Davis, and again rejected.[33]

The importance of these points of debate is to be

found in their relationship to future legislative changes in

the Radio Act, and they lie chiefly in two areas. First,

the very real problem of just how much discretionary power

should be given to the Secretary of Commerce (or later, to

the regulatory commission having under its jurisdiction the

licensing of radio stations); and second, the provision hav-

ing to do with violations of the antitrust laws, which is

significant in the light of the recurrent problems it pre-

sents today.

Up to the present time no solution has been found for

either of these problems, particularly for the problem arising

out of the antitrust laws. In consequence the Commission has

generally preferred to avoid all entanglement with the rather

---

[31]_Ibid._, p. 5557.    [32]_Ibid._, p. 5560.
[33]_Ibid._, pp. 5563, 5564, 5565.

vague antitrust and anti-monopoly provisions contained in
the Act.

### 5. Other Points of Debate in Connection with the Passage of the Radio Act -- Its Passage and Approval by the President

H. R. 9971 passed the House on March 15, 1926. A
similar bill (S. 1754) was introduced in the Senate, where
the Committee on Interstate and Foreign Commerce held hearings on its several provisions. The Senate amended the
House bill by striking out all the provisions that came after the enacting clause, and inserting in their place, provisions of their own. One which was added stated there should
be no discrimination as to charges, terms, or service to ad-
vertisers, and stated in language that is still largely to
be found in Section 315 (a) of the present Act that --

> If any licensee shall permit a broadcasting station to
> be used by a candidate or candidates for any public office,
> it shall afford equal opportunities to all candidates for
> such public office, and the use of such broadcasting
> station.[34]

The Senate also engaged in considerable debate whether
or not the broadcaster should be considered a common carrier.
Since it was reasoned that radio transmission was interstate
commerce, some Senators felt that Congress therefore had the
right to control rates. This provision was not included in
the final version however, except that "for the purpose of
nondiscrimination as to political candidates the broadcaster

---

[34]Congressional Record, 67th Cong., p. 12502.

shall be considered a common carrier."[35]  The bill passed the
Senate and was sent to conference on July 2.

There were a number of striking similarities in the
House and Senate bills as well as a number of important differences. Both provided for the establishment of a Federal Radio
Commission. The House bill placed original licensing authority in the hands of the Secretary of Commerce. He could, however, refer any matter to the Commission, to which any person
affected by the action of the Secretary might appeal. The
Senate bill placed the original licensing authority in the
Commission. Both bills agreed, insofar as they placed administrative authority in the hands of the Secretary of Commerce. Licensing authority included the fixing of wave
lengths, power, and time of operation. Administrative authority included the inspection of stations at land or sea, the
licensing of operators, and the assignment of call letters.
The House bill placed a limitation of five years upon licenses; the Senate amendment carried a limitation of two
years upon all licenses. Both versions carried a privilege
for renewal of license.

A compromise was worked out on the question of appeals
from Commission decisions. By the terms of the House bill
all appeals were to the Court of Appeals of the District of
Columbia. Under the Senate version appeals upon questions of
revocation could be taken either to the Court of Appeals of

35Ibid., p. 12505.

the District of Columbia or to the district court of the
United States in the district in which the station covered by
the license was located.[36]

The conferees were unable to reach an agreement in the
current session since time had grown very close to adjournment. It was felt, however, that there should be some form
of legislation in effect during the interim period before
Congress reconvened. Throughout the entire debate there had
been concern shown by Congress over the possibility that licensees might attempt to establish property rights in the
radio frequencies which would seriously inhibit the functioning of any regulatory authority. Therefore, Senate Joint
Resolution 125 was adopted by both Houses on July 3, stating
that until otherwise provided by law no original license
for operation of any radio broadcasting station and no renewal of a license of an existing station should be granted
for a period longer than 90 days, and only then if the applicant would sign a waiver of any right to any wave length,
or the use of the ether in radio transmission. The resolution had been passed so late in the session, however, that
it was not possible for it to be presented to the President
for his signature before the adjournment of Congress. Actually it was not approved until December 8, after the convening
of the following session.

The second session of the 69th Congress met on

---

[36]S. Doc. 200, 69th Cong., 2d sess., to accompany
H. R. 9971; p. 18, sec. 16.

December 6, 1926, and the conferees reached agreement on January 27, but the two Houses did not ratify the action of the conferees for several weeks.[37] The bill setting up the Federal Radio Commission was approved by the President on February 23, 1927 (44 Stat. L., 1162).[38]

### 6. A Brief Analysis of the Radio Act of 1927

Between the years 1921 and 1927, twelve bills had been introduced in Congress which, if passed, would have replaced the Radio Act of 1912 with more up-to-date legislation. In addition to these, an additional four were introduced which would have amended the law.[39] Now, after six years of effort, Congress finally succeeded in passing a comprehensive broadcasting act. Drafting of the legislation had not been an easy task. The field of radio broadcasting developed so rapidly after the end of World War I that few men outside the newly created broadcast industry itself had even the vaguest understanding of it. Yet Congress was faced with the problem of having to draft a new law which somehow would deal sensibly with its complexities.

---

[37]H. Rept. 1886; S. Doc. 200, 69th Cong.

[38]Public Law No. 632, February 23, 1927, 69th Cong.

[39]Bills to "regulate" broadcasting included: 67th Cong., 2d sess., S. 31, S. 1627, S. 1628, H. R. 1432, H. R. 5889; 68th Cong., 1st sess., S. 2796; 69th Cong., 1st sess., S. 3968, S. 4057, S. 4156, H. R. 5589, H. R. 9108, H. R. 9971. Bills to "amend" the Radio Act of 1912 included: 67th Cong., 2d sess., S. 2290; S. 3694, H. R. 11964; 68th Cong., 1st sess., S. 2524.

Although the debates on the 1927 Act had been marked
with lengthy arguments on proper parliamentary procedure, confusion over radio terms and technicalities, and constant ir
relevancies, the resulting legislation would, in the years to
come, prove adequate enough for the licensing function that
the Commission had been given. The way Congress had sur-
mounted the problem of having to deal with a subject about
which it had little or no knowledge was to turn the entire
matter over to the agency it was creating. This it did by
conferring broad power on the Commission and telling it its
task was to regulate all interstate and foreign transmissions
originating in the United States. Except that it could not
censor radio communication and that it was required, in the
performance of its licensing function, to distribute radio
service to all parts of the country on an "equal" basis,
the Commission was given "carte blanche" to do whatever it
felt the "public interest" required relative to the licensing
and regulation of broadcast stations.

The Radio Act of 1927 was then basically nothing more
than a licensing act although, in one area at least (that of
anti-monopoly), there was a rather vague provision looking
toward the disqualification of a licensee under what might be
termed qualitative grounds.[40]

---

[40]Section 13 contained the anti-monopoly provision
which was the subject of extended floor debate and attempts
at amendment during the passage of the bill. Its language
was as follows:

The Act created a Federal Radio Commission, which for a period of one year was to be the original licensing authority.
At the expiration of this time the Secretary of Commerce was
to succeed to that function, and the Commission was to become
an appellate body.[41]

---

The licensing authority is hereby directed to refuse
a station license and/or the permit...for construction...
to any person, firm, company, or corporation, or any
subsidiary thereof, which has been finally guilty by a
Federal Court of unlawfully monopolizing or attempting to
monopolize, after this Act takes effect, radio communication, directly or indirectly, through the control of the
manufacture or sale of radio apparatus, through exclusive traffic arrangements, or any other means, or to
have been using unfair methods of competition.  The
granting of a license shall not estop the United States
or any person aggrieved from proceeding against such
person, firm, company, or corporation for violating the
law against unfair methods of competition or for a violation of the law against unlawful restraints and monopolies...or from instituting proceedings for the dissolu-
tion of such a firm, company, corporation.  (Emphasis
supplied.)

Schmeckebier states that the wording of the provision
caused some confusion as to whether it applied to a civil
or a criminal judgment. (See the Federal Radio Commission
by Lawrence F. Schmeckebier, (Washington: Brookings Institution, 1932), p. 18)

The act also provided (sec. 15) that all antitrust laws
would be applicable to the manufacture and sale of and trade
in radio apparatus and devices entering interstate commerce,
and that if any licensee should be found guilty, either in
civil or criminal proceedings, of a violation of the antitrust
laws, the court could decree that the license shall be revoked. (Settlement by consent decree, of course, had no
effect on the provisions of the Act.)

[41]The licensing power of the Commission was extended
to March 16, 1929 (45 Stat. L., 373), then to December 31,
1929 (45 Stat. L., 1559), and finally it was made of
indefinite duration (46 Stat. L., 50).

It was the intention of Congress that the Commission would regulate both interstate and foreign transmissions originating in the United States, and that it would maintain governmental control over all channels by providing for the licensed use of those channels for limited periods of time. For this purpose the nation was divided into five geographical zones. Each of the five members of the Commission was required to be an actual resident within the zone from which he was appointed, with no more than one commissioner being from any zone and not more than three commissioners being members of the same political party. The President was to make the appointments, with the advice and consent of the Senate. Initially, he was to designate the chairman with all subsequent chairmen being chosen by the Commission itself. Terms of appointment were to be for two, three, four, five, and six years at the outset, with all successors to be appointed for terms of six years except for those appointed to fill a vacancy of a term yet unexpired. The powers of the Commission were that it could "...from time to time, as public convenience, interest, or necessity requires..." classify as to power and hours of service and assign frequencies to stations; locate stations and regulate the types of apparatus they might use; make regulations to prevent or at least lessen interference between stations and establish zones which they were to serve; and require that stations keep accurate records of all the programs broadcast by them. The Act required the equal distribution of radio service to all parts of the country (a practical impossibility because of geography and economic factors) and allowed the Commission to license broadcast stations for a maximum period of three years after which time licenses could be reviewed upon Commission approval. No license, wave length or frequency could be sold or transferred without the Commission's passing on the transaction.

Although the Commission had no power of censorship over radio communications or signals and none of its regulations or conditions were to be permitted to interfere with the right of free speech by means of radio communication, it was empowered to revoke station licenses (a) where there had been failure to operate in accordance with the terms by which the license had been granted, (b) where there had been instances of violation of the Act or Commission regulations, (c) in instances where any Federal body having jurisdiction should certify to the Commission that the licensee had failed to afford reasonable facilities, or (d) was guilty of discrimination in service and charges (this latter provision was directed primarily against stations engaged in the point to point transmission of commercial messages). Under the law, all Commission actions and decisions could be appealed to the Court of Appeals for the District of Columbia.

### 7. The Federal Radio Commission, 1927-1934.

The Radio Act was approved and signed by the President on February 23, 1927, only nine days before Congress was to adjourn. During this short space of time, nomination and confirmation of the five Commissioners had to be made. The five nominations were made and sent to the Senate on March 1. Three of the Commissioners had been confirmed by March 4, with recess appointments being given to the other two. However,

> ...as the vacancies existed when the Senate was in session, no salary could be paid to the unconfirmed appointees.[42]
>
> One of the confirmed Commissioners died on October 8, and another on November 24, 1927. The successor to the latter was not appointed until March 29, 1928, being confirmed the following day. Therefore, from November 24 1927, to March 29, 1928, there were only four Commissioners, and of these only one had been confirmed by the Senate.[43]

No money had been appropriated for the new Commission, which nevertheless was enabled to function due to a clause in the Radio Act making it possible for it to utilize the unexpended balance existing in the appropriation made to the Department of Commerce under the item "Wireless Communication Laws."

It was decided immediately upon the organization of the Commission that its greatest task lay in the field of broadcasting, due to the chaotic condition that had existed since the decision of the United States Court for the Northern

---

[42]One of the unconfirmed Commissioners resigned October 31, 1927, before being confirmed; payment of salary was provided by a special joint resolution approved March 23, 1928 (45 Stat. L., 1712). The other appointee to the original Commission was not confirmed until March 30, 1928, and received no salary prior to that date (R. S. 1761).

[43]Schmeckebier, op. cit., p. 22.

District of Illinois in the Zenith case. When the Commission
took office there were 732 stations under license, and only
90 channels in the standard or broadcast band available for
use by them. Some distribution of these 732 stations over
the 90 channels had to be accomplished as quickly and
efficiently as possible.[44] This could be done only by
dividing broadcast time, allocating frequencies, creating
various classes of stations according to assigned frequency
and power and eliminating some fringe stations altogether.
While this was taking place, an attempt had to be made to
secure "a fair and equitable distribution" of stations to
the five geographical zones. These steps the Commission
immediately proceeded to take.

The results at the end of some few months showed a
certain improvement but were by no means definitive, as is
imported in the Commission's annual report for 1928:

> ...Radio-reception conditions were far from satis-
> factory as the result of the commission's allocation
> of June 15, 1927. The reallocation had succeeded to a
> marked extent in reducing interference arising from con-
> gestion in the larger metropolitan centers, where
> stations had been crowded together without adequate
> frequency separation; it had not, however, succeeded in
> remedying heterodyne interference (resulting from two or
> more stations operating simultaneously on the same
> channel), which was ruining reception in rural areas, and
> indeed in all parts of the country. The complaints
> which deluged the Commission made it apparent that
> changes would have to be effected.[45]

------

[44]The Secretary of Commerce had (prior to the Zenith
case) assigned stations to specific wave lengths -- but following the Zenith decision, stations had moved at will to
other wave lengths, regardless of the assignment given.

[45]Federal Radio Commission, Annual Report, 1938, p. 8.

At the same time these steps were being taken, concern began to grow in Congress that all parts of the country
were not getting their share of stations. It was particularly charged that discrimination had been exercised against the
South and West, and that preference had been given to high
power stations in the North and East. At the time the nominations of three Commission-members were pending in the Senate,
it was stated on the floor that there was "great doubt with
regard to their confirmation, not by reason of anything particularly against them, but for reasons which appealed to us."[46]
It was further reported that many Senators were willing to
vote for confirmation for two years but not for six. Therefore, in order to make the provision for zonal allocation
more definite the House proposed to change the wording of
section nine of the Radio Act which read:

> In considering applications for licenses and renew-
> als of licenses, when and insofar as there is a demand
> for the same, the licensing authority shall make such a
> distribution of licenses, bands of frequency of wave
> lengths, periods of time for operation, and of power
> among the different States and communities as to give
> fair, efficient, and equitable radio service to each of
> the same.

In making this change, it was planned to substitute the
words:

> The licensing authority shall make an equal alloca-
> tion to each of the five zones established in section 2
> of this Act...and within each zone shall make a fair and
> equitable allocation among the different States thereof
> in proportion to population and area.

---

[46]Congressional Record, 69th Congress, 1st sess.,
Pt. 3, p. 2533.

This amendment, which came to be called the Davis amendment because it had been drafted by Representative Edwin L. Davis, of Tennessee, was adopted after prolonged debate by a vote of 235 to 135, largely based on a sectional division of East against South and West. The language of the amendment was changed and added to, being adopted in the Act as follows:

It is hereby declared that the people of all the zones established by section 2 of this Act are entitled to equality of radio broadcasting service, both of transmission and reception, and in order to provide such equality the licensing authority shall as nearly as possible make and maintain an equal allocation of broadcasting licenses, of bands of frequency or wave lengths, of periods of time for operation, and of station power, to each of said zones when and insofar as there are applications therefor; and shall make a fair and equitable allocation of licenses, wave lengths, time for operation, and station power to each of the States...within each zone, according to population. The licensing authority shall carry into effect the equality of broadcasting service hereinbefore directed, whenever necessary or proper, by granting or refusing licenses or renewals of licenses, by changing periods of time for operation, and by increasing or decreasing station power, when applications are made for licenses or renewals of licenses: Provided, That if and when there is a lack of applications from any zone for the proportionate share of licenses, wave lengths, time of operation, or station power to which such zone is entitled, the licensing authority may issue licenses for the balance of the proportion not applied for from any zone, to applicants from other zones for a temporary period of ninety days each, and shall specifically designate that said apportionment is only for said period. Allocations shall be charged to the State, District, Territory, or possession wherein the studio of the station is located and not where the transmitter is located.[47]

---

[47]Public Law No. 195, 70th Cong., March 28, 1928. The language of the last sentence of the amendment was adopted in the present form mainly to settle the allocations problem arising from stations with transmitters in New Jersey and studios in New York.

In addition to the more stringent allocation proceedings called for in the Davis amendment, the Act of March 28 also extended the life of the Commission as the licensing authority for broadcasting until March 16, 1929. It further provided that the Commission should grant no license or license renewal for a period longer than three months. (In the original Act, the period of licensing for broadcast stations was three years.)

Another unusual provision was one which stated that

> The term of office of each member of the Commission shall expire on February 23, 1929, and thereafter commissioners shall be appointed for terms of two, three, four, five and six years, respectively, as provided for in the Radio Act of 1927.

This put the commissioners somewhat on the spot, insofar as the short period elapsing between the passage of the amendment and their reconfirmation was concerned, putting them, in effect, on probation for a year, and their "uncertain tenure" was cited by the House committee as a source of embarrassment to them.[48]

On March 4, 1929, a further Act was passed "...continuing the powers and authority of the Federal Radio Commission under the Radio Act of 1927...."[49] It continued the Commission's powers until December 31, 1929, but again legislated all the Commissioners out of office after one year. It also added to the Commission's staff the positions of General

---

[48]H. Rept. 800, 70th Congress, p. 2.

[49]Public Law No. 1029, 70th Congress.

Counsel (at $10,000 per year) and three legal assistants
(at salaries of $7,500 each). Thus, "by July 1, 1929, the
staff of the Commission, with the exception of the commissioners and their secretaries, had reached 80 persons, an in-
crease of 59 over the number a year earlier."[50]

Meanwhile, the provisions of the Davis amendment were
creating some confusion and difficulty for the Commission,
so that the President, in his annual message to Congress on
December 2, 1929, criticized it in the following words, and
recommended at the same time that the Commission be given
permanent status:

> I recommend the reorganization of the Radio Commission
> into a permanent body from its present temporary status.
> The requirement of the present law that the Commissioners
> shall be appointed from specified zones should be abol-
> ished and a general provision made for their equitable
> selection from different parts of the country. Despite
> the effort of the Commissioners, the present method
> develops a public insistence that the Commissioners are
> specially charged with supervision of radio affairs in
> the zone from which each is appointed. As a result
> there is danger that the system will degenerate from a
> national system into five regional agencies with vary-
> ing practices, varying policies, competitive tendencies,
> and consequent failure to attain the utmost capacity
> for service to the people as a whole.[51]

This recommendation was rejected by the Congress, but, on
December 18, 1929, it once again renewed the life of the
Radio Commission, this time in language that attested to its
increasing permanence: "...all powers and authority vested
in the Federal Radio Commission...shall continue...until

---

[50]Schmeckebier, op. cit., p. 33.

[51]Congressional Record, 71st Cong., 1st sess.

otherwise provided by law....[52] The Act further provided
for the appointment of a chief engineer with two assistants
to the Commission.

An important amendment (H. R. 12599), changing the
process for making appeals, passed and was signed into law
on July 1, 1930.[53] Under the provision of the original Act
of 1927, an appeal relating to a new license, a renewal, or
a modification, could be made to the Court of Appeals of
the District of Columbia, but an appeal from revocation proceedings could be made either to a district court or to the
Court of Appeals of the District of Columbia. The new amendment provided that all appeals could be made only to the
Court of Appeals of the District of Columbia. It further
provided that an appeal could be taken "by any other person, firm, or corporation aggrieved or whose interests are
adversely affected by any decision of the Commission." By
this amendment, another station, if adversely affected by
the assignment of a channel to a station, could now appeal
the decision.

One of the difficulties of court procedure in appeals
cases up to this time centered around the question as to
whether the court could review testimony, as well as
questions of law and findings of fact by the Commission.

---

[52]Public Law No. 25, 71st Congress. (S. 2276).

[53]Public Law No. 494, 71st Congress, an act to amend
sec. 16 of the Radio Act of 1927.

Section 16 (d) of the amendment stated:

> Review by the court shall be limited to questions of
> law and...findings of fact by the Commission, if supported
> by substantial evidence, shall be conclusive unless it
> shall clearly appear that the findings of the Commission
> are arbitrary and capricious.

Another change was made, in that

> the court's judgment shall be final, subject, however,
> to review by the Supreme Court of the United States
> upon writ of certiorari on petition therefor under
> section 346 of title 28 of the Judicial Code by appellant,
> by the Commission, or by any interested party interven-
> ing in the appeal.

The amendment thereby prevented the Court of Appeals

of the District of Columbia from considering a case <u>de novo</u>,

required a ruling on the record as sent up by the Commission,

and provided for review by the Supreme Court of the United

States, which had refused to review a decision of the Court

of Appeals of the District of Columbia on the grounds that

such a review would be essentially legislative or administra-

tive.[54]  After these laws were passed, no further legislation

vitally affecting radio broadcasting was enacted until the

passage of the Act creating the Federal Communications Com-

mission in 1934.

Thus, with little in the way of Congressional direct-

ive to guide it other than the fair and equitable distribu-

tions of frequencies to all parts of the nation according

to what it should consider to be in the public interest --

the Radio Commission was given the task of providing broadcast

---

[54]Federal Radio Commission <u>v</u>. <u>General Electric Company</u>,
<u>et al</u>., 281 U. U. 464-70.

service to the public. From the years 1928 to 1934, its
major efforts were in this direction. The Commission was
required to form a smooth and integrated national engineering
picture out of the jig-saw pieces that already happened to
exist, and that had come into being as the result of economic
rather than engineering factors. If it had been empowered to
call in all the licenses that had been distributed over the
years in order to redistribute them for the purpose of providing service to all parts of the country, using competent
engineering knowledge as a criterion and prepared to ignore
the anguished cries of broadcasters thus deprived of their
frequencies, it might have achieved saturation coveration
within two or three years. But even if it had succeeded in
such a plan, the results would probably have been the birth
of great numbers of economic cripples since out of the commercial system of broadcasting which had begun to evolve during those years, the economic factors which had ruled in the
first instance would have been bound to prevail in the end.

Questions relating to the broadcaster's competence or
eligibility to be a broadcaster were seldom considered. Although the Radio Act of 1927 gave the Commission the power to

> prescribe the nature of the services to be rendered...
> establish the areas to be served by each station...re-
> quire records of programs...prescribe as to...the purpose
> for which the station was to be used....

the Act was not at all clear as to what was actually intended
by this language, and indeed in a later paragraph the Act stated
that the Commission was under no circumstances to "censor"

programs. Nevertheless, Llewellyn White, in that portion of his book which delineates in brief form the history of Government regulation of radio, calls the span of years from 1927 to 1932 the "cleanup period," which indeed it was.[55] Whatever its other failings may have been, the newly formed and precariously maintained Commission did not lack courage or energy. It immediately began to follow up the "broad powers" concept of its enabling legislation by beginning to establish standards in specific cases which gave notice to broadcasting interests concerning the type of service they might be expected to provide. Indeed, in establishing certain of these standards, the Commission may have gone somewhat beyond the powers with which it had been provided. The Act was not at all clear on the question of whether the Commission might establish its own programming standards, yet, the Commission immediately attempted to exercise control over program content under the public interest interpretation.

The first of these precedent setting cases occurred in August 1928, when the Federal Radio Commission took positive action against "overcommercialization" by refusing license renewal to station WCRW (location not known). In its decision, the Commission stated that

> ...it is clear that a large part of the program is distinctly commercial in character, consisting of advertiser's announcements and of direct advertising. A very limited amount of educational and community civic service (is provided), but the amount of time thus employed is

---

[55]White, op. cit., pp. 126-127.

negligible. Manifestly this station is one which exists
chiefly for the purpose of deriving an income from the
sale of advertising of a character which must be objectionable to the listening public and without making
much, if any, endeavor to render any real service to
the public.[56]

We might conclude from this license deletion case that the
Federal Radio Commission had established a ruling that a
station which existed only to provide commercial programs and
which had largely failed to provide community service was not
entitled to renewal of its license to broadcast. Such a conclusion would indeed seem to be made on valid grounds, since
only a few days later, several additional stations were placed
on temporary license for similar "overcommercialization" --
though less extreme in character.

Although no court had been as yet called upon to decide whether or not the Federal Radio Commission possessed
the power to revoke a station's license on grounds dealing
with program content, a court ruling was soon to be made on
the question as to whether the Commission was within its
rights in refusing to renew the license of a station which
had broadcast a program on which indecent and profane language was used; such language being specifically proscribed
by the terms of the Act. This decision was made in what is
now known as the Schaeffer case (KVEP - Portland, Ore.). In
this proceeding the Commission decided that a radio licensee

---

[56]Federal Communications Commission, Public Service
Responsibilities of Broadcast Licensees (Washington:
Government Printing Office, 1946).

had full authority over, and full responsibility for, the
content of programs broadcast over his station. Because the
licensee had permitted the broadcasting of vicious and profane attacks on individuals or groups, on paid programs, the
Commission considered he had given sufficient cause for its
refusal to renew the station's license.

What had occurred in this instance was that, both prior
to and following an Oregon primary election in which he was
defeated as a candidate for Congress, Robert G. Duncan
broadcast a two hour program on paid time, six days a week
over station KVEP of Portland, Oregon, owned by William D.
Schaeffer. On receipt of complaints from various leading
Portland citizens concerning the content of the broadcasts,
the Radio Commission ordered a hearing on renewal of the
station's license. Evidence was brought out at the hearing
that Duncan had made vitriolic attacks on various individuals
and groups who had opposed him, using such terms as "damned"
and "by God" repeatedly in his attacks, including those made
in the series of broadcasts which followed the election.
Schaeffer contended that since he had sold time to Duncan,
he had no authority under the law to censor Duncan's material.
The Federal Radio Commission refused to support this contention, and in June 1930, terminated the station's license,
holding that Duncan had defamed and maligned "the character
of decent citizens by the direct use of profane and indecent
language" and that Schaeffer was responsible, since "as pro-
prietor of the station, he had full authority over all

programs broadcast." The station was thus taken off the air in 1930 -- the first station to lose its license as a result of the character of programs broadcast.

Duncan was later found guilty in a Federal District Court of using profane language in a radio broadcast, in violation of the Radio Act of 1927, and sentenced to serve six months in prison. Appeal was taken to the Federal Circuit Court of Appeals, which in March 1931 upheld the verdict of the lower court, denying Duncan's contention that the "no censorship by the Commission" clause in the Radio Act prohibited the assessment of any penalty for use of profane or indecent language in a broadcast.[57]

Again, in the Dr. Norman Baker (KTNT - Muscatine, Iowa, 1931) and Dr. John R. Brinkley (KFKB - Milford, Kansas, 1931) proceedings the FRC was successful in making its opinions stand in instances where it considered "indecent advertising" sufficient cause for refusal to renew a station license. In the Brinkley case the Commission was again upheld by the United States Court of Appeals, which ruled it might properly consider the "past performance" of a station licensee in passing upon a license renewal.[58] This case is of considerable importance since it gave court approval to the philosophy that the Commission had power to consider the

---

[57]Duncan v. United States, 48 F. (2d) 128, C.C.A. 9th (1931).

[58]KFKB Broadcasting Assoc. v. Federal Radio Commission, 47 F. (2d) 670, App. D. C. (1931).

past programming record of a station as relevant in cases of license renewal, and further gave the Commission opportunity to define and standardize what it expected "good programming" would comprise.

To examine the two cases briefly: In the <u>Dr. Norman Baker Case</u>, complaints had been filed with the Commission (during 1930) by the Iowa State Board of Health, the Iowa State Medical Association, and the American Medical Association, that station KTNT of Muscatine, Iowa, was being used by its owner, Dr. Norman Baker, to advertise a "cure" for cancer in his Muscatine hospital, and to "malign, abuse and falsify" the medical profession in talks delivered by Baker himself. Following a hearing in the spring of 1931, the Federal Radio Commission refused in June of that year to renew the station's license, stating:

> The record discloses that he (Baker) continually and erratically over the air rides a personal hobby, his cancer cure ideas and his likes and dislikes of certain persons and things. Many of his utterances are vulgar, if not indeed indecent...(His) personal and bitter attacks on individuals, companies and associations, whether warranted or unwarranted...have not been in the public interest.[59]

The station was taken off the air in 1931.

In the <u>Dr. John R. Brinkley Case</u>, station KFKB, of Milford, Kansas, had been used by its owner, Dr. Brinkley, to advertise his "goat gland" operation; also to present a "Medical Question Box" program in which Brinkley prescribed medicines for listeners who wrote to him describing their

---

[59]Louis G. Caldwell, <u>Annals of the American Academy</u>, Jan. 1935, p. 179.

symptoms by letter. Brinkley's unorthodox medical practices resulted in the revocation of his license to practice medicine by the State Medical Board in July 1930, and complaints filed by the American Medical Association caused the Federal Radio Commission to order a hearing on renewal of the license of his station the same year. Following the hearing, the FRC refused in the autumn of 1930 to grant renewal of the KFKB license, holding that Brinkley had broadcast "obscene and indecent" materials in advertising his "goat gland" operation, and that the practice of giving prescriptions over the air was "personal communication" rather than broadcasting, in violation of the station's license.

Brinkley appealed the FRC's decision to the federal courts. In 1931, the United States Court of Appeals for the District of Columbia upheld the Commission's ruling, finding that the views of the FRC on the medical programs of the station were "reasonable," and that the Commission has the right to consider past performances of a licensee in ruling on renewal of a broadcast license, without such consideration violating the censorship provisions of the Act.[60]

The last of the important cases in which the FRC, in refusing renewal of a license, objected to the nature of the materials broadcast by the licensee was the so-called Shuler Case, in which station KGEF, of Los Angeles, licensed to the

---

[60]Supra, KFKB Broadcasting Assoc. v. Federal Radio Commission (1931).

Trinity Methodist Church, South, was used chiefly to broadcast sermons and talks by the Pastor of the Church, Rev.
Robert P. Shuler.  Reverend Shuler had carried over the air
a continuous campaign against individuals or organizations
of which he disapproved -- the Jewish race, the Catholic
Church, Christian Science, the local Chamber of Commerce, and
the Salvation Army, among others.  In 1930, he was convicted
of contempt of court for attempting, by his radio broadcasts,
to influence the court's decision in a pending criminal
action.  In 1931, the Federal Radio Commission held a hearing
on renewal of the station's license; following the hearing,
in November 1931 the FRC refused to grant license renewal to
the station, one ground of action being that Shuler had
"repeatedly made attacks upon public officials and the courts"
and "had vigorously attacked by name all organizations,
political parties, public officials and individuals whom he
conceived to be moral enemies of society."

Shuler appealed the FRC decision to the courts,
charging that the FRC's denial of the station's license
violated the Constitutional guarantee of free speech.  In a
1932 decision, the United States Court of Appeals for the
District of Columbia upheld the Radio Commission, ruling that

> ...denial of license was neither censorship nor pre-
> vious restraint.  Appellant may continue to indulge his
> strictures upon the characters of men in public office,
> may criticize religious practices of which he does not
> approve, may even indulge private malice or personal
> slander -- but he may not, as we think, demand of right,

the continued use of an instrument of commerce for
such purposes.[61]

Shuler appealed next to the United States Supreme Court,
which, in January 1933, denied his petition for review of the
decision of the lower court.

It is to be noted in these cases, that while the FRC's
record in court was good in all instances, at least one or two
of the reasons that the Commission gave for refusing to renew
in each case were specifically listed as grounds for revocation in the Act. The Act specifically forbade broadcast
stations to indulge in "point to point," or "personal" communication, to employ "obscene or indecent" language, or to
deviate from assigned frequencies or fail to employ the prescribed technical equipment provisions of the Commission.
But in addition to reliance on these points, it is equally
clear from our analysis that the Commission was attempting to
go beyond grounds for revocation specifically listed in the
Act, and to provide a set of programming standards of its
own.

More important yet, in one of its earliest cases
which came to be known as the Great Lakes Application
Decision, the Federal Radio Commission at least laid the
groundwork for a development of a set of standards in relation
to programming. The opinion in the Great Lakes case provides
one of the best statements of the Federal Radio Commission's

[61]Trinity Methodist Church South v. Federal Radio
Commission, 62 F. (2d) 850, App. D. C. (1932).

concept of the responsibilities of a station licensee.

Similar philosophies have been followed by the Federal Com-

munications Commission since 1934. Excerpts from the

opinion follow:

> Broadcasting stations are licensed to serve the public
> and not for the purpose of furthering the private inter-
> ests of individuals or groups of individuals. The only
> exception to this rule has to do with advertising...be-
> cause advertising furnishes the economic support for the
> service and thus makes it possible. (But) the amount and
> character of advertising must be rigidly confined within
> limits consistent with the public service expected of the
> station...if a broadcasting station (like a telegraph
> company) had to accept and transmit...anything and every-
> thing any member of the public might desire to communi-
> cate to the listening public...the public would be de-
> prived of the advantages of the self-imposed censorship
> exercised by the program directors of broadcasting sta-
> tions who, for the sake of the  popularity and standing
> of their stations, will select entertainment and educa-
> tional features according to the needs and desires of
> their invisible audiences....
>
> The service rendered by broadcasting stations must be
> without discrimination as between its listeners...the
> entire listening public within the service area of a
> station is entitled to service from that station. If,
> therefore, all the programs transmitted are intended for,
> and interesting or valuable to, only a small portion of
> that public, the rest of the listeners are being dis-
> criminated against....The tastes, needs and desires of
> all substantial groups among the listening public should
> be met, in some fair proportion, by a well rounded pro-
> gram in which entertainment...religion, education and
> instruction, important public events, discussions of pub-
> lic questions...news, and matters of interest to all
> members of the family find a place. With so few channels
> in the spectrum and so few hours in the day, there are
> obvious limitations on the emphasis which can be appro-
> priately placed on any portion of the program....
>
> In such a scheme there is no place for the operation
> of broadcasting stations exclusively by, or in the private
> interests of, individuals or groups so far as the nature
> of the programs is concerned. There is not room in the
> broadcast band for every school of thought, religious,
> political and economic, each to have its separate broad-
> casting station....Propaganda stations...are not consistent

with the most beneficial sort of discussion of public questions....[62]

In the early 1930's, the Federal Radio Commission gave effect to the standards it had laid down in the Great Lakes case in numerous comparative hearings. Prior to 1930, most stations had been licensed to operate on a part-time basis, sharing a channel with one or more other stations in the same or in nearby communities. By 1930, stations began to apply to the FRC for authority for full-time operation -- usually on the channel assigned to them for part-time operation. In each case, if full-time authorization was given, it could only be at the expense of other stations authorized for part-time operation on the same channel, and such stations had to be taken off the air. Consequently, the FRC inaugurated the practice of holding comparative hearings to determine which one of the two to four competing licensees for part-time operation on a given channel should be allowed to continue on that channel on a full-time basis, and which other or others should be taken off the air. Typical of these were the so-called Brooklyn cases; important too, was the deletion of station KWBG in Nebraska -- partially on the basis of advertising carried by the station; highly important also was one case in which WOW, Omaha, had asked for full time, involving the deletion of a non-commercial educational station owned by Nebraska Wesleyan University in Lincoln which was actually

---

[62]Great Lakes Broadcasting Co., Federal Radio Commission Docket 4900 (1928).

on the air only an hour or so a day.  The FRC concluded that
the WOW service was "superior" to that of the Lincoln station
and deleted the latter.[63]

Taking all these factors into consideration then,
it can be concluded that the 1927 Act did in fact lay down
only "broad principles" for the Federal Radio Commission to
employ, and that the Commission did make a beginning at least
in working out the "detailed standards" that were implied in
its passage.  Even though about one in ten of the many hundreds of cases it considered and decided upon underwent subsequent court appeal, the Commission's record of success
emanating from these appeals was a good one, clearly
demonstrating to both Congress and the industry the absolute
necessity of its continuance as a permanent regulatory body.

---

[63]This one action was heavily used by those advocates
of the 25% of-all-broadcast-channels-to-education bill (the
Wagner-Hatfield group) which will be discussed in the
following chapter.

CHAPTER III

THE EVENTS LEADING UP TO THE ABOLITION OF THE
FEDERAL RADIO COMMISSION AND THE ESTABLISHMENT
OF THE FEDERAL COMMUNICATIONS COMMISSION

### 1. First Attempts at Passage of a Comprehensive Bill - H. R. 7716

In an article appearing in the American Political
Science Review, Carl J. Friedrich and Evelyn Sternberg
state:

> For some years, various Government officials had ex-
> pressed an interest in the establishment of an overall
> commission concerned with communications. The existing
> setup was unsatisfactory, since authority was divided be-
> tween the ICC and FRC and the Department of Commerce.
> In 1932-33, a legislative attempt to combine the Radio
> Division of the Department of Commerce with the Commis-
> sion was stymied by President Hoover's pocket veto after
> the bill had been passed by both Houses.[1]

This attempted legislation marks a most important step
along the way toward establishment of the FCC in 1934. The
bill which President Hoover refused to sign was H. R. 7716,
and a great many of the provisions of the Act of 1934 derive
from it. H. R. 7716, as it came from the House of Representatives, provided for the amendment of twelve different sections
of the Radio Act of 1927.[2] An examination of the Senate

---

[1]"Congress and the Control of Radio Broadcasting,"
The American Political Science Review, vol. 27, no. 5,
(October 1943), p. 801.

[2]Report to accompany H. R. 7716, submitted by Mr.
Davis (H. Rept. 221, 72d Cong., 1st sess.).

62

report will suffice to study the bill both as it emerged from
the House and as it was amended by the Senate since the Senate report gives both House and Senate versions.[3]

The bill as it left the House amended the Radio Act
of 1927 by clarifying and amplifying provisions dealing
chiefly with Commission procedure and administrative function.
It also contained several entirely new provisions. The most
important changes recommended in H. R. 7716 pertained to the
following:

a) A fixed term for the Chairman of the Commission.
The amendment of section 3 of the Act provided for a fixed
term for the Chairman instead of an indefinite period and also
provided for a Vice Chairman to function in the event of ab-
sence or disability of the Chairman.

b) Changes in the wave length of power of a station
could no longer be made without a hearing. (Sec. 4, par. (f)
of the existing law. Under this section no hearing was required.)

c) An outline of procedure for hearings. Paragraph (k)
of section 4 was amended by setting forth more particularly
the methods the Commission should employ in the conduct of its
hearings. It specifically authorized holding of public hearings, provided that they could be held at any designated
place, and designated who might hold such hearings and the
limits of their authority in so doing. This amendment, as

---

[3]Senate report to accompany H. R. 7716, submitted by
r. Dill (S. Rept. 1045, 72d Cong., 2d sess.).

further revised by the Senate, was the subject of prolonged
debate in both Houses, and considerable comment in the press.[4]

The Senate committee had amended the House text of the
bill by striking out those words which authorized all hearings to be held by "examiners or other employees of the Commission" and restricted the use of examiners in the holding
of hearings. (Under existing law at the time the amendment
was offerred, the Commission had assumed authority to empower the examiners it had appointed to hold hearings, since
the Radio Act of 1927 simply provided that the Commission
"should hold hearings," and stated that "examiners are among
those that may be appointed by the Commission.") In offering
the revised amendment, the Senate report commented:

> During recent months the Commission has directed that
> examiners hold practically all hearings. In some cases
> parties to contests before the Commission have found it
> impossible to secure hearings before the Commission after
> an examiner had taken all the testimony. Under present
> procedure there seems to be little justification for the
> continuation of five Commissioners unless the Commission-
> ers are to conduct the hearings and do the work originally
> intended by the law. If this policy is to continue, it
> would seem to be in the interest of economy to cut the
> Commission to three members or to a director of radio.
>
> Your committee believes it more desirable that the
> Commission should hold all important hearings and secure
> more personal knowledge of contests by this method, and
> for that reason has provided that all hearings on major
> radio questions shall be held by the Commission, or by a
> Commissioner, or by a number of the Commissioners as the
> Commission may designate.
>
> An amendment to the House text provides that the Com-
> mission may authorize an examiner to hold certain hearings,
> but that in such cases the Commission shall permit an oral
> argument on the request of either party.

---

[4]Broadcasting Magazine, January 1, 1933, p. 5.

H. R. 7716 also provided for the levying of fines in
cases of law violation by the Federal Radio Commission. In
regard to an amendment of section 14 of the Radio Act, relating to the revocation of licenses, the Senate report stated:

> The House language provided for revocation, modifica-
> tion, or suspension. Your committee believes that a fine
> is preferable to modification or suspension, and has pro-
> vided that licenses may be revoked or the owners fined,
> not to exceed $1,000, in case of violation of the law.

This amendment, along with the amendment providing for the
elimination or reduction of Commissioners, was bitterly fought
by the radio industry. In testimony before the Senate Interstate Commerce Committee on December 22 and 23, Henry A.
Bellows, CBS vice president, stated:

> New and most alarming powers to suspend stations would
> be given the Commission under the proposed amendment
> authorizing it to suspend stations as well as revoke or
> modify licenses. Stations survive on their advertising
> revenues, and a 30-day suspension would mean termination
> of contracts and probably the "ruin" of certain stations.
> The public would be the obvious victim, since it would
> be deprived of the station's service....

Mr. Bellows concurred in a statement by Chairman Couzens
(Republican of Michigan) that "A fine would be preferable to
a suspension and would serve the same purpose."[5]

In addition to the foregoing provisions, H. R. 7716
also provided for a revision in the procedure for appeals.
Section 10 substituted for section 16 of the radio law a
stipulation very similar to that which had existed when the
Act was originally passed in 1927 "in order to provide a more
efficacious procedure in appeals." Provisions were added

---

[5]Ibid., p. 15.

that gave the licensee, whose license had been revoked, or
the owner, who had been fined, the right of appeal in the
lower district court. Thereby, he would no longer have been
required to bring the case to Washington, D. C., to prosecute
his appeals in the Court of Appeals of the District of Columbia. It was stated that this kind of provision would result
in submittal of questions of radio law to judges of the
district courts and circuit courts of appeals instead of all
radio law questions having to be passed upon by the Court of
Appeals of the District of Columbia. The committee report
stated: "This is especially important from the standpoint of
building up a series of legal interpretations of radio law
by different inferior courts of the United States."

Section 13 contained a new provision requiring that
no person should broadcast "any information concerning any
lottery, gift enterprise, or similar scheme, offering prizes
dependent in whole or in part upon lot or chance, etc." The
committee report stated:

> The committee does not think that the United States
> should permit any radio station, licensed and regulated
> by the Government, to engage in such unlawful practices.
> Furthermore, the broadcast of such information is unfair
> to the newspapers, which are forbidden the use of the
> mails, if they contain such information.

Section 14 of H. R. 7716 struck out section 18 of the
Radio Act of 1927 in regard to treatment of political candidates
for public office, and substituted for it the following intent:

> The purpose of this amendment is to extend the re-
> quirement of equality of treatment of political candidates
> to supporters and opponents of candidates, and public
> questions before the people or a legislature or city

council for a vote.  It also prohibits any increased charge for political speeches.

No station owner is required to permit the use of his station for any of these purposes, but if a station permits one candidate or the supporters or opponents of a candidate, or of a public question upon which the people are to vote, then the requirement of equality of treatment and of no higher rates than the ordinary advertising rates shall be charged.

These in summary form are the more important changes in the text of the Radio Act of 1927 that were suggested in the separate House and Senate versions of H. R. 7716.

The conference report on the bill removed many of the more controversial provisions.[6]  These major revisions involved:

a) The provision in the House bill which authorized any examiner or other officer or employee, when designated by the Commission, to hold hearings without limitation.  In lieu of this, an amendment was inserted authorizing the Commission to empower examiners to hold hearings in certain restricted instances, and further provided "that in all cases heard by an examiner the Commission shall grant oral arguments on request of either party."

b) A provision was added (sec. 10) requiring that all opinions or memorandum opinions filed by the Commissions in support of its decisions be entered on record, and such record made public on request of any party interested.

c) The Commission was empowered to grant additional

---

[6]Conference report to accompany H. R. 7716, submitted by Mr. Davis of Tennessee (H. Rept. 2106, 72d Cong., 2d sess.).

licenses for stations not exceeding 100 watts, "if the public interest would be served thereby and interference with
other stations would not result" (sec. 16, amending sec. 9 of
the 1927 Act).    The report stated:

> The purpose of this amendment is to permit the Com-
> mission to license local stations in areas which, on
> account of topography, distances from existing broadcast-
> ing stations, or their conditions, are without adequate
> radio service....

d) The provision that a station license could be modified or suspended, as well as a fine imposed, was changed so
that no more than a fine, not to exceed $1,000 for each day's
violation, could be handed down.

e) Fifteen days was substituted for the wording "a
reasonable opportunity" with respect to the time allowed to
show cause why a revocation should not be issued or a fine
imposed.

f) The conferees substituted the Circuit Court of
Appeals for the District Court in regard to the filing of
appeals to any order of the Commission revoking a station
license or fining a station owner.

As was mentioned earlier, once the bill had passed in
final version in both the House and Senate it was pocket vetoed
by the President.  Although he did not divulge his reasons for
vetoing the bill officially, an unofficial interpretation of
his reasons for doing so is given in Broadcasting:

> It was ascertained at the White House that, following
> usual practice, the retiring President inquired of the
> Radio Commission whether there were objections to the bill....
>
> The Commission, it was learned, replied among other
> things that the provision limiting the authority of the

examiners would require that the Commission or a Commissioner hold probably 80 percent of all hearings; that the provision for new 100-watt stations was ambiguous since it was not clear as to whether the Davis amendment applied, and that the new court provisions permitting appeals from Commission decisions to circuit courts throughout the country would necessitate additional employees.[7]

Regardless of its ultimate failure to become law, however, H. R. 7716 had an extremely important effect upon the legislation that was to be enacted by the Congress and to be signed by the new President in just a few months' time. The debate in connection with H. R. 7716 and the legislative compromises that marked its passage in both Houses would serve to put in better focus the issues before the Congress in the new session.

## 2. The President Requests Congress to Enact Comprehensive Broadcast and Communications Legislation

In the summer of 1933, at the suggestion of the President, the Hon. Daniel C. Roper, then Secretary of Commerce, appointed an Interdepartmental Committee on Communications to consider a national communications policy. The committee was to conduct

...what the President stated should be a study -- not an investigation -- of the present condition of what we are accustomed to call "the communications" related primarily to interdepartmental service.[8]

---

[7]Broadcasting Magazine, March 15, 1933, p. 30.

[8]Statement of Hon. Daniel C. Roper, Secretary of Commerce, before the House of Representatives Committee on Interstate and Foreign Commerce hearings on H. R. 8301, Tuesday, April 10, 1934, pp. 1-2.

In its report that Committee recommended the establishment of
a Federal Communications Commission to which should be transferred (a) the jurisdiction of the Interstate Commerce Commission over common carriers by wire or wireless; and (b)
the jurisdiction of the Federal Radio Commission, and of the
Postmaster General over telegraph companies and telegraph
lines.[9]

After consideration of the confidential report of the
Committee, which was submitted to him in December, 1933, Mr.
Roosevelt, on February 26, 1934, sent the following message
to Congress:

> I have long felt that for the sake of clarity and
> effectiveness the relationship of the Federal Government
> to certain services known as "utilities" should be divi-
> ded into three fields: Transportation, power, and com-
> munications. The problems of transportation are vested
> in the Interstate Commerce Commission, and the problem
> of power, its development, transmission, and distribution,
> in the Federal Power Commission.
>
> In the field of communications, however, there is today
> no single Government agency charged with broad authority.
>
> The Congress has vested certain authority over certain
> forms of communications in the Interstate Commerce Com-
> mission, and there is in addition the agency known as the
> "Federal Radio Commission."
>
> I recommend that the Congress create a new agency to
> be known as the "Federal Communications Commission,"
> such agency to be vested with the authority now lying in
> the Federal Radio Commission and with such authority over
> communications as now lie with the Interstate Commerce
> Commission -- the services affected to be all of those
> which rely on wires, cables, or radio as a medium of
> transmission.
>
> It is my thought that a new Commission such as I sug-
> gest might well be organized this year by transferring

---

[9]Broadcasting Magazine, December 15, 1933, p. 5.

the present authority for the control of communications
of the Radio Commission and the Interstate Commerce Commission. The new body should, in addition, be given full
power to investigate and study the business of existing
companies and make recommendations to the Congress for
additional legislation at the next session.

Franklin D. Roosevelt.

THE WHITE HOUSE, February 26, 1934.[10]

The letter of the President contained two key phrases:
that the "present authority" of the FRC and ICC should be
transferred to the new Commission, and "the new body should
be given full power to investigate and study...and make recommendations to the Congress for additional legislation at the
next session." Because of this language, many Congressmen,
in particular Congressman Rayburn, chairman of the House committee which would consider any bill, felt that what the
President wanted and what Congress should give him was minimum legislation, leaving the more controversial issues open
for the new Commission to study with a view to further legislation. Therefore, "With the approval of the President, Senator Dill (D. of Washington) and Representative Rayburn (D. of
Texas) started drafting bills, after agreement that controversial subjects should be omitted."[11]

In fact, after a White House conference with the
President, Senator Dill said:

---

[10]Message (of the President) recommending that Congress
create a new agency to be known as the FCC. 1 p. (S. Doc. 144,
73rd Cong., 2d sess.)

[11]Friedrich and Sternberg, op. cit., p. 801.

It is far wiser to let the proposed Commission have
power to make these studies than try to have Congress
legislate on intricate and complex aspects of the communications program at this time. If we leave out the
controversial matters, the bill can be passed at this
session of Congress; otherwise it cannot.[12]

### 3. S. 2190

In line with the wishes of the President, both Houses

of Congress immediately set to work drawing up separate bills

calling for the creation of a new Commission. The Senate

bill, originally S. 2190 but later designated S. 3285, was

given the most extensive hearings, but the version which

passed both Houses and was signed into law by the President

more closely approximated the non-controversial companion

House bill, H. R. 8301. In spite of all intentions to the

contrary, the Senate bill (S. 2190) immediately became a

center of debate. Dr. Friedrich states that the major reason

for this controversy arose out of the fact that "it called

for the repeal of the Radio Act of 1927." And that "under

this act, the industry had jockeyed itself into a position

of legal security which would be lost if the act were re-

pealed."[13]

As early as March 1, 1934, Broadcasting indicated the

concern of the industry toward the Senate bill in an article

which stated:

Despite previous announcements that the proposed legislation would simply consolidate the present Radio Act

---

[12]Broadcasting Magazine, February 15, 1934, p. 5.
[13]Friedrich and Sternberg, op. cit., p. 801.

with those provisions of the Interstate Commerce Act
relating to wire and radio communications, the measure
introduced by Senator Dill...of Washington, is regarded
as far from "uncontroversial" insofar as the broadcasting industry is concerned....

The Dill measure embodies practically every amendment
proposed in the last few years in Congress against which
broadcasting interests have protested. That the NAB, in
behalf of the industry, will vigorously resist passage of
the bill as introduced is a foregone conclusion.

In the hearings held in the Senate committee on March 9, 10,
13, and 15, 1934, the following provisions of the bill were
a subject of controversial testimony:[14]

a) Section 307 (b) of the Senate bill, which provided
that no channel should be reserved for the use of one station
for a distance of more than 2,200 airlines miles. It provided further that such additional stations as might have
licenses granted them should not be charged to the quota of
the States in which they were located.[15] Witnesses complained
in committee hearings that this provision would automatically
delete all clear-channel stations operating on the Nation's
coastlines, and that it would allow the indiscriminate
licensing of 250-watt stations throughout the country. Additional testimony was elicited that the Davis amendment had not
effectively brought about an equal division of broadcast

---

[14]U. S. Congress, Senate, Committee on Interstate and
Foreign Commerce. For Regulation of Interstate and Foreign
Commerce by Wire or Radio, (S.2190), Part III, 73rd Cong., 2d
Sess. (Washington: Government Printing Office, 1934).

[15]Public Law No. 195, 70th Cong., created the so-called
Davis amendment, which required allocation of radio stations
in equal amounts to all zones in the Nation.

stations to each geographical area in the Nation and should, itself, be repealed instead of retained.

b) The license terms of stations were to be decreased according to the Senate bill from a three-year period allowed by the Radio Act of 1927, to a one-year period. (Licenses at that time ran only six months, although the Commission could, if it chose, take advantage of the three-year provision.) The industry, naturally, preferred a longer provision of license tenure and, therefore, opposed a legislative provision limiting license span to one year.

c) Authorization was made to the Commission to fine stations a maximum of $1,000 per day for making false statements in applications, and to levy such fines without hearings.

d) A new provision (sec. 315 (b) and (c)) tightened up the rules for political speeches, against which many stations had been protesting because of existing libel laws. It provided that speeches and discussions of public questions could not be censored by station owers, and further specified that the rates charged by stations would be regular commercial rates.

e) A further provision in the Senate bill, in addition to the provision enabling a fine to be levied, gave the Commission power to suspend station licenses in instances of violation of regulations, if it was felt that license revocation would be a too drastic punishment.

f) The procedural and administrative provisions of the Act were entirely rewritten and made to conform more nearly

to Interstate Commerce Commission procedure. District courts
throughout the country, instead of the Court of Appeals of
the District of Columbia were again to become the appellate
bodies.[16]

To a very considerable extent, the testimony of Henry
A. Bellows, former Radio Commissioner and subsequent vice
president of CBS, typified the type of industry opposition
toward this version of the bill. Similarly, Chairman Sykes,
of the Federal Radio Commission, pointed out where that body
stood in connection with certain of its provisions.[17]  Mr.
Bellows based his testimony principally on the grounds that
the radio section of the Senate bill was in direct conflict
with the suggestion of President Roosevelt that the measure
be uncontroversial.[18]  He thereupon suggested that the
whole radio section of S. 2190 be stricken out and that the
provision of the Rayburn bill (H. R. 8301) which would simply
abolish the Radio Commission and transfer its functions to
the new agency be substituted.  Mr. Bellows went on to criticize the clear-channel breakdown proposal, stating:

> If it fixes by statute the mileage separation between
> highpowered stations, why not do exactly the same thing

---

[16]Both procedures had been recommended earlier at one
time or another in the drafting and amending of the Radio Act
of 1927, as has been discussed earlier, but, from the time of
passage of Public Law No. 494 of the 71st Cong., appeals had
been brought to the Court of Appeals of the District of Columbia.

[17]Hearings on the "broadcasting phase" of S. 2190 were
held and completed on March 9, 1934.  See testimony of Henry
A. Bellows and E. O. Sykes.

[18]Supra, p. 70, see the President's message.

for the regionals and locals? We have no specific quar-
rel with 2,200 miles, but we do protest most earnestly
against this basic change in the whole theory of the
Radio Act....We believe that the new Commission should be
free to deal with its technical engineering problem in its
own way....What this section actually does is to put Congress into the electrical engineering profession, with a
provision which may be a serious burden upon the new Commission before Congress can possibly get round to changing it.[19]

The same objection, the witness asserted, applied to the

250-watt station provision. He pointed out that the Commis-

sion, under the present Act, was free to do approximately what

the provision suggested, and that the "quota" system was not

mentioned, as such, in the existing Act, but was purely

...a bit of administrative machinery set up by the
Commission -- and a bit of machinery, be it said in passing, which already creaks so much that the Commission is
now in the process of overhauling it.[20]

Mr. Bellows attacked the provision which would have re-

duced the maximum term of broadcasting licenses from three

years to one year in these words:

The short-term license has been a serious barrier to
the technical advance of radio, but at least there has
always been the consolation that Congress recognized the
ultimate desirability of giving some semblance of stab-
ility to the business by authorizing licenses for as
much as three years....

Now, after seven years, it is proposed to destroy that
hope, and to tell the new Commission that broadcasting
must remain unstable, hazardous, unable to look ahead with
any assurance or confidence.[21]

---

[19]Ibid., Hearings before the Committee on Interstate
Commerce, U. S. Senate, 73rd Cong., 2d sess., on S. 2910, a
bill to provide for the regulation of interstate and foreign
communications by wire or radio, and for other purposes,
March 9, 10, 13, 14, and 15, 1934, pp. 56-57.

[20]Ibid., p. 57.     [21]Ibid., p. 58.

On the subject of the controversial "revocation" clause, the
witness stated the bill seemed to reverse the entire theory
of the Radio Act that a licensee should have his "day in
court." He asserted that the measure did not provide for a
hearing. Senator Dill objected to this interpretation, and
declared that a hearing was provided for. Mr. Bellows nevertheless asked that the provisions then in effect in the Radio
Act of 1927 be retained and the amendment deleted. He
stated: "We feel that it is utterly foreign to the whole
spirit of the Radio Act to set up such an arbitrary power of
radio life and death as is provided in this section." Vigor-
ous objection was also voiced by the same witness to the provision for a $1,000-a-day fine for violation of radio regu-
lations. The allegation was made that it would turn the Commission into a "radio police court."

On the political section of the bill, the witness
testified it would prohibit debate of public questions on
the air, and damage the usefulness of radio. In the light of
practical experience, he said that the present political
section needed revision, either to safeguard the right of
free speech or to protect the broadcasters,

> ...but, certainly, we do not want to see our liability
> for slander increased to a point where we shall have to
> bar all candidates for public office and all their sup-
> porters, and all discussion of public questions to be
> voted on at an election from the air.[22]

When the time came for Chairman Sykes to testify, he

---

[22]Ibid., p. 63.

informed the committee that the Radio Commission endorsed the
proposal for a Communications Commission, but he, too, opposed
the provision having to do with the breakdown of clear
channels, and similarly opposed the additional licensing of
250-watt stations without charging them up to quota.[23]  Chairman Sykes further recommended a revision of the jurisdiction
of the three divisions proposed in the Senate bill.[24]  He suggested that the radio division be called the radio broadcast
division and that its jurisdiction be limited to broadcasting
and amateur service.  (The Senate bill added mobile services.)
Where the Senate bill proposed that each division of the
Commission should have specialized jurisdiction and that the
whole Commission should have jurisdiction over all matters
which did not fall under one or more of the divisions, Judge
Sykes proposed that the full Commission handle the assignment
of frequencies or bands of frequencies to the various radio
services rather than let such allocations rest with any
single division.  "All radio services," he said in explanation, "must use a common medium and the type of service is
not necessarily the criterion of interference.  This change
will avoid conflicts of jurisdiction between divisions."[25]

---

[23]Ibid., pp. 37-47.

[24]The Senate bill would have created a Commission of
seven members which would take over all of the functions of
the Radio Commission, Interstate Commerce Commission, and other agencies dealing with radio, cables, and telegraph, the
Chairman to be a general member, with the three divisions, radio,
telephone, and telegraph, to be presided over by two Commissioners, one of whom would be a Vice Chairman.  A similar provision
was contained in H. R. 7716.

[25]Ibid., p. 38.

He recommended the deletion of the "Davis amendment"
in the following words:

> The provision of the bill which contains the Davis
> amendment to the original section 9 of the Radio Act of
> 1927 is contrary to natural laws and results in concen-
> tration of the use of frequencies in centers of popula-
> tion and a restriction of facilities in sparsely popu-
> lated States, even though interferences would permit the
> operation of one or more additional stations. Because
> of the size of the zones this distribution results in
> providing ample broadcasting service in small zones and
> lack of service in large zones. Experience has provided
> that the section as proposed is very difficult of admin-
> istration and cannot result in an equality of radio
> broadcasting service. In the provision suggested, service
> is made an important criterion, making it possible to
> carry out the statutory provisions of public interest,
> convenience, and necessity without artificial
> restrictions.[26]

Finally, in connection with the proposed shift of
appeals cases from the Court of Appeals of the District of
Columbia to other Federal Courts, the witness said the Commission had experienced good results under section 16 of the
old bill and that he felt it was essential in the new bill:

> A consistent body of radio jurisprudence has grown up.
> A single court has become well informed concerning a
> technical subject. It would seem desirable to continue
> to afford a direct method of appeal in the two instances
> provided for and such continuance would not give rise to

---

[26]Ibid., pp. 39-40. The Davis amendment, passed in
1928 as an amendment to the Radio Act of 1927, required the
Federal Radio Commission to allocate radio frequencies and
license broadcast stations on such a basis as would provide
equal broadcast service to all parts of the Nation. For this
purpose, the amendment divided up the Nation into five zones.
Because of the arbitrary manner in which these zones had been
established -- one which ignored the density of population in
the respective zones, consequent economic factors, and geographical realities, the Commission experienced considerable
difficulty in making the so-called zonal allocation system
come out right, and there were always great numbers of
complaints from sections which claimed they were being deprived of broadcasting service.

any claim of discrimination by other persons or carriers
subject to the jurisdiction of the proposed Communications
Commission.[27]

After the testimony had been presented in the five
days of hearing on the bill, it was evident that the industry
felt it had done an adequate job of refuting its more controversial provisions.  On March 15, Broadcasting stated:

Bearing out predictions made immediately after the
bill was introduced last month, new broadcasting provisions of the measure were sharply criticized in behalf of the broadcasting industry and, in some instances,
by the Radio Commission itself.  The result was that a
conciliatory attitude was taken by committee members,
notably Chairman Dill (D. of Washington), author of the
measure, and it seemed apparent that most, if not all,
of the amendments would be deleted or altered so as to
minimize opposition.[28]

### 4.  The Wagner-Hatfield Amendment

In the article "Congress and the Control of Radio
Broadcasting" Friedrich and Sternberg state:

The greatest controversy (over S. 2910, which had
been amended and changed to S. 3285) was over the so-
called Wagner-Hatfield amendment, which would require
that 25 percent of facilities be allotted to religious,
cultural, agricultural, cooperative, labor, and similar
nonprofit organizations.[29]  Variety reported that "the
NAB were in a panic checking off names of Senators and
trying to pull wires to get votes."  The NAB wrote to
all Senators asking them "not to destroy the whole
structure of American broadcasting."[30]

The wording of the amendment, which was offered from

---

[27]Ibid., p. 44.

[28]Broadcasting Magazine, March 15, 1934, p. 7.

[29]Friedrich and Sternberg, op. cit., p. 802.

[30]Variety, May 22, 1934.

the Senate floor on May 15, 1934, was as follows:[31]

To eliminate monopoly and to insure equality of opportunity and consideration for educational, religious,
agricultural, labor, cooperative, and similar non-profit-
making associations, seeking the opportunity of adding
to the cultural and scientific knowledge of those who
listen in on radio broadcasts, all existing radio broadcasting licenses issued by the Federal Radio Commission,
and any and all rights of any nature contained therein,
are declared null and void 90 days following the effective date of this act, anything contained in this act to
the contrary notwithstanding.

The Commission shall, prior to 90 days following the
effective date of this act, reallocate all frequencies,
power, and time assignments within its jurisdiction among
the five zones herein referred to.

The Commission shall reserve and allocate only to
educational, religious, agricultural, labor, cooperative,
and similar non-profit-making associations one-fourth of
all the radio broadcasting facilities within its jurisdiction. The facilities reserved for, or allocated to,
educational, religious, agricultural, labor, cooperative,
and similar non-profit-making associations shall be
equally as desirable as those assigned to profitmaking
persons, firms, or corporations. In the distribution of
radio facilities to the associations referred to in this
section, the Commission shall reserve for and allocate
to such associations such radio broadcasting facilities
as will reasonably make possible the operation of such
stations on a self-sustaining basis, and to that end the
licensee may sell such part of the allotted time as will
make the station self-supporting.

Senator Dill, chairman of the Interstate Commerce

Committee, opposed the measure, although he himself claimed

to be in favor of educational broadcasting, and argued that

the so-called noncommercial stations, in order to be self-

supporting, would have to sell about 75 percent of their

time. His solution was to require commercial stations to

---

[31]Congressional Record, vol. 78, pt. 8, p. 8828.

give a certain percentage of their time to nonprofit organizations.[32] After four hours of heated debate, the amendment
was defeated on the floor by a vote of 42 to 23.[33] Upon its
defeat there was no further opposition to the Senate bill and
S. 3285 was thereupon passed by the Senate without a record
vote.[34]

### 5. The Senate Report on S. 3285

In order to see more clearly what were the major
differences between Senate and House versions of the Federal
Communications Bill both Senate and House hearing committee
reports on the bill will be analyzed in the following pages.
This analysis is important in our study of the evolution of
congressional intent in the drafting of this legislation
because it will serve to point out what the major points of
view were and how these were later modified by the conference
committee.

The report on the Senate bill (originally designated
as S. 2910, later changed to S. 3285) was issued on April 17,
1934, after many changes made as the result of conferences

---

[32]Congressional Record, 73rd Cong., 2d sess., May 15,
1934, p. 8828 ff. In lieu of the Wagner-Hatfield proposal,
the Senate adopted a provision proposed by Senator Dill authorizing the new Commission to study the proposal that Congress by statute allocate fixed percentages of facilities to
particular types of nonprofit activities, and report to Congress not later than February 1, 1935, its recommendations.

[33]Ibid., p. 8846.     [34]Ibid., p. 8854.

with representatives from the ICC, Radio Commission, and the State Department.[35] The Senate report states that, in the original framing of the bill, two courses were open -- one would have been "to prepare a detailed and practical bill which incorporated all legislation pertinent to the subject." The other was "to draft a short bill creating the Commission and delegating to it...the powers now vested in the Radio Commission, the Interstate Commerce Commission, and the Postmaster General."[36]

The Senate bill chose to "take the longer, more detailed course" so as to give "definite statutory provisions" to the new Commission.[37] It was also felt that there were certain inherent weaknesses in the Interstate Commerce Act insofar as it applied to radio communications, that these weaknesses would continue if legislation merely transferred the powers of the ICC to the new Commission. Those who drafted the bill were particularly concerned that "under existing provisions of the Interstate Commerce Act the regulation of the telephone monopoly has been practically nil," and that "this vast monopoly which so immediately serves the needs of the people in their daily and social life must be effectively regulated." The report went on to say that

no Government organization can provide such regulation without a full knowledge of the contractual relations between the parent, subsidiary, and affiliated corporations engaged in the telephone, telegraph, and cable business.

---

[35]S. Rept. 781, 73rd Cong., 2d sess., 11 pp.
[36]Op. cit., p. 1.    [37]Ibid., p. 2.

It finally stated that "It may be...necessary to give the
Commission power to void or modify contracts between these
corporations."[38]

The bill reported out by the Senate expressly directed
the Commission to make any recommendations that it might feel
necessary involving amendments to the proposed Act before
February 1, 1935. It also expressly directed the Commission
to investigate "certain important phases of the communications
business" and report its findings to Congress. These investigations were provided for in section 220, which called upon
the Commission to make recommendations regarding the desirability of permitting State regulation of systems of accounts and
rates of depreciation charges. In section 307 (c), a provision
was contained which authorized the Commission to study the
proposal that Congress legislate a fixed percentage of broadcasting facilities for nonprofit programs by educational,
religious, fraternal, labor, and charitable groups.

A brief analysis of the Senate bill (which did not
become law until after considerable modification in conference
committee) follows:

Title I. General Provisions

The bill's general provisions were practically identical to those contained in the earlier H. R. 7716 vetoed by
President Hoover with the exception that section 5 divided

--------------------

[38]Ibid., p. 2.

the Commission into two divisions, the Radio Division and
the Telephone Division.  The Chairman of the Commission was
to be designated by the President as a member of both.  The
Senate report commented:

> One reason for this statutory division is a desire to
> achieve effective regulation of the telephone and tele-
> graph business.  Experience has shown that commercial
> broadcasting takes the attention of all the members of
> the Radio Commission....Your committee believes that un-
> less the law provides a clear division of powers, broad-
> casting problems being so numerous, the Commission would
> give most of its attention to radio and neglect the prob-
> lems of telephone and telegraph regulation.  The study
> and regulation of the telephone and telegraph business
> must be a full-time task if it is to be effective.[39]

## Title II.  Common Carriers

This portion of the bill, for the most part, followed
the provisions of the Interstate Commerce Act then in effect
with respect to communications, or adopted the same provisions of that Act which were then only applicable to trans-
portation.

## Title III.  Special Provisions Relating to Radio

The Senate Report stated:

> Most of the changes from the present Radio Act of
> 1927 are changes carried in H. R. 7716 of the 72d Congress
> which passed both Houses of Congress, but failed to be-
> come a law because of the failure of President Hoover to
> sign the bill.[40]

Those portions of the Senate bill which added to or

---

[39]Ibid., p. 3.        [40]Ibid., p. 6.

differed from the Radio Act of 1927 were the following:

Section 303 (g), which directed the Commission to study new uses for radio and to encourage the more effective use of radio in the public interest.

Section 303 (q), which required the painting or illumination of radio towers which constituted a menace to air navigation.

Sections 307 (a) and (b) preserved the Davis amendment of March 28, 1928, dealing with allocation procedures; the (b) paragraph also preserved the language contained in H. R. 7716, which authorized additional licenses for stations not exceeding 100 watts, "when they will not interfere with the efficient service of other licensed stations."[41] (This provision was designed to permit additional service to those parts of the country that were then being inadequately served.)

Section 307 (c) was mentioned earlier as being that section which authorized the Commission to make studies to ascertain whether it would be feasible to set aside a certain percentage (as high as 25 percent) of the broadcast channels for the use of nonprofit organizations.

Section 307 (d) of the Senate bill, in line with H. R. 7716, modified section 9 of the Radio Act of 1927 and limited maximum terms of broadcast licenses from three years to one year. The report stated: "Reduction of the maximum

---

[41]Ibid., p. 6.

term of licenses will assist the Government in retaining
control over these valuable privileges."[42]

The language of section 315 of the Senate bill, involving facilities for candidates for public office, is the
same as that contained in H. R. 7716.

Section 316, dealing with information pertaining to
lotteries, gift enterprises and games of chance was also
adopted in toto from H. R. 7716.

Section 325 (a) was in the same language as the original Act, but paragraphs (b) and (c) were adopted from
S. 2660, a bill that had been passed by the Senate in the
72d Congress under which the Commission was to be given control of all studios in the United States used in connection
with a broadcast station in a foreign country for the purpose
of furnishing programs to be transmitted back into the United
States.[43]

Finally, section 326 of the Senate bill, prohibiting
censorship of programs, was modeled after section 29 of the
Radio Act of 1927.

### 6. The House Report to Accompany S. 3285, and Final Passage of the Bill

From the hearings on H. R. 8301 (a companion bill to
the one originally introduced in the Senate), the Committee

---

[42]Ibid., p. 6.

[43]Supra, pp. 66-68. This idea was also contained in
H. R. 7716.

on Interstate and Foreign Commerce, under the chairmanship
of Mr. Rayburn, worked out a substitute bill which eliminated
the controversial portions of the Senate version by carrying
over in toto into the new law breadcast provisions of the
Radio Act.  This bill was reported out in House Report
No. 1850 on June 1, 1934.

The Senate bill and the amendment of the House
(H. R. 8301) were alike in many respects, except, as the
House report stated:  "There are three principal differences
which may be noted as follows:"[44]

a) As passed by the Senate the bill (S. 3285) repealed the Radio Act of 1927, "although including in Title III
provisions which were substantially the same as the provisions
of the Act."[45]  The amendment the House committee added
eliminated this title from the bill and substituted a provision (Title III, sec. 301) which transferred to the new
Commission all the functions of the Federal Radio Commission,
but left the provisions of the Radio Act of 1927, as amended,
unchanging adding no provisions to supplement that Act.[46]

---

[44]Interstate and Foreign Commerce Committee, House of
Representatives, Rept. No. 1850, 73rd Cong., 2d sess., to
accompany S. 3285, submitted by Mr. Rayburn, 9 pages.

[45]Ibid., p. 2.

[46]Both the Senate bill and the House amendment provided
for the abolishment of the Radio Commission.  The conference
report (H. R. 1918) later adopted the provisions of the Senate
bill, except that most of the changes in the Radio Act of
1927 that were not contained in H. R. 7716 as pocket vetoed
by President Hoover were omitted.  In other words, the controversial parts of S. 3285, i.e., those which would have reduced station licensing periods from three years to one year,

b) The Senate bill (S. 3285) included an amendment
adopted on the floor of the Senate exempting carriers engaged
in interstate or foreign communication solely through physical
connection with the facilities of a nonaffiliated carrier.
The House amendment retained this provision except that it
made these carriers subject to the regulation of charges and
prohibited any discrimination.

c) The Senate bill (S. 3285) provided for two divisions within the Commission, the "Radio Division" and the
"Telegraph Division," and prescribed the jurisdiction of each
division.  Under the Senate bill, "these divisions would
function practically as separate commissions without their
action being subject to review by the full Commission."[47]
The amendment reported by the House rejected this provision
and substituted for it one patterned on section 17 of the Interstate Commerce Act, authorizing the Commission to provide
for the performance of any of its work, provisions, or functions through such divisions or through individual commissioners or boards of employees.  The action of these divisions
was to be subject to rehearing at the discretion of the
Commission.[48]

---

ould have permitted issuance of fines and suspensions, and
would have split the Commission into two sections -- one to
andle broadcasting, another to deal with point-to-point
ommunication, were taken out.

[47]Ibid., p. 2.

[48]This provision was adopted in the conference report
H. Rept. No. 1918, 73rd Cong., 2d sess.)

The bill (H. R. 8301) passed the House without a record vote on June 2, 1934, but not without some opposition. Among the first to comment on the bill was Representative McFadden (R. of Pennsylvania) who alleged radio censorship and sought consideration of his own measure for an investigation of the Commission and of chain broadcasting. He asserted:

> The strong hand of influence is drying up the independent broadcasting stations in the United States and the whole thing is tending toward centralization of control in...two big companies.. (CBS and NBC).[49]

It is interesting to note that even during this period when the old Radio Commission was dying and a new one being born, that there were three resolutions to investigate it that were introduced in the Congress.[50] While these were pending, a new bill emerged from a conference committee of House and Senate as substitute for the Senate and House bills.[51] After more debate in the House the conference report was adopted by both Houses, the bill was signed by the President, and went into effect on July 1, 1934.[52] The conference bill, when passed, became the Communications Act of 1934.

---

[49]Congressional Record, 73rd Cong., 2d sess., June 2, 1934, debate in House of Representatives on S. 3285.

[50]Resolution to investigate the FRC, S. 250, S. Res. 260, and S. Res. 275, investigation of censorship of broadcasting.

[51]Conference report on S. 3285, H. Rept. No. 1918, 73rd Cong., 2d sess.

[52]Congressional Record, 73rd Cong., 2d sess., June 4, 1934, debate in the House of Representatives on the conference report on S. 3285.

An examination of the Communications Act of 1934 thus
demonstrates its close affiliation with the Radio Act of
1927. It too gave broad powers to the Commission. However,
it went no further toward providing the Commission with a
standard to follow in the creation of its policy other than
"the public interest, convenience, and necessity," which
conferred an almost unlimited area for administrative judgment and discretion. But again it was expected that this
admittedly broad language would furnish the Commission with
an effective means by which it could formulate its own firm
policy in a rapidly developing area where Congress still
claimed to have little knowledge. The Commission's "broad
powers" were not in any way more limited in the Communications
Act of 1934 than they had been in the Radio Act of 1927. It
was still largely up to the Commission itself to decide what
its policies would be relative to their implementation.

One important difference, however, is to be noted
between the manner of the debate that looked toward passage
of the Radio Act of 1927 and the one which resulted from the
drafting of the Communications Act of 1934 -- that is the
emergence of a strong and vociferous broadcast lobby. This
lobby was largely successful in eliminating all the more controversial issues from the Act of 1934. One might expect to
see and hear more of this lobby in the future. It would be
logical to expect that it might make the formulation of
regulatory policies by the Commission a somewhat more difficult
task for it in the times to come, and that Congress, because

of the pressures of this lobby and other varying types of
broadcast lobbies, would be increasingly called upon to examine, criticize, and sometimes prod the actions and policies
of the Commission.

# CHAPTER IV

## AN ANALYSIS OF THE FEDERAL COMMUNICATIONS ACT

Having traced the development of congressional intent
with respect to broadcasting up to the time of the passage of
the Federal Communications Act of 1934, it is necessary now
to enumerate the more important provisions of that Act in
order to obtain a clearer picture of the powers laid down by
Congress upon the Commission. There follows, therefore, an
examination of the purposes for which the Act was passed,
the subject to which the Act applies, and the kinds and extent of power it bestows.

## 1. Purpose

The purpose for which the Act was passed is contained
in "Title I, General Provisions," as being the regulation of
interstate and foreign commerce in communication by wire and
radio,

> ...so as to make available, so far as possible, to all
> the people of the United States, a rapid, efficient,
> nationwide, and worldwide wire and radio communication
> service with adequate facilities at reasonable charges....[1]

Although the word "television" does not appear in the Communications Act, the Commission, by common consent, has
exercised its regulatory privilege over any and all forms of
broadcasting.)

---

[1]"Radio Laws of the United States," 1953 edition,
compiled by Elmer A. Lewis, superintendent, document room, House
of Representatives, p. 49. (Public Law No. 416, 73rd Congress)

The Federal Communications Commission has been created
to perform this function acting as a "central authority" over
wire and radio communication, taking those powers which had
been "previously granted by law to several agencies."

## 2. General Provisions

The provisions of the Act (sec. 2) apply only to
"interstate" (as opposed to intrastate, over which the Commission has no control) "and foreign communication by wire
or radio, which originates and/or is received within the
United States." Furthermore, its powers extend to persons
engaged in this communication, and to the licensing and regulating of all radio stations used for this purpose.

Section 3 provides definitions for the terms used in
the Act.

Section 4 contains provisions relating to the composition of the Federal Communications Commission. Paragraph (a)
states that there shall be "seven Commissioners, appointed by
the President, by and with the advice and consent of the Senate, one of whom the President shall designate as Chairman."[2]

---

[2]The Senate bill provided for a Federal Communications
Commission with five commissioners and terms of six years.
The House amendment provided for seven commissioners with
terms of seven years. As is obvious, the House amendment was
adopted. The Act setting up the Interstate Commerce Commission,
in many ways the model on which the FCC was laid out, does
not contain a provision whereby the President appoints the
Chairman. Instead the Act is silent on the method to be followed in the choosing of a Chairman, although it implies that a
Chairman shall be chosen. However, in 1946, the practice which
had developed of selecting the Chairman on the basis of senior-
ity was formally adopted by that Commission.

Paragraph (b) carries in it the provisions that all commissioners shall be United States citizens; that none shall have any financial interest whatsoever in any aspect of communication by wire or radio, including the manufacture and sale of radio apparatus. Nor should the commissioners "engage in any other business, vocation, or employment."[3] A further provision is made that no more than four out of seven commissioners be members of the same political party.

Paragraphs (c), (d), (e), (f), and (g) stipulate that the commissioners shall be appointed for terms of seven years, provide for the salary to be paid them, the place where Commission meetings shall be held, what officers, assistants, and secretaries may be hired, as well as what other types of expenditures may be made.

Paragraphs (k) and (l) require that "the Commission shall make an annual report to Congress," and that reports of all investigations shall be entered of record.

Section 5 was one of the portions of the bill where there had been a major difference of opinion between Senate and House as to what the law should require.[4]

---

[3]Recently, a Commissioner was asked to resign on the ground, among others, that he was engaged in another business or vocation besides that of his duties as a Commissioner. (See testimony of Richard Mack before the House Committee on Legislative Oversight.)

[4]The Senate bill provided for two designated divisions of the Commission, and fixed the jurisdiction of these divisions and of the Commission over various subjects of the bill, while the House amendment followed the provisions of sec. 17 of the Interstate Commerce Act, as amended, providing that the Commission may fix its own divisions (not in excess of three)

As finally carried, paragraphs (a), (b) and (c) authorize division of the Commission into not more than three sections, each to consist of not less than three members, with each division choosing its own chairman. Each division has power to hold hearings and hand down orders, decisions, and reports, subject to rehearing by the full Commission.

Paragraph (e) gives the Commission authority to assign any portions of its workload to any individual commissioner, "or to a board composed of an employee or employees of the Commission..." except that

This authority shall not extend to investigations instituted upon the Commission's own motion or, without the consent of the parties thereto, to contested proceedings involving the taking of testimony at public hearings, or to investigations specifically required by this Act.

Provision is made for the rehearing of any case by the Commission, upon filing of a petition in accordance with section 405 of the Act.

### 3. Common Carriers

Title II, dealing with common carriers, was essentially the same in both Senate and House versions, and followed procedures provided for in the Interstate Commerce Act and proposed in H. R. 7716. It gives the Commission power to govern service and charges of common carriers, as well as to set

---

and make its own assignment of work thereto, as well as assign certain of its work to individual Commissioners and employees. The House amendment was adopted in the final version of the bill, and passed.

echnical standards, authorize extension of lines, and make
aluations of property owned by the companies under its con-
rol.

## 4. Provisions Relating to Radio

Title III contains "special provisions relating to
adio." While abolishing the Federal Radio Commission,
ongress, as was pointed out earlier, kept many of the pro-
isions of the Radio Act of 1927.   Sections 301, 302 (a),
04, 306, 309, 313, 314, 315, 317, 318, 319, 320, 321, 322,
23, 324, 325 (a), 326, 327, 328, and 329 are, respectively,
ubstantially identical with sections 1, 2, 5, 11, 15, 17, 18,
9, 20, 21, 22, 23, 24, 25, 26, 29, 30, 35, and 36 of the
adio Act of 1927.

Section 301 states it is the purpose of this act

...to provide for the use of (the channels of interstate and foreign radio transmission)...but not the ownership thereof, by persons for limited periods of time,
under licenses granted by Federal authority, and no such
license shall be construed to create any right, beyond the
terms, conditions, and periods of the license. No person
shall use or operate any apparatus for the transmission
of energy or communications of signals by radio...within
any State when the effects of such use extend beyond the
borders of said State...except under and in accordance
with this Act and with a license in that behalf granted
under the provisions of this Act.

Section 302 retains the zonal division of the United
tates into five parts.

Section 303 combines sections 4 and 5 of the Radio Act.
t outlines the general powers of the Commission, which are
o issue licenses, classify stations, assign frequencies,

determine locations, and inspect apparatus, and to make
special regulations in regard to chain broadcasting. New
provisions are contained in paragraphs (f), which adds the
requirement of a public hearing in cases involving changes in
the frequency, authorized power, or times of operation of any
station; (g), which directs the Commission to study new uses
for radio and to encourage the more effective use of radio in
the public interest; and (q) which requires the painting or
illumination of radio towers which constitute a menace to air
navigation.[5]

Section 304 merely repeated the provision contained in
the earlier Radio Act which stipulated that no license shall
be awarded until the licensee shall sign a waiver of any
claim to the frequency because of previous use of the same,
whether by license or otherwise.

Section 305 was copied from section 6 of the Radio
Act, stating that stations owned and operated by the Government
shall not be subject to FCC control, except that they
shall conform to such rules and regulations as have been designed to prevent interference and to protect the rights of
others.[6]

Section 307 (a) and (b), dealing with the allocation
of facilities, were taken from section 9 of the Radio Act, as

[5]Pars. (f) and (q) were contained in H. R. 7716.

[6]The provision in the old Radio Act permitting the taking over of a station in time of war was transferred to
sec. 606 (c) of the new law.

amended, paragraph (b) being that paragraph which pertains to the "equal allocation of broadcast licenses" according to zones,[7] except that a second proviso to this paragraph was added, authorizing additional licenses for stations not exceeding 100 watts of power when they will not interfere with the efficient service of other licensed stations.

Paragraph (c) directs the Commission to study the proposal that Congress, by statute, allocate fixed percentages of broadcasting facilities to particular types of nonprofit programs or to persons identified with particular kinds of nonprofit activities.

Paragraph (d) sets the three-year limit on licenses, as provided for in the original Radio Act, and adds the further provision taken from H. R. 7716 that the Commission, in granting the renewal application of a license, should be governed by the same considerations which affected the granting of original applications.[8]

Section 308, dealing with procedure for filing applications for licenses, followed section 10 of the Radio Act

---

[7]This provision would not have a long life after the Act was passed, however. This rigid rule for allocation of licenses would be repealed by an act of Congress on June 5, 1936 (Public Law. No. 652, 74th Congress).

[8]The provision of the Senate bill which reduced the maximum terms of broadcast licenses from three years to one year was rejected in the conference committee. A further paragraph (f), which was contained in the Senate bill, carried a provision requiring that the Commission distribute broadcast licenses so that no one licensee or organization of licensees could exercise dominant control over the broadcasting facilities of any locality. This provision also was dropped from the final version of the bill.

as proposed to be modified by H. R. 7716, which added the requirement that modifications and renewals of licenses may be granted only upon written applications, a practice which was even then being followed by the Federal Radio Commission.

Section 309 deals with the process to be followed in case the Commission is unable to decide whether to grant a license, license renewal, or modification from an examination of the application, in which case the Commission must notify the applicant and fix a time and place for hearing. Paragraph (b) of the same section treats of the form of licenses and conditions attached to licenses.

Section 310 (a), is adapted from section 12 of the Radio Act, with certain modifications proposed by H. R. 7716 included. Section 12 of the Radio Act provided that radio station licenses may not be granted or transferred to any corporation of which any officer or director is an alien, or of which more than one-fifth of the capital stock may be voted by aliens, their representatives, a foreign government or a company organized under the laws of a foreign country. Section 310 (a) (4) modifies this provision by making the restriction apply also where one-fifth of the capital stock is owned of record by the designated persons, and altered the words "may be voted" to "is voted." Further, section 310 (a) (5) provides that such licenses may not be granted to or held by any corporation controlled by another corporation, of which any officer or more than one-fourth of the directors are aliens, or of which more than one-fourth of the capital stock is owned of

record or voted by aliens or their representatives...if the
Commission finds that the public interest will be served by
the refusal or revocation of such license.[9]

Paragraph (b) of that section requires the Commission
to decide whether any transfer of control of a station license,
including transfer of stock control, is in the public interest before allowing such transfer to take place; to secure
full information before the transfer is made; and to give
its consent in writing.[10]

---

[9]An interesting interpretation of this rule was given
by the Commission in the so-called "Latter Day Saints Application Denial" (Kansas City Broadcasting Company, Inc.,
5 R. R. 1057, 1952) in a case involving a construction permit,
filed by the Reorganized Church of Jesus Christ of Latter Day
Saints, a branch of the Mormon Church with headquarters in
Independence, Mo. Following a hearing, the hearing examiner
recommended that no license be given, primarily on the
ground that a license issued to a religious body would, in
effect, call for the operation of a "propaganda station."
FCC's opinion, in denying the application, however, stressed
other grounds -- that the application had failed to indicate
the citizenship status of the 17 members of the joint council,
governing board of the church, one of whom was known to be an
Australian citizen. The Church argued that since it was a
"voluntary association," it did not fall within provisions of
sec. 310 of the Act. FCC, however, held that in intent, the
section applied equally to unincorporated "voluntary associations." The application was accordingly denied. See also
Loyola University, 12 R. R. 1017 and St. Louis Telecast, 12
R. R. 1289 (1956), where a similar argument by competing applicants for TV licenses were disallowed on the ground that where
a major stockholder is a Jesuit University, where the university is an independent entity and not subject to direction
and control from an outside authority the interests of other
Jesuit institutions are not deemed relevant in ascertaining
ownership of mass communications of local ownership by an
applicant.

[10]Par. (b) is substantially sec. 12 of the Radio Act with
the modifications proposed by H. R. 7716. As in H. R. 7716,
the authority to approve or disapprove such transfers is extended to cover transfer of stock control in a licensee corporation. The new law was also modified to require the Commission to secure full information before reaching a decision
on the transfer.

Section 311, based upon section 13 of the Radio Act, directs the Commission to refuse a station license or permit to anyone whose license had been revoked by the court under section 313 of the Act, and authorizes, but does not direct, the Commission to refuse a license to any other person (or to any person directly or indirectly controlled by such a person) which has been

> finally adjudged guilty by a Federal court of unlawfully monopolizing or attempting unlawfully to monopolize, radio communication, directly or indirectly, through the control of the manufacture or sale of radio apparatus, through exclusive traffic arrangements, or by any other means, or to have been using unfair methods of competition....

Thus the provision was modified to leave the Commission discretion in refusing a license where the applicant has been adjudged guilty of a violation of the antitrust laws by a court, but where judgment by the court has not extended to the revocation of existing licenses.

Section 312, outlining the procedure for the revocation of station license, is based upon section 13 of the Radio Act, with modifications proposed by H. R. 7716 to reduce from 30 to 15 days the period within which a licensee may take exception to the Commission's action in revoking his license.[11] Paragraph (b) provides for the modification of station licenses and construction permits in cases where the

---

[11]The Senate provision which authorized the Commission itself to suspend licenses for cause was dropped from the final version of the bill.

Commission finds such action in the public interest.[12]

Section 313 and 314 provide for the application of the antitrust laws and the preservation of competition in commerce respectively. The first makes those laws applicable to the manufacture, sale of, and trade in radio apparatus. It provides that, upon the finding of any guilt of a civil or criminal violation of those laws the court may revoke the broadcast licenses of the guilty party. The second makes it unlawful for any broadcaster or other person to

> acquire, own, or control any part of the stock or other capital share or any interest in the physical property and/or other assets or any such cable, wire telegraph, or telephone line or system, if in either case the purpose is and/or the effect thereof may be to substantially lessen competition or to restrain commerce... or unlawfully to create monopoly in any line of commerce.[13]

Section 315, on facilities for candidates for public office is the same as section 18 of the Radio Act.[14]

-------

[12]This provision is along the lines of one proposed by H. R. 7716.

[13]According to the 1943 decision of the Supreme Court in the Chain Rules case, National Broadcasting Company v. United States, 319 U. S. 190, pp. 222-223, the "public interest" criterion read in the light of its legislative history, authorizes the Commission to revoke or to refuse a license to anyone whose conduct in its judgment is in violation of the antitrust laws.

[14]Sec. 315 contains the language: "If any licensee shall permit any person who is a legally qualified candidate for any public office to use a broadcasting station, he shall afford equal opportunities to all other such candidates for that office in the use of such broadcasting station....Such licensee shall have no power of censorship over the material broadcast under the provisions of this section."

This provision has a long history of somewhat confusing

Section 316 provides that no person shall broadcast
by means of any radio station any information concerning any
lottery, gift enterprise, or similar scheme offering prizes
dependent in whole or in part upon lot or chance.  This
section was not a part of the original Act, but was taken

---

and varying interpretations as to what the broadcaster's
liabilities are under existing laws of libel.  Recently the
Supreme Court of North Dakota ruled a station was immune from
libel damages because of sec. 315's restriction against
censorship.  (The aforementioned decision has been appealed
to the Supreme Court, which has not as yet handed down its
ruling in the matter.)  This has not always been the case,
however.  The precedent setting case in this area was the
Sorenson v. Wood decision, 123 Neb. 348, 243 N. W. 82, 1932
(upheld by the U.S. Supreme Court), in which it was the
court's opinion that a broadcasting station is liable for
defamatory statements broadcast over its facilities by a
qualified political candidate, even though it has no power
of censorship over material broadcast by such a candidate.
Then, in Josephson v. Knickerbocker Broadcasting Co., 38
N. Y. S. (92d) 985, 1942, a New York court decided -- If a
station exercises "due care" it should not be held liable for
defamatory statements made in political speeches which it is
forbidden to censor; "due care" includes advance inspection
of the script.  In the Port Huron political censorship opinion (Port Huron Broadcasting Co., 12 FCC 1069, 4 R. R. 1,
1948) the Commission itself ruled a licensee of a broadcasting station may not censor a political speech by a qualified
candidate to eliminate statements which the licensee
believes to be libelous; however, it said, the licensee does
have the right to eliminate materials the broadcasting of
which would violate Federal statutes.  This ruling was re-
stated and reemphasized by FCC in the WDSU Broadcasting Corp.,
7 R. R. 769, 1951, except that in WDSU the Commission did not
restate the latter part of its ruling which gave licensees
the right to eliminate material contrary to Federal law.
Instead it stated that from that time on stations would be
expected to abide strictly by the wording given by the Communications Act of 1934.

        In the light of the judicial results of this legisla-
tion and the jeopardy in which it places licensees who are
attempting to program talks of political candidates "in the
public interest," it becomes obvious that the Congress should
reexamine and perhaps clarify the wording of this section to
provide protection for a licensee in cases of libel and
defamation by a qualified political candidate.

from H. R. 7716.[15]

Sections 317 to 325 were taken from the Radio Act of 1927. They provide: That announcements shall be made in cases of all broadcast matter that is paid for; for the method of operation of transmitting apparatus; for the issuance of

---

[15]The Commission and the courts have often been at variance as to what constitutes a "lottery" under the provisions of the Act. (See early cases, FCC decisions WRBL Radio. Station, Inc., 2 FCC 687, 1936. Metropolitan Broadcasting Corp., 5 FCC 501, 1938.) In the cases of Public Clearing House v. Coyne, in 1904, the United States Supreme Court had ruled that for a "gift enterprise" to be a lottery, it must meet all three of the following tests: A prize must be given to the winning contestant, selection of the winner must be made on the basis of chance, and the contestants eligible to win the prize must provide some sort of consideration.

In 1949, FCC held, in a hearing involving station WARL of Arlington, Va., that a program broadcast by that station giving a prize for a correct answer to a difficult question asked over the telephone was a lottery, since participants were selected from the telephone book by chance, and since the questions asked were so difficult that they could not be answered except by those who had been listening to the station for two or three minutes prior to the telephone call, at which time the correct answer was announced in one of the station's programs. The Commission held that the requirement of listening to the program constituted consideration.

At the same time, complaints were being received by the Commission that certain telephone quiz programs broadcast over the national radio networks -- "Stop the Music" among them -- were lotteries, since participants to be called on the telephone were chosen by chance, a prize was given, and to participate, a contestant was forced to listen to a radio program to hear a musical number which he was expected to identify.

To clarify the situation, the Commission in August, 1949, announced a proposed regulation dealing with lotteries, in which "consideration" was defined to include any requirement that a participant was forced to listen to a particular radio program at a certain time, or that he had to answer a telephone call, in some prescribed manner. Three networks -- ABC, CBS, and NBC -- filed suits in Federal courts challenging the regulation as an illegal form of censorship being exercised by the FCC. In February, 1953, the Federal District

construction permits; the designation of stations liable to
interfere with distress signals; the transmission and
reception of distress signals and communications; for inter-
communication in mobile service; for cases of interference
between Government and commercial stations; the use of minimum power; and the sending of false distress signals.

Paragraphs (b) and (c) of section 325 were designed
to give the Commission control of all studios or apparatus
in the United States used in connection with a broadcasting
station in a foreign country for the purpose of furnishing
programs to be transmitted back into the United States.[16]

Section 326 prohibits censorship in the same language
as that provided in section 29 of the Radio Act, specifically
stating that neither the Commission nor anyone else shall

---

Court for the Southern District of New York declared the
regulation invalid, because the court felt that the Commission
gave too broad an interpretation to the requirement of "consideration" in a lottery.

The FCC appealed to the Supreme Court which on April 5,
1954, upheld the lower court's decision (FCC v. American Broadcasting Co., Inc., 347 U. S. 284, 1954.) The Supreme Court's
1954 decision held that the lottery regulations proposed by
the FCC were invalid, and an unauthorized attempt by the FCC
to legislate. The proposed regulations never were in effect,
since their effective date was held up until their validity
had been finally determined by the courts. (See also Caples
Co. v. United States, U. S. D. C. of Appeals, 1957, in 15 R. R.,
2005.)

[16]During the same session of Congress as that when the
Federal Communications Act was passed (73rd Cong., 2d sess.)
the House Committee on Merchant Marine, Radio, and Fisheries
favorably reported a bill (S. 2660) which contained provisions
similar to these.

"interfere with the right of free speech by means of radio
communication," but that, "No person within the jurisdiction
of the United States shall utter any obscene, indecent, or
profane language by means of radio communication."

Sections 327, 328, and 329 complete that portion of
the law (title III) pertaining to special provisions relating to radio, by a delineation of what use may be made of
naval stations in the carrying of commercial messages, the
making of special provisions for the Philippine Islands and
Canal Zone, and the administration of the radio laws in the
Territories and possessions.

## 5. Procedural and Administrative Provisions

Title IV treats of procedural and administrative
provisions of the law, with section 401 (a) and (b) outlining
the jurisdiction to enforce the acts and orders of the
Commission.  These first two paragraphs give the district
courts of the United States jurisdiction

> ...upon application of the Attorney General of the
> United States at the request of the Commission,
> alleging a failure to comply with or a violation of
> any of the provisions of this act by any person, to
> issue a writ or writs of mandamus commanding such
> person to comply with the provisions of this act.

The paragraphs also provide that the courts shall enforce
obedience to any such orders "regularly made and duly served"
by the Commission.  Paragraph (c) provides that any district
attorney of the United States shall, upon the Commission's
application, institute proceedings in the proper court for

the enforcement of the provisions in the Act, and that the costs shall be borne out of the "expenses of the courts of the United States."

Section 402 treats of appeals and proceedings to set aside the Commission's orders in certain cases. For the purposes of cases involving carriers, section 402 carries forward the then existing method of review of order of the Interstate Commerce Commission, and, in the main, for radio cases, carries forward the existing method of review of orders of the Federal Radio Commission; but in radio cases involving affirmative orders of the Commission entered in proceedings initiated upon the Commission's own motion in revocation, modification, and suspension matters, review is to be by the method applicable in the case of orders of the Interstate Commerce Commission.

According to the section, appeals may be taken in the Court of Appeals of the District of Columbia in any of the following cases (402 (b)):

a) By an applicant for a construction permit for a radio station, a radio station license, or a renewal or modification of an existing license, if that person's application has been denied by the Commission.

b) "By any other person aggrieved or whose interests are adversely affected by any decision of the Commission granting or refusing any such application."

Section 402 (c) states that any appeal shall be filed with the court within 20 days after the decision complained of is effective, and the Commission shall not later than five

days after,

>...mail or otherwise deliver a copy of said notice of
appeal to each person shown by the records of the Commission to be interested in such appeal and to have a
right to intervene therein under the provisions of this
section, and shall at all times thereafter permit any
such person to inspect and make copies of the appellant's
statement of reasons for said appeal at the office of
the Commission in the city of Washington.

Within 30 days the Commission shall file with the

court all pertinent records and evidence upon which the

decision was based and shall within 30 days thereafter

>file a full statement in writing of the facts and grounds
for its decision as found and given by it, and a list
of all interested persons to whom it has mailed or otherwise delivered a copy of said notice of appeal.

Finally, section 402 (d) provides that within 30 days

after filing of appeal any other "interested person" may

intervene and participate by filing with the court notice of

such intention "and a verified copy showing the nature of

the interest of such party." An "interested party" is

defined as "any person who would be aggrieved or whose inter-

est would be adversely affected by a reversal or modification

of the decision of the Commission complained of...."

>(e) At the earliest convenient time the court shall
hear and determine the appeal upon the record before it,
and shall have power, upon such record, to enter a
judgment affirming or reversing the decision of the
Commission, and in event the court shall render a decision and enter an order reversing the decision of the
Commission, it shall remand the case to the Commission
to carry out the judgment of the court:  Provided however,
That the review by the court shall be limited to questions
of law and that findings of fact by the Commission, if
supported by substantial evidence, shall be conclusive
unless it shall clearly appear that the findings of the
Commission are arbitrary or capricious.  The court's
judgment shall be final, subject, however, to review

by the Supreme Court of the United States...by appellant, by the Commission, or by any interested party intervening in the appeal.

Section 403 permits the Commission to institute inquiries on its own motion and to make and enforce any order or orders resulting therefrom (excepting orders for the payment of money), and section 404 makes it the duty of the Commission to report the results of any of its investigations in writing, together with its decision.

Section 405 provides for rehearings before the Commission where "sufficient reason" can be shown by any party thereto, provided that application is made within 20 days of the effective date thereof and by an aggrieved party or one whose interests are adversely affected. However,

no such application shall excuse any person from complying with or obeying any decision, order, or requirement of the Commission, or operate in any manner to stay or postpone the enforcement thereof, without the special order of the Commission.

Upon results of such hearing the Commission "may reverse, change or modify" its original decision, order or requirement if it appears to be "in any respect unjust or unwarranted."

Sections 406 to 416 provide for the issuance of writs of mandamus to compel furnishing of facilities, petitions for enforcement of order, general provisions relating to Commission proceedings, the use of joint boards and cooperation with State commissioners, joinder of parties, documents to be filed as public records and their use in proceedings, the designation of an agent for service, limitations as to action, and provisions relating to orders.

## 6. Penal Provisions and Forfeitures

Section 501 provides a fine of not more than $10,000 or imprisonment for a term of not more than two years or both for any person who knowingly and willfully violates the Act.

Section 502 pertains to violation of any "rule, regulation, restriction, or condition made by the Commission under the authority of the Act," or that of any treaty or convention, and provides a fine of $500 for each day's offenses.

Section 503 pertains to commercial carriers and provides for forfeiture of license in cases of rebates and offsets, while section 504 delineates the provisions relating to forfeitures.

Finally, section 505 states that "trial of any offense under this Act shall be in the district in which it is committed."

## 7. Miscellaneous Provisions

Section 601 transfers to the new Commission the duties, powers, and functions of other agencies under then existing law; section 602 repeals the Radio Act of 1927, certain provisions of the Interstate Commerce Act, and other pertinent acts; section 603 transfers pertinent records, property, appropriations, and employees to the Communications Commission; section 604 states that the effect of all transfers, repeals,

and amendments made previously would be the same until changed
by the new Commission; and section 605 forbids any unauthorized publication of communications by a common carrier.

Section 606 implements the wartime powers of the
President. It authorizes him, during the continuance of a
war in which the United States is engaged, should he find it
necessary for the national defense and security, "to direct
that such communications as in his judgment may be essential
to the national defense and security...have preference or
priority with any carrier subject to this Act." Further (b),

> it shall be unlawful for any person during any war in
> which the United States is engaged to knowingly or will-
> fully...obstruct or retard or aid in obstructing or re-
> tarding interstate or foreign communication by wire or
> radio.

It authorizes the President, "whenever in his judgment the
public interest requires, to employ the Armed Forces of the
United States to prevent any such obstruction or retardation
of communication."

Paragraph (c) gave the President power to "suspend or
amend, for such a time as he may see fit, the rules and regulations applicable to any or all stations within the jurisdiction of the United States..." and to "cause the closing of
any station for radio communication and remove therefrom its
apparatus and equipment," or authorize its control or use "by
any department of the Government under such regulations as he
may prescribe, upon just compensation to the owners."

Finally, section 607 provided the effective date of
the Act; 608, a separability clause in the case that any of

its provisions were held invalid, and 609, a short title,
"Communications Act of 1934."

## 8. Conclusions Based on an Analysis of the Federal Communications Act

From our further detailed examination of the Communications Act of 1934, we can again draw the conclusion that the Act conferred "broad powers" upon the Commission, and did not attempt any closely drawn definition of how these powers were to be employed.

The Commission's major function was to remain that of a licensing body, one which employed the broad measure of the "public interest" to decide who was to broadcast, and under what conditions and at what hours such broadcasting was to be done. The Act required that certain procedural steps be followed by the Commission in each case where it granted or renewed a license but, except for the proviso that such licenses be distributed on an equal basis to all five of the broadcast zones it established, in only one instance did it go so far as to state in plain language what it considered the desired qualities in a potential licensee to be.[17]

Even in those provisions dealing with attempts to monopolize radio communication or the manufacture or sale of radio apparatus, (sections 311, 313) except where the court

---

[17]This single instance was in section 310, of the Act, which forbade the Commission to award a license to any corporation in which a certain specifically stated degree of alien control was present. (Supra, pp. 100-101.)

had already revoked the license, the Commission was given complete discretion as to whether license revocation was in order where an applicant had been judged guilty of a violation of the antitrust laws.

Thus, while it may be argued that a strong prejudice existed in the mind of Congress against a licensee or applicant who had been adjudged guilty by a court of attempted monopoly of the broadcast industry, Congress did not make such conviction in itself a disqualifying factor, and it was not until the Supreme Court's decision in the Chain Rules case that an unequivocal statement was made that the Commission did indeed have the right to revoke or refuse a license to anyone whose conduct "in its judgment" was in violation of the antitrust laws.[18]

Apart from its delineation of the licensing function of the Commission, the Act was no more clear in its other sections as to the amount or degree of "regulation" of broadcasting it considered optimum. Section 326 stated that the Commission could undertake no regulatory action which would "interfere with the rights of free speech," but left the question open as to what constituted such "interference." The Act proscribed the broadcast of "lotteries" and schemes offering prizes dependent in whole or in part upon lot or chance (section 316), but again left the question of definition of terms (such as, for example, the word "lottery") to the

---

[18]Supra, p. 106, Footnote 13.

Commission and the courts. The Act was quite clear in its
provisions dealing with rules and regulations that the Commission might designate in order to prevent interference
between stations (as it was indeed in all cases which dealt
with the technical performance of a broadcasting station), but
left the matter open to debate as to how much power the Commission possessed to perform any kind of qualitative or even
quantitative appraisal of a station's programs, (i.e., for
example, its "past performance" and programming record.) In
only one part of the Act does it seem to permit the Commission any form, loose or otherwise, of program review --
paragraph (d) of section 307 states that in granting the renewal application of a license, the Commission should be
governed by the same considerations which affected the granting of the original application. Thus, the Commission could
argue, (as it was to argue later or when the question of so-
called "ex post facto censorship" was to arise), that since
it considered an applicant's proposed programming as a factor
in the original granting of a license, it had equal right to
consider what his programming service had been at time of
license renewal. This whole area was and has remained somewhat open to interpretation. Congress has never succeeded in
providing any further definition of how the "public interest"
was to be looked upon as it might affect such program review.
While the Commission has, as will be outlined in subsequent
chapters of this study, frequently attempted to obtain a clearer positive directive from Congress in regard to this question,

the broadcast industry has done everything in its power to
prevent such a directive from being forumlated into law.
(Of course, it would be perfectly content with any directive
which, instead of being positive, clearly denied the Commission the right of program review.)

Congress had failed to provide the President with an
Act which would avoid the more controversial broadcast
issues during the time of its debate and passage, just as it
had in an equal degree failed (if indeed that had been its
intention) to provide the Commission with an enabling law
that would be free from controversial interpretations as to
its intent after it had become law. What it had done, it is
clear, was to continue the philosophy of the Radio Act of
1927 into the Communications Act of 1934, in relationship to
its "broad powers."

## CHAPTER V

## TEN YEARS OF OPERATION OF THE FEDERAL
## COMMUNICATIONS ACT, 1935-45

After the passage of the Federal Communications Act
of 1934, except for the repeal of the so-called "Davis
Amendment" in 1936 (to be discussed later in this Chapter)
and certain other very minor revisions, it remained unchanged
for a period of 18 years.  Although, admittedly, it had been
passed in a rush of debate and hurried congressional action,
and at the same time was considered to be minimum legislation which would have to be further refined at the next and
in succeeding Congresses, there was in actual fact no prolonged or concerted attempt to provide any further definition
of its broad legislative powers on the part of Congress.
Instead, there was for this period of years a steady drumfire
of criticism of the activities of the Commission from both
legislative branches.  There was an increasing realization
of the inadequacies of the Act, and there is every indication that, had it not been for the advent of war, Congress
would have devised and enacted further refinements of its provisions.[1]  But the war and the fast succession of events that
followed demanded continued attention, with the result that

---

[1]See Chapter VI, Part 1, for a delineation of the
attempts on the part of both the Legislative and Executive
branches to rewrite the Communications Act and to reorganize
the Commission prior to World War II.

all relatively less pressing domestic issues such as broadcast reform were put aside until a later time.

Irrespective of these considerations, a brief examination of the most recurrent broadcast issues before the Congress
will serve to demonstrate where certain of its members believed
the Act to be most in need of revision, as well as where it
seemed to many that the Commission was failing to employ its
broad powers to best advantage.

The most often discussed issues before the Congress
revolved in a general way around the Commission's licensing
function. The first of these to be taken up was the equitable distribution of radio frequencies and service to all the
states; next came the extremely involved question of program
content, so-called "balanced programming," and the delicate
problem of censorship; and finally, the always present possibility of broadcast monopoly.

### 1. The Fair and Equitable Distribution of Broadcast Frequencies by the Commission. S. 2243

One of the earliest enacted amendments to the Communications Act was S. 2243. It was introduced in the 74th Congress,
2d session (1936), and related to the allocation of radio
frequencies. As pointed out in the preceding pages, passage
of the Davis amendment in 1928, and its reaffirmation in the
Communications Act of 1934, made it necessary for the Commission to divide the available radio frequencies on an equal
basis among the various zones and States within the zones,

in accordance with their population.

There were five zones. The first zone had an area of 129,000 square miles. It consisted of northeast New York and a narrow strip of land down the Atlantic coast. By comparison, the fifth zone, consisting of the Rocky Mountain and Pacific Coast States, had an area of 1,250,000 square miles, exclusive of Alaska and Hawaii, which were included in the zone.

Because of wider areas and geophysical factors, more stations could be accommodated without objectionable interference in the fifth zone than in the first. In accordance with the law, however, it was necessary to limit the larger zone, and by this arrangement the larger zones were restricted to the facilities that could be crowded in the smaller. As one early writer and critic of the system put it:

> Considerable doubt exists as to the soundness of the
> zone system provided in the Act. The zones are similar
> only in point of population, and, in determining their
> boundaries, no consideration was given to such potent fac-
> tors as geographical characteristics, available capital,
> or program talent....[2]

Many ridiculous occurrences arose as a result of this arbitrary system, as when, in late 1931, the Commission ordered two time-sharing Chicago stations operating on 560 kilocycles off the air on the ground that they were over quota according to the allocation plan. The 560 kilocycle regional channel was then given to a Gary, Indiana, radio station, not more

---

[2]Paul R. Olson, "Regulation of Broadcasting in the United States (unpublished Ph.D. dissertation, University of Iowa, 1931), p. 205.

than 10 miles away from the former holders of the radio frequency. The Commission's action was appealed, and in 1933 the Supreme Court of the United States upheld the Commission ruling, granting absolute power in the distribution of radio facilities to the regulatory agency.[3]

Over the years, however, pressure for repeal of the provisions grew ever stronger until, when the bill repealing the zonal allocation procedure came up for consideration in the 74th Congress, the western Senators and Representatives who had originally insisted upon the amendment and upon whom it had backfired led the fight for its repeal. Senator Wheeler (D. of Montana), in urging passage of S. 2243, stated from the floor that

> ...myself and other Senators from the West were very anxious that the bill should become law....We found... that the operation of the so-called Davis amendment had discriminated against the West, because of the fact that the zones in the West are so large and zones in the East are small. Consequently, the big cities of the country, such as those in New York, have found that the law works all right; but in the case of the larger zones in the West and Midwest it has hampered us in securing the facilities we ought to have to meet the demands of that section of the country....[4]

In quoting from the report of the Interstate Commerce Committee of the Senate, Mr. Wheeler made the further statement that

> The legislation is recommended for practical reasons of administration by the Communications Commission, which has found that the drawing of artificial zone lines for guides in allocating facilities cannot satisfactorily be applied because of the physical laws governing radio transmission. As a consequence, the policy of Congress to

---

[3]Broadcasting Magazine, May 15, 1933.

[4]Congressional Record, 74th Cong., 2d sess., 1936, p. 6032.

distribute radio facilities so that every section of the country will be adequately supplied, has been very difficult of effectuating.[5]

The bill passed the Senate and House and was signed into law by the President on June 5, 1936. It restored the provisions of the original Act which created the Federal Radio Commission in the following language:

Sec. 2. Subsection (b) of section 307 of such Act is amended to read as follows:

(b) In considering applications for licenses, and modifications and renewals thereof, when and insofar as there is demand for the same, the Commission shall make such distribution of licenses, frequencies, hours of operation, and of power among the several States and communities as to provide a fair, efficient, and equitable distribution of radio service to each....[6]

2. Freedom of Speech and the Broadcaster
Censorship -- Ex Post Facto and Otherwise, and
Regulation Affecting Program Content

The Federal Communications Act, as it passed the Congress in 1934, contained the language that "Nothing in this Act shall be understood or construed to give the Commission the power of censorship over the radio communications...." nor could the Commission fix any rules "which shall interfere with the rights of free speech."[7]

A number of very perplexing problems arose as a result of this language. Although censorship had always been overlooked upon as an evil to be avoided at all costs, at

---

[5]Ibid.    [6]Public Law No. 652, 74th Congress.

[7]Federal Communications Act, sec. 326, 48 Stat. 1091.

times the apparent "costs" seemed much too high and threw
members of Congress into deep consternation. They were concerned, for example, over programs that were thought to be
"obscene and indecent." They deplored the broadcasts of
such men as "Doc" Brinkley, who, when refused renewal of his
broadcast license by the Federal Radio Commission,[8] continued
to beam programs to the United States from a very powerful
transmitter in Mexico;[9] they decried the high degree of
suggestivity contained in a Sunday night broadcast over a
major network, which featured Mae West.[10]

---

[8]Station KFKB, of Milford, Kans., owned and operated
by Dr. John R. Brinkley, was used to advertise his "goat
gland" operations as well as to broadcast a Medical Question
Box program in which he prescribed medicines for listeners who
wrote to him describing their symptoms. His unorthodox medical practices resulted in the revocation of his license to
practice medicine by the State Medical Board in July 1930.
Complaints were then filed by the American Medical Association
which caused the Federal Radio Commission to order a hearing
on renewal of his radio station license that same year. Following the hearing, the Commission refused to grant renewal
on the ground that he had broadcast "obscene and indecent"
material in advertising his goat gland operations, and that
the practice of giving prescriptions over the air constituted
"personal communication" instead of broadcasting, in violation of the station license. The Commission's decision was
appealed to the Federal courts (KFKB Broadcasting Assoc. v.
Federal Radio Commission, 47 F. (2d) 670 App. D. C. 1931).
The U. S. Court of Appeals for the District of Columbia upheld the Commission in a 1931 ruling stating that the Commission had the right to consider past performances of a licensee; in ruling on renewal of a broadcast license, without such
consideration violating the censorship provisions of the Act.

[9]Congressional Record, 72d Cong., 1st sess., April 11,
1932, p. 7862.

[10]In a broadcast of the Charlie McCarthy program over
the NBC network, in December 1937, an "Adam and Eve" sketch
was presented with the role of Adam taken by Charlie McCarthy
and that of Eve played by Mae West. The program resulted in

Most affected, however, by the problems of censorship versus free speech were the fields of religious broadcasting, the broadcasting of public issues, and talks by candidates for public office. A bill introduced in 1934 by Representative McFadden (R. of Penna.) had as its subject matter the abolishment of radio censorship and the provisions of equal treatment for political aspirants.[11]

Beginning in 1935 and continuing up to the outbreak of war a number of bills were introduced to clarify the confusion over censorship.[12] These would have required stations to devote certain hours to unrestricted discussion of public issues, on a free-time basis, and would have protected licensees from libel suits on matters which concerned the broadcasting of

---

widespread criticism, and hundreds of letters were received by NBC and by the Communications Commission complaining that the sketch presented was vulgar and indecent. (See news stories in Broadcasting, December 20, 1937, and January 25, 1938.)

Letters and articles were also sent to Members of Congress, and the Congressional Record for the 75th Cong., 3rd sess. (January 14, 1938, p. 560; January 26, 1938, p. 357), contains materials relevant to the incident.

After an informal investigation, the Commission decided that the sketch was in fact "vulgar and indecent," and against all "proprieties," and in January, 1938, sent a letter of reprimand to NBC and to each of the stations which carried the program, stating that the Commission would take into account the carrying of offensive program materials in passing on applications for license renewals. No station lost its license as a result of the incident, however, and the Commission took no further action on it.

[11]H. R. 7986, 73rd Congress, 2d session, p. 3543.

[12]H. R. 9229, 74th Cong., 1st sess.; S. 2755, S. 2756, S. 2757, 75th Cong., 1st sess.; S. 3515, 76th Cong., 3rd sess.; H. R. 1082, 77th Cong., 1st sess.

public questions. For example, there were three bills introduced in the 74th Congress (1935), which dealt with this
topic.[13] Representative Scott (D. of California), in remark-
ing on the subject matter of the proposed legislation, stated:

The three bills would deprive the Communications Commission of censorship powers and relieve radio stations
from liability for remarks made in any broadcasts on
public, social, political, or economic issues; would compel radio stations to set aside regular periods for un-
censored discussion of social problems, with an equal
opportunity for both sides of a controversial issue to
expound their points of view; and would compel all radio
stations to keep accurate records of rejected applications for time and reasons therefore.[14]

Another frequent cause of irritation to the Congress
in regard to programming was the amount and type of advertising on the air. Of bills submitted in this respect, those to
prohibit the advertising of alcoholic beverages have been the
most prevalent. From 1934 to the end of World War II, no
less than 12 bills to prohibit the advertising of liquors
were introduced.[15]

Censorship over program materials again became a
popular subject, but for an entirely different reason, in 1940,
when a bill introduced by Representative Ditter (R. of Penna.),
if passed, would have completely denied the Commission the

---

[13]H. R. 9929, H. R. 9230, H. R. 9231, 74th Cong.,
1st session.

[14]Congressional Record, 74th Cong., 2d sess., p. 973.

[15]S. 3015, March 10, 1934; H. R. 8404, S. 541, June 7,
1935; H. R. 3140, January 18, 1937; S. 3550, February 25,
1938; H. R. 9624, February 25, 1938; H. R. 251, H. R. 252,
January 3, 1939; S. 517, January 10, 1939; S. 575, January 12,
1939; H. R. 123, January 3, 1941; H. R. 6785, March 13, 1942.

right to consider programming offenses (as it obviously
had considered the John R. Brinkley and Mae West cases) in
passing on license renewals.  Ditter contended that program
standards should be set up in advance and objected to what
Commissioner Craven called "ex post facto censorship" at
hearings on license renewals.  Ditter declared that the "public convenience, interest, or necessity" clause was being
used as an excuse to censor programs.[16]  Thus the question
of censorship, whether indirect or direct, remained a controversial issue, as it is today; one frequently debated but
always unresolved in the halls of Congress.  Interestingly
enough, even the Supreme Court has not been able to agree
with its own former decisions (see below) on the Act's interpretation in this regard, for the Act of '34, by way of contrast with transmitters of telephonic, telegraphic and wireless  messages for pay, stated that "...a person engaged in
radio broadcasting shall not be deemed a common carrier."[17]
This led Justice Roberts to state in the Saunders Bros. case:

> Thus the Act recognizes that the field of broadcast-
> ing is one of free competition...the Act does not essay
> to regulate the business of the licensee.  The Commission
> is given no supervisory control of the programs, of busi-
> ness management or of policy...."[18]

Only three years later, in the important National

---

[16]Congressional Record, 76th Cong., 2d sess., pp. 806 ff.
(appendix).

[17]U. S. Code, sec. 153 (h).

[18]FCC v. Saunders Bros. Radio Station, 309 U. S.
Reports 470 at 474-75 (1940).

Broadcasting case in 1943, a somewhat contradictory principle was established. The case was fought because the FCC
had issued regulations which, besides obtaining the separation of the Red and Blue Networks without first holding a
court contest, broke up various exclusive arrangements between the stations and the networks that were considered to
be abuses contrary to the public interest. These new regulations were held by the Supreme Court to lie within the
broad statutory powers of the Commission. Justices Murphy
and Roberts dissented, thinking that specific Congressional
authority was needed for such action. Justice Frankfurter,
for the Court, however, stated:

> The Act itself establishes that the Commission's pow-
> ers are not limited to the engineering and technical
> aspects of regulation of radio communication. Yet we
> are asked to regard the Commission as a kind of traffic
> officer, policing the wave lengths to prevent stations
> from interfering with each other. But the Act does not
> restrict the Commission merely to supervision of the
> traffic. It puts upon the Commission the burden of
> determining the composition of that traffic. The facil-
> ities of radio are not large enough to accomodate all
> who wish to use them. Methods must be devised for choos-
> ing among the many who apply. And since Congress itself
> could not do this, it committed the task to the
> Commission.[19]

The Commission took full advantage of this wording
when it issued its now famous "Blue Book" in 1946, which
stated:[20]

> not only that the Commission has the authority to concern
> itself with the programming service, but that it is under

---

[19]NBC., Inc. v. U. S., 319 U.S. Reports 190 at 215-216
(1943).

[20]Op. cit., Public Service Responsibilities of Broadcast
Licensees, 1946, p. 12.

an affirmative duty, in its public interest determinations, to give full consideration to program service.

Even so, however, no supervision of particular programs was
suggested, and it was stated that the evaluation of total program performance would do no more than require minimum standards of quality for the purpose of giving the available wave
lengths to stations which met those standards.

After describing in detail the existing defects of
then current radio programs the "Blue Book" stated:

> Primary responsibility for the American system of
> broadcasting rests with the licensee of broadcast sta-
> tions, including the network organizations. It is to the
> stations and networks rather than to Federal regulation
> that listeners must primarily turn for improved standards
> of program service. The Commission, as the licensing
> agency established by Congress, has a responsibility to
> consider overall program service in its public interest
> determinations, but affirmative improvement of program
> service must be the result primarily of other forces....[21]

Therefore, it was suggested that the industry, through self
regulation, and the public, through what it termed in hopeful
language to be "responsible criticism," would together be enabled to "stimulate the free and unfettered development of
radio as a new medium of artistic expression." Publication
of the "Blue Book" created a new furor over the question of
possible censorship, and it was to become an even greater issue
for a time in the various reorganization acts that were to come
before the Congress in the late 1940's, finally to be once
more taken out of the final version of the 1952 amendments in
favor of the usual "noncontroversial" bill.

---

[21] Ibid., p. 54.

## 3. The Monopoly Issue

In his article in the <u>American Political Science Review</u>, Professor Friedrich makes the statement:

> ...From the point of view of time consumed in hearings and debates, Congress has been more concerned with the problems of monopoly than with any other aspect of the radio industry. Competition has always been considered desirable in the American economy, but particularly in radio has Congress been vigilant to preserve competition because of the nature of radio as a molder of public opinion and an instrument of political power.[22]

Practically every year since the passage of the Communications Act has brought its share of bills and resolutions relative to monopolies or the threat of monopolies in broadcasting. In 1935 Representative Monaghan (D. of Montana) introduced a bill for Government control of radio, and cited the radio monopoly as the chief abuse of the present system.[23] In a long debate advocating passage of the bill, he called it an "effort to curb the growing power of money in our country," and stated that "the power interest, or Radio Trust, has successfully imposed upon the Government and secured from a Government agency of the Congress (the FCC)...virtually dominant control of the radio structure." He scathingly attacked the "big business control of radio," its "power of censorship," its "trafficking in radio licenses," "monopoly of news," and "influence of the networks."

---

[22]Friedrich & Sternberg, "Congress and the Control of Radio Broadcasting," <u>American Political Science Review</u>, Vol. 27, No. 5, October, 1943.

[23]H. R. 8475, 74th Congress, 1st sess., p. 9253.

In the course of the debate, one Congressman stated:

The president of NBC publicly admitted that the primary purpose for which his company was organized was not to serve the public interest but to serve the radio manufacturing industry and the Bell Telephone Co.[24]

Unable to maneuver legislation limiting the power of big business in broadcasting through the Congress, a group of members of both Houses next attempted to force the Communications Commission to play a more active part in keeping the channels of broadcasting out of the hands of the "powerful interests" and the "Radio Trust." In 1936, Representative Connery (D. of Massachusetts) introduced a resolution (reintroduced for several years thereafter) to permit Congress to investigate the Communications Commission, especially in regard to alleged abuses in the granting of licenses, the broadcasting of obscene programs, and monopolistic practices.[25] He recommended that Congress

...appoint a select committee to investigate the charges of irregularities in the granting and renewal of radio licenses, the broadcasting of obscene and indecent utterances by radio stations, the charges of alleged monopolies, and to investigate and report on charges made or which may be made as to charges of alleged misconduct and alleged corruption on the part of certain persons officially connected with said Commission, and to investigate the acts and activities of said Commission.[26]

Concern over control reached an all time high in 1937,

---

[24]Congressional Record, 74th Cong., 1st sess., pp. 14310-14316.

[25]H. Res. 394, 74th Cong., 2d sess., p. 456. (Introduced again in 1937 as H. Res. 61, at that time the Rules Committee refused to report it out.)

[26]Congressional Record, 74th Cong., 2d sess., p. 417.

when no less than four resolutions for investigation of monopolistic practices were pending at the same time.[27] Representative McFarlane (D. of Texas) claimed that

> we have dictatorship in America when 300 or less persons
> have an absolute monopoly in the molding of public opin-
> ion through undisputed use of radio stations, newspapers,
> and motion pictures....[28]

He charged that a monopoly was enjoyed by the three big
broadcasting networks and that the Commission itself had been
guilty of fraudulent practices. McFarlane attacked "trafficking," the RCA consent decree, and strongly criticized the
Commission for playing favorites in the issuance of an experimental license to a radio station. Of the station itself, he
had this to say:

> In order to promote science and to encourage inventors,
> we authorized the FCC to issue experimental licenses to
> radio stations....A manufacturer in Cincinnati...having
> a better knowledge of how to secure concessions apparent-
> ly than some of his competitors...was permitted to obtain...
> an experimental license to use a total of some 500,000
> watts power, the largest station in America. Nine-tenths
> of this power was experimental, so, I understand, he immed-
> iately raised the price of his radio advertising some 50
> percent and has continued to collect handsome commercial
> profits on the basis of experimentation for these 39
> months.[29]

---

[27]H. Res. 61, 75th Cong., 1st sess., p. 216; H. Res. 92,
p. 542; S. Res. 149, pp. 6785-6786; H. Res. 321, p. 9295;
(debated, 9405).

[28]Congressional Record, 75th Cong., 1st sess., p. 7280.

[29]Evidently the complaints of some members of discrimination in regard to the issuance of experimental licenses had
some effect, for in June, 1938, a Senate resolution that broadcast power in excess of 50 kilowatts would be against the public interest effectively removed superpower from FCC consideration. In October of that year the FCC superpower committee
recommended ending WLW's license for 500 kilowatts. (Broadcasting, June 15, 1938, and November 1, 1938.)

McFarlane's conclusion was that "a colossal fraud was being perpetrated on the American people," that the radio monopolies controlled all 40 clear channels, all stations of over ,000 watts operating at night, and 93 percent of the transmitting power.[30] Representative Wigglesworth (R. of Massachusetts) concurred in the statements made by Mr. McFarlane,[31] as apparently did Senator White (R. of Maine) in the Senate Chamber.[32]

Failing passage the previous year, House Resolution 02 was revived in the next session of Congress, and when the time came for floor debate on the resolution, Representative O'Connor (D. of New York) charged:

> I have never seen a situation just like this. I have never in my life seen such lobbying against a resolution.... You can walk out in that lobby tonight and you will find difficulty in getting through the lobby because of the crowd of radio lobbyists from New York and all over the country....We shall have a roll call and see who is for the Radio Trust.[33]

The House voted down the resolution for an investigation of monopoly in radio by an overwhelming vote of 234 to 101.[34] However, even though none of the resolutions for such investigations, whether of the FCC or the industry, were ever passed, congressional pressure and discontent did bring about

---

[30] Congressional Record, 75th Cong., 1st sess., pp. 7280-7282.

[31] Ibid., p. 7851, pp. 8651-8657.  [32] Ibid., p. 2332.

[33] Congressional Record, 75th Cong., 3rd sess., p. 9314.

[34] Broadcasting Magazine, June 15, 1938.

a final result in the Commission, which began its own investigation (the Chain Monopoly Hearings), in November 1938.[35]

In 1940 the Chain Monopoly Committee reported its findings in a recommendation that called for drastic changes in network operations, such as (a) limiting network ownership of stations and the duration of affiliation contracts; (b) the removal of networks from the transcription and talent booking business; and (c) the requirement that they serve remote and sparsely populated areas whether it was profitable to do so or not. The final report, when adopted by the full Commission in 1941, called for a major reorganization of radio network operation. This included a ban on network option time, exclusive affiliations, ownership of more than one station in a market, and operation of more than one network by the same interest.[36]

---

[35]Congress did, however, pass a bill creating a Congressional Monopoly Investigating Committee to investigate monopolies in all lines of industry, and it appropriated $600,000 to perform the task. As might be expected, with such a broad scope of investigation as this committee enjoyed it had very little time to spend in any one area. (See Congressional Record, 76th Cong., 1st sess., p. 4806.)

[36]See the Report on Chain Broadcasting, Federal Communications Commission Order No. 37, Docket No. 5060, (Washington: Government Printing Office, May 1941) 139 pages. In 1943 a U. S. Supreme Court decision upheld the action of the Commission in adopting the "Chain Broadcasting Rules," thereby forcing NBC to sell its "Blue Network" and the networks to work out new contracts with their affiliates by the June 14 deadline, in which exclusivity was forbidden and option time curtailed. (See National Broadcasting Company v. FCC, 319 U. S. 190, 1943, and story in Broadcasting of May 17, 1943.)

## 4. The So-called "Cox Investigation"

Movements in Congress to investigate the Commission's conduct in regard to the broadcast industry did not come to an end merely because the Commission had itself undertaken such a study; in fact, long before the final version of the "Report on Chain Broadcasting" had been approved, Congress had begun to lose patience with the slowness of the investigation. Senate Resolution 149 and House Resolution 92 were still being offerred and debated. Mr. Connery was again asking that Congress conduct an

> immediate investigation of the entire subject of radio, particularly the apparent inability of the members of this Commission to protect the public and to eliminate or set aside the present radio monopoly.[37]

Representative Cox (D. of Georgia) countered, however, that, "What we probably need more than anything else is an investigation of the Broadcasters Trust. It is time they were stopped from monopolizing the air."[38]

Impatience with the "slowness of the Commission to authorize the setting up of a television service was another subject for concern, and an investigation was recommended by Senator Lundeen (Farmer-Labor of Montana).[39] Mr. Cox once more rose to the defense of the Commission and charged that the industry was trying to rush it into an approval of television

---

[37]Congressional Record, 76th Cong., 1st sess., p. 9313.

[38]Congressional Record, 76th Cong., 3rd sess., p. 433.

[39]S. Res. 251. See also Congressional Record, 76th Congress, 3rd sess., p. 5572.

standards before they could be adequately tested and the best means discovered:

> An attack is being made on the FCC on the ground that the Commission is retarding the growth of TV. The investigation I have made discloses the fact that the reason for the attack is that the Commission will not permit the Broadcasters Trust to exploit the public through the sale of near obsolete TV sets.[40]

Finally, however, it was not any of these events which brought matters to the climax which culminated in a congressional investigation. Instead, certain actions by the Commission itself contributed directly to the creation of an atmosphere whereby such a resolution was finally assured of passage. The first of these was its Chain Broadcasting Investigation and the publication of the Commission's "Report." As has been previously pointed out, this more than any other action in the history of the Commission enraged a powerful group within the broadcast industry. As one writer has put it:

> Prior to 1941 the FCC rarely made the headlines. At the annual convention of the NAB (National Association of Broadcasters) in May 1941, the Commission and its Chairman received its first real flaying. Ex-President Mark Etheridge accused the FCC of having gone beyond its delegated powers and having cleared the way for Government ownership of radio.[41]

At its May convention that year the NAB, in a loud and stormy attack on the Commission, (a) voted a fight to the finish against its "Monopoly Rules"; (b) backed a plan for a Senate

---

[40] Congressional Record, 76th Cong., 3rd sess., p. 433.

[41] Henry Hottman, "Some Problems of Federal Regulation of the Broadcast Industry," unpublished Ph.D. dissertation (Univ. of Colorado, 1947), p. 116.

investigation of the FCC;[42] and (c) requested legislation to
aid broadcasters. Mr. James Lawrence Fly, then Chairman of
the Commission, angered by the accusations directed against
that agency and himself, gave a rebuttal in which he described
the NAB and its leaders as akin to "a mackerel in the moon-
light...it both shines and stinks."[43] The radio industry
thereafter left no stone unturned to see that it got an "investigation" underway.

The second Commission action that was to bring about
a change of attitude in the Congress was the one it brought
against the newspaper industry. On March 20, 1941, it issued
order No. 79, which directed that an investigation be made
concerning a determination of

> What statement of policy or rules, if any, should be
> issued concerning applications for high frequency broad-
> cast stations (FM) with which are associated persons also
> associated with the publication of one or more newspapers...
> such investigations and public hearings shall also in-
> clude a statement of policy or rules, if any, which
> should be issued concerning future acquisition of broad-
> cast stations by newspapers.[44]

In July, 1941, the Commission went beyond the scope of the
earlier order and ruled that it would also investigate the
operation and conduct of the newspapers themselves, and that
the resultant orders would not only apply to FI but to the
then present system of broadcasting.[45]

---

[42]S. Res. 300, 76th Cong., 3rd sess., p. 10788.

[43]Broadcasting Magazine, May 19, 1941.

[44]Broadcasting Magazine, March 24, 1941.

[45]Commission Order No. 79A. (At that time 292 of the
country's 893 broadcasting stations were newspaper affiliated.)

The newspaper industry, disturbed by the Commission's actions, accused it of attempting to punish those newspapers which were not in sympathy with the administration by threatening to take away their radio licenses. A Newspaper-Radio Committee was formed for the purpose of bringing to the FCC the point of view representative of those newspapers which had interests in radio stations. The Committee felt that the orders of the Commission and the proposed investigation

> involved questions of deep importance to a democratic nation, such as...the preservation of newspapers and radio as a safety valve for the uncontrolled and free source of information for the growth of independent public opinion.[46]

As the political climate turned in an increasing degree toward the sanctioning of what was felt, for a number of often somewhat contradictory reasons, to be a much-needed investigation, new complaints were being made to the Congress. These new complaints charged that the Commission had, on occasions, (a) been guilty of an abuse of its licensing powers, (b) that it had shown political favoritism in certain licensing cases, and (c) that it had, on numerous occasions, particularly in connection with its activities in relationship to the war effort, gone beyond the powers vested in it by the Communications Act of 1934. All of these events contributed to the feeling in Congress that an investigation was due.

The final act of the Commission bringing on an investigation was that it had, sometime before, lost the friendship

---

[46]See Freedom of the Press prepared and released by the Newspaper-Radio Committee, 370 Lexington Avenue, N. Y., N. Y., 105 pages.

of a Representative who had been one of its staunchest de-

fenders. This occurred when it charged Representative Cox

of having received pay for representing a radio station be-

fore it. Mr. Cox retaliated by calling Chairman Fly

> the most dangerous man in the Government....He maintains
> an active and ambitious Gestapo and is putting shackles
> on freedom of thought, press and speech without restraint....
> He is taking advantage of the stress of the moment to
> federalize all means of communication....[47]

Mr. Cox later referred to the entire FCC in the following

words: "His (Fly's) whole outfit is a nest of reds...."[48]

Mr. Cox introduced a resolution, quickly passed by

the House by an almost unanimous vote, calling for the forma-

tion of a select committee

> ...to conduct a study and investigation of the organi-
> zation, personnel, and activities of the Federal Communi-
> cations Commission with a view to determining whether or
> not such Commission, in its organization, in the selection
> of personnel, and in the conduct of its activities, has
> been, and is, acting in accordance with the law and the
> public interest.[49]

The resolution provided that the select committee was to be

composed of five members of the House, to be appointed by the

Speaker, one of whom was to be designated as chairman. Re-

presentative Cox was appointed to this position. There

followed what, without a doubt, has been the most controver-

sial investigation in the history of the Communications  Com-

mission.

---

[47]Congressional Record, 77th Cong., 2d sess., p. 794.

[48]Congressional Record, 78th Cong., 1st sess.,
pp. 234-235.

[49]H. Res. 21, 78th Cong., 1st sess., pp. 233-235 (first
introduced the previous session as H. Res. 426).

The Cox investigation, unlike previously proposed
resolutions to investigate which had no success in passage
in the Congress, was an inquiry oriented around conservative
lines. It found fault with the FCC for actions that it had
taken, rather than for actions it had failed to take. Instead of criticizing the Commission because it had not taken
an active roll in riding herd on the "radio monopolies," it
was criticized because some members of Congress felt that it
had, through the publication of its "Chain Monopoly Rules,"
gone much too far. As one member stated, it had tried "to
put radio stations in the same category as public utilities."[50]
Many Committee members believed and stated that the Commission had no right to mix into the program and business affairs of a station; and that it had erred when, in 1941, it
began consideration as to whether it should prohibit the
further issuance of broadcast licenses to newspaper owners;
that it had no right to place a numerical limit on the number
of stations a single owner might possess; and that it had no
business meddling in considerations of prices paid for stations in matters of transfer.

In addition to these broad questions of policy, specific charges were also levied against the Commission. There
were charges brought that the Commission had (a) practiced
political favoritism in the performance of its duties; (b)
that it had sought to punish newspapers that were politically

---

50H. Rept. 2095, 78th Cong., 2d sess., p. 55.

opposed to the Administration by seeking to restrain certain of them from owning and operating radio stations; and (c) that the Commission had arrogated to itself powers not granted by the Congress and invaded the wartime fields of operation within the sphere belonging to the Army and Navy. The Commission's Chairman, Mr. Fly, was accused of "completely dominating the rest of the Commission," and of helping certain of his friends to obtain radio stations.[51]  Although evidence was introduced which in varying degrees substantiated each of the charges laid against the Commission, the majority report of the Committee states in precise and lucid terms what was really at the bottom of the entire investigation:

> It is apparent that members of the Commission have interpreted their duties as set forth in the Communications Act according to their different philosophies of government. The predominating group of the Commission, in the main led by Chairman Fly, represented the more liberal interpretation of the Act as to the broad powers conferred on the Commission. Under this interpretation, powers that might be of debatable validity were claimed for the Commission. The other viewpoint believed in the strict construction of their powers with a view of restricting the Commission's activities and the exercise of caution in the exercise of debatable powers. This difference in governmental viewpoint is perhaps the basic explanation of the differences among the Commission members which have been more or less notable for many years.

In respect to the Commission's most controversial figure the report stated:

> Mr. James Lawrence Fly came to the chairmanship of the Commission when there was undoubtedly a necessity for better organization and efficient administration, notably

---

[51]*Ibid.*, p. 54.

as affecting the broadcasting phases of the Commission's powers. Mr. Fly is a very able, resourceful man, strong in his convictions, aggressive and persistent in advancing them, and assumed an unquestioned leadership in the activities of the Commission. His zeal for his work met with increasing opposition. Sometimes he was arbitrary in the conduct of hearings, to the irritation of persons appearing before the Commission and to some members of the Commission itself. His general assertion of the full powers of the Commission that might be claimed under the Act was from time to time a matter of bitter criticism directed at his activities.

It is probably true that Mr. Fly contributed materially to the better functioning of the Commission. He left it better than he found it. His resignation from the Commission has removed him as an element of controversy from its future activities.[52]

In closing, the majority report made the following recommendation:

The basic need now, from a congressional standpoint, is for a reexamination of the provisions of the Communications Act with a view to their modification to conform to the requirements of administration as demonstrated by the needs of the industry and the Commission since the original acts were enacted.[53]

By the time the smoke of battle had cleared, a great many changes in personnel had been made on both sides of the controversy. Since the investigation's beginning, Chairman Fly had resigned from the Commission; Commissioner Craven had publicly declined renomination; Commissioner Payne had failed to be reappointed; and Dr. Robert D. Leigh, Director of the Foreign Broadcast Intelligence Service, had resigned immediately following the conclusion of his testimony before the Committee.

The Committee had seen the resignation of its original

[52]Ibid., p. 52.    [53]Ibid., p. 53.

Chairman, Representative Cox.  Its original General Counsel,
Mr. Eugene L. Garey, and its subsequent General Counsel,
Mr. John J. Sirica, had both resigned charging the investigation had been turned into a "whitewash."  By the time the investigation was over, the Committee staff through various
resignations had shrunk in size from an original 19 to five.

In the final outcome, the record of the hearings and
the resultant recommendations of the Committee did not have
as great a legislative effect upon Congress as would have
been the case had not the issue of politics and personalities
been so predominant.  It had become far too controversial a
topic of discussion for anyone, in Congress or out, to make
a cool appraisal of the legislative weaknesses and failures
that it brought to light and the remedies it afforded.  However, it did furnish further proof of the need of clarification of the Communications Act of 1934, and certain of its
recommendations were echoed in future legislative attempts to
amend the Act.  Two of the more comprehensive bills which
owed their origins at least in part to the revelations of the
Cox investigation were S. 1333 and H. R. 3595, introduced in
the 80th Congress, 1st session (the so-called White-Wolverton
bill), and S. 1973, 81st Congress, 1st session, first introduced by Senator McFarland in 1949.  Each of these bills will
be discussed and analyzed at a later point in our study.[54]

The investigation seemed to mark something of a turning

_____

[54]See Chapters VI and VII.

point in the attitude of Congress toward the Federal regulatory agencies. From this time until the passage of the Communications Act Amendments of 1952 and thereafter, there seems to have been a gradual postwar swing of the pendulum away from a congressional attitude which called for a stricter governmental supervision of broadcasting (a characteristic of the 1930's), to a gradual return of a philosophy which called for a greater degree of self-regulation. Along with this came an attempt to provide a more explicit enumeration of the Commission's powers and duties by means of clarifying changes in the law.

# CHAPTER VI

## ATTEMPTS ON THE PART OF CONGRESS
## TO REORGANIZE THE COMMISSION

On January, 1939, the President wrote letters to the
chairmen of the Committees of Interstate Commerce of both
Houses, in which he expressed dissatisfaction with the manner in which the Communications Commission was organized.

> I have come to the definite conclusion that new legis-
> lation is necessary to effectuate a satisfactory reorgani-
> zation of the Commission. New legislation is also needed
> to lay down clearer congressional policies on the sub-
> stantive side -- so clear that the new administrative
> body will have no difficulty in interpreting and adminis-
> tering them.[1]

This statement sparked the submission of a number of reorganization bills to Congress over the next few years. The first
of these was introduced approximately one month after the
Presidential letter was sent. On February 8, 1939, a bill
(S. 1268) was submitted by Senator Wheeler (D. of Montana).[2]
The proposed legislation would have (a) created a new Commission of three members, (b) provided for the hiring of administrative assistants, and (c) the creation of a Department
of Research and Information.

Another bill was introduced on February 21 of that
year by Senator White (R. of Maine), which proposed to amend

---

[1]Carl J. Friedrich and Evelyn Sternberg, "Congress and
the Control of Radio Broadcasting," The American Political
Science Review, vol. 27, No. 5 (October 1943), p. 1016.

[2]S. 1268, 76th Cong., 1st sess., Congressional Record,
p. 1275.

sections one through six inclusive of the Act of 1934,
basically changing the administrative structure and functioning of the Commission.

> Summarized, the bill proposes in the first six
> sections a Commission composed of eleven members, separ-
> ated into two permanent divisions of five members each,
> not including the Chairman.[3]

This was merely an early example of a long line of reorganization bills, stretching to the present time, in which it was
recommended that the Commission be divided into two divisions,
a Common Carrier Division and a Broadcast Division.  Bills
such as this were introduced because experience had indicated
that the problems which had to be faced in the common carrier
field were basically different from the problems of broadcasting.  If one was to be treated as a public utility and
the other, by law, was not, it was necessary not only to provide different solutions but a different point of departure
for both.  For this reason many members of Congress believed
there should be two separate and distinct divisions, each
with its own duties, in order that, over a period of time,
each would acquire the capability of understanding and dealing with its own peculiar problems.  In addition to this,
there was some feeling in Congress that far too much of the
Commission's time was taken up by the problems of broadcasting,
and far too little of it given to the common carrier field,

---

[3]Congressional Record, 76th Cong., 1st sess., p. 1673.
S. 1520, an act to amend the Communications Act, introduced
by Mr. White.

with the result that the latter was not being properly regulated.

Had S. 1520 passed Congress it would have vested the
judicial and quasi-judicial functions of the Commission in
the two divisions, a Division of Public Communication for
all broadcasting, and a Division of Private Communication for
all common carriers.  Each division would have had authority
to make its own decisions and act upon questions under its
jurisdiction without taking them before the full Commission.

A similar bill (to S. 1520) was again introduced by
Senator White in 1941.[4]  That same year brought forth the
so-called Saunders bill (Rep. Jared Y. Saunders, Jr., D. of
Louisiana) which contained many similar provisions and was
introduced in the House.[5]  Again, a similar bill for reorganization of the Commission was introduced at the beginning of
the session in 1943 by Representative Holmes (Pehr G. Holmes,
R. of Massachusetts).[6]  In the same year Senators Wheeler and
White produced another bill, S. 814, which paralleled the
Holmes bill in certain respects but which, in addition,
carefully defined the limits of FCC authority.  All bills,
however, either failed to emerge from committee, or failed in
passage, marking an end until postwar days of congressinnal
attempts to reorganize the Commission.

---

[4]S. 1806, 77th Cong., 1st sess., p. 6641.

[5]H. R. 5497, 77th Cong., 1st sess., p. 6802.

[6]H. R. 1490, 78th Cong., 1st sess., p. 175.

## 1. The White-Wolverton Bill, S. 1333

The most interesting and pervasive of the postwar
attempts at reappraisal and reenactment prior to passage of
the McFarland Acts was a bill introduced by Senator White in
the first session of the 80th Congress (1947),[7] (the companion
bill, H. R. 3595, was introduced in the House by Rep. Wolverton (R. of New Jersey). Senator White was one of the few remaining members of Congress who had been present and had
played a part in the enactment of the original legislation
affecting radio broadcasting (the Radio Act of 1927). Now
that he was about to retire from Congress, he announced his
intention to propose passage of this new bill revising Commission procedures as a kind of final effort on his part in the
broadcast field.

Senator White stated that the bill was the "result of
more than seven years of congressional investigations, studies,
and hearings by committees in both Houses of Congress...."
Its "immediate source (was) in S. 1268, a bill introduced by
Senator Wheeler in the 76th Congress (1939); S. 1520, introduced by me in the 76th Congress"; and "S. 814, introduced
by me, for myself and Senator Wheeler, in the 78th Congress
(1943)."[8] The Senator claimed the bill was not intended to

---

[7]S. 1333, a bill to amend the Communications Act of
1934, and for other purposes (House version, H. R. 3595).

[8]Congressional Record, vol. 93, 80th Cong., 1st sess.,
p. 5707.

constitute a complete overhaul of the existing law; instead,

The purpose of the bill is largely to clarify the meaning and intent of the existing Act and to rectify some of the defects which have become obvious during the last twelve years of administration of the law.[9]

The bill was also intended to deal with "alleged ambiguities," "asserted conflicts," and "with administrative and legal interpretations which have led to sharp differences of opinion among and between licensees, the Federal Communications Commission, the Congress, and the courts."[10]

### 2. An Analysis of the More Important Provisions Contained in S. 1333, as It Was Originally Proposed to the Congress

#### a. The Organization of the Commission

The White bill contained a number of provisions that had been previously proposed before Congress. Regarding the organization of the Commission, it would have made the following changes:

Sections 4 and 5 would have changed sections 4 and 5 of the Communications Act by eliminating the provision which gave the President the authority to name the chairman of the Commission. It would have provided, instead, for the annual election of the chairman. In addition, the Commission of seven members would have been split into two statutory divisions of three members each, a Common Carrier Division and a Broadcast

---

[9]Ibid., p. 5707.

[10]S. Rept. 1567, to accompany S. 1333, 80th Cong., 2d sess., p. 2.

Division. The chairman was to serve as the executive
officer and coordinator of each division, except in the
determination of contested matters. These were to be made
the exclusive business of each division.

### b. Policy in Station Transfers

Section 13 proposed to change section 310 (b) of the
Communications Act to provide for the observance of a definite procedure by the Commission in cases which involved the
transfer or sale of a station license. The new proposed provision outlined definite standards which were to control the
ultimate decision in each case.

### c. The Right to Issue Cease-and-Desist Orders

Section 14 would have amended section 312 to authorize the Commission to issue cease-and-desist orders, subsequent violation of which would give cause for license
revocation.

### d. Prohibition Against "Discrimination" in Licensing

Section 25 proposed a new requirement be added to
Title IV, section 418, of the Communications Act, to deal
with "discrimination." It would have prohibited the Commission from taking any action which might result in its "discriminating between any applicant because of race, religion,
business, or political affiliation."[11] The provision was

---

[11]Such a provision would, for instance, prevent the
Commission from adopting any rule, regulation, or policy which
would deny or mitigate against the award of broadcast

also designed to prevent the Commission from holding certain applications or classes of applications in an inactive status.

## e. The Handling of News and Public Issues

In regard to the handling of news, public issues, and broadcasts by political candidates, the following proposed revisions were offered by the White bill.

Section 15 revised section 315 (which dealt with broadcasts by candidates for public office) clarifying the existing statute and exempting licensees from charges of libel or slander by any person speaking under the provisions of that section. The proposed new section would also have considerably broadened the meaning of the statute, to give "equal opportunity" not only to legally qualified candidates for the same office, but also persons designated by them as spokesmen. Finally, it would have prohibited any broadcasts by candidates or their representatives for 24 hours prior to the time that an election was to be held.

Section 17 was to amend sections 330 and 331 of the Communications Act to require equal opportunity to be afforded to the discussion of all public issues once one side had been given or sold time. Full information was to be furnished to the listener concerning the speaker, his subject, the capacity in which the speaker appeared, under what circumstances the time was made available, and, if paid for,

___

licenses to newspapers. Since the time of the Commission's investigation into newspaper ownership of radio (1941), newspaper-radio interests had been attempting to obtain passage of an amendment similar to the one above.

by whom. In regard to this proposal, Senator White charged
that "Too often, advocates of a particular policy or issue
have appeared under false colors."[12]

Section 18 would have further required that editorials and interpretive news should be identified as such, and
the source of news items disclosed. Mr. White stated: "It
is common knowledge that, in many so-called news broadcasts,
not even the most discerning of listeners is able to separate fact from opinion."[13]

### f. Chain Broadcasting

The bill would have added two major amendments to the
Communications Act having to do with "chain broadcasting."
Section 7 was designed to change subsection (i) of section
308 to expressly limit the Commission's rulemaking power

---

[12]Congressional Record, vol. 93, 80th Cong., 1st
sess., p. 5710.

[13]Ibid., p. 5710. The comment is in order that,
while little valid objection can be raised in respect to the
proper differentiation between news and commentary, the requirement in regard to identification of a news source could
be reasonably interpreted as a possible infringement of the
constitutional privilege of freedom of the press. As anyone
engaged in the dissemination of news will readily state, the
source or informant in a story often cannot be revealed without a breach of confidence in regard to the manner in which
the story is given. (See New York Times, June 15, 1947,
Jack Gould, which states: "To ask a commentator to identify,
item by item, the 'source and responsibility' for his views
can only be regarded as implied censorship. If a journalist...
were required as a matter of law to identify always the source
of his views, the blunt truth is that a great deal of news
never would see the light of day. The protection of the
source of news, in fact, is a cardinal principle of journal-
istic integrity.")

with respect to stations engaged in chain broadcasting to only the physical and technical phases of regulation. This would have narrowed down, to a considerable extent, the effect of the Supreme Court opinion in NBC, Inc., et al. v. U. S. et al. (319 U. S. 190 (1943)).

Section 9 proposed to add a totally new provision to the Act (sec. 333) which would have supplied positive and unequivocal statutory prohibitions against certain kinds of contractual relationships between the licensees of broadcast stations and networks, as well as certain limitations on ownership of radio stations. The new amendment would have prevented a single licensee or corporation from owning stations which served more than 25 percent of the Nation's population.[14]

. The Power to Examine the "Overall Operation" of a Station

Section 16 would have revised section 326 to specify that the Commission should have no power to regulate the business of the licensee, except when such power is specifically conferred by the Act itself. However, the new provision also clearly stated the Commission did have authority, in any case where application for renewal of license is made, to examine the overall operation of the licensee to determine

---

[14]In effect, the new provisions adopted the FCC'S Chain Broadcasting Rules, and made them law.

whether or not the operation had satisfied the statutory
standard.  Senator White stated:

> The proposed language of this section does not take
> away the Commission's authority to make a finding
> whether or not a licensee has operated in the public
> interest; it is, in fact, affirmed.  But it also makes
> clear that the Commission does not have the authority to
> tell a licensee, directly or indirectly, what he can
> broadcast or cannot broadcast, or how he shall run his
> day-to-day business.[15]

### 3.  The Testimony on the Bill

Senate hearings on the White measure were held from
June 17-20, and 23-25, 1947.  During this period, strong
opposition to its passage became apparent from the testimony
by representatives of the National Association of Broadcasters (NAB).  The broadcasting interests, while approving
some of the bill's provisions, were in violent opposition to
those provisions which connoted an espousal of the so-called
"Chain Broadcast Rulings" and the "Blue Book" philosophy of
the FCC.  Some of the strongest objections were made in connection with amending section 326 to allow the Commission to
review "past performance" of a station at the time of license
renewal.  Other strong objections were directed against
(a) any numerical limitation on ownership of stations, and

---

[15]Ibid., p. 5709.  This portion of the bill, in
effect, embraced the philosophy the Commission had adopted in
its issuance of the Blue Book (Public Service Responsibilities
of Broadcast Licensees, Washington: Government Printing
Office, 1946, 139 pages.)  It was to this portion of the proposed legislation that the broadcast industry would object
most strongly.

(b) the amendment which called for identification of the
source of a news item.[16]

Criticism of the White bill was not limited to that
expressed by broadcasters, however, for the very first witness before the committee was FCC Chairman Charles R. Denny,
who raised the following objections to parts of the bill:

First, he proposed that there be three divisions of
the Commission instead of two -- one for safety and special
services as well as those for broadcast and common carriers.
Each division should have more than three members, to avoid
the possibility of two-to-one votes on major policy matters.
Enlargement of the Commission should be undertaken if it was
considered necessary in order to achieve the larger divisions. Mr. Denny stated:

> Each division would have a chairman, who would serve on
> that division only. In that way, you would have on each
> of those divisions one man who would be completely free
> of all other work, and who would be able to devote his
> entire time to supplying leadership in that particular
> field of activity. All other Commissioners would serve
> on two divisions. And it has been suggested that the
> Chairman of the Commission might serve on all three
> fields of Commission activity.
>
> Where a division is evenly divided -- two to two --
> the matter automatically would be referred to the entire
> Commission. Such a system would insure executive leader-
> ship in each field and at the same time would preserve

---

[16]The evidences are many that from the time of publication of the Commission's Blue Book, strong pressures had been
building in the industry against any further occurrences of
what was termed to be "outside interference" by Government in
the business and programming practices of station owners.
Any kind of espousal of "Blue Book" philosophy by the Congress
was thus bound to be extremely unpopular.

the advantage of securing the judgment of the full Commission on all important questions of policy.[17]

Although he did not criticize the proposal to have the chairman elected annually by the Commission instead of appointed by the President, he was opposed to the bill's plan calling for the placement of any limitation on the activities of the chairman, who he said would become nothing more than a "ceremonial figurehead."

Chairman Denny found "serious objection" to the bill's prohibition against FCC regulation of multiple ownership, and pointed out that the Act would write the Commission's present network broadcasting regulations into law, but would forbid future rules. Mr. Denny was of the opinion that the Commission would be seriously hampered if it were deprived of that right.[18]

The Commission Chairman viewed the controversial amendment on license renewal with approval (sec. 326), as an "improvement in existing law." He declared:

> It makes explicit what is now implicit, namely, that there is a distinction between censorship of radio program material, in which the Commission does not and should not indulge, and the consideration of the overall service of a station, including its program service, in determining whether a station has operated in the public interest.[19]

Mr. Denny stated that he regarded the Commission's AVCO "auction" rule as the main target of the bill's transfer

---

[17]Hearings of the Senate Interstate and Foreign Commerce Committee on S. 1333, 80th Cong., 1st sess., p. 23.

[18]Ibid., p. 54.    [19]Ibid., p. 58.

section. He explained that under the present law, section
310 (b) provided that no license could be transferred unless the Commission "after securing full information" should
decide that the transfer was in the public interest. The
proposed amendment would have eliminated that requirement
and substituted for it a mere finding that the proposed
transferee possessed the qualifications of an original licensee. He described what he called a "basic defect" in the
Commission's handling of transfer cases, and gave the following explanation of why the "AVCO" procedure had been adopted.

...prior to AVCO...a man retiring from the radio business had the power, for all practical purposes, to
select his successor, and his selection was final except in the very rare case where he elected to sell to a
party who was subsequently found to be unqualified. The
difficulty with this is that a person who on retiring
from radio is selecting a purchaser, is naturally influ-
enced by the size of a prospective purchaser's pocket-
book, and not by the type of service which the purchaser
intends to offer the public. Thus, once he finds the
highest bidder, he sells to that person even though
there may be many other better qualified persons willing
and anxious to take over the operation of the station
on the same terms and conditions.

We thus had the anomalous situation that entirely
different procedures were followed in transfer cases
than is customary in the handling of applications for
new stations, although the standards prescribed by the
Act were substantially identical. For in the case of
licensing new stations the procedure followed, and which
would continue to be followed if these amendments are
enacted, is designed to insure that everyone who is
interested in applying for a particular broadcast frequency had an opportunity to do so. This has usually
resulted in a competitive situation where the Commission
has a choice between applicants. It is difficult to
reconcile procedures which on the one hand take such
pains to insure the fullest competition among applicants
for new stations and on the other hand permit a licensee
to transfer to whomever he pleases -- provided the transferee selected is qualified. This is particularly difficult to understand when the section under consideration

specifically provides for following the same procedure in transfer cases as for original applications but changes the substantive standards.

In order to cure this discrepancy, the Commission adopted the so-called AVCO procedure for dealing with transfers....Under this procedure when a transfer application is filed with the Commission, it is held in abeyance for 60 days during which time an advertisement is carried in the Federal Register and in the newspapers of the community served by the station to the effect that the existing licensee proposes to transfer his station license and the terms and conditions of the sale. The notice provides that any other person wishing to apply for the facilities on the same terms may do so. If no one applies, the Commission acts on the transfer application on its merits. But if other parties come in, the Commission gives comparative consideration to all applications, granting the application of the original proposed transferee if it appears from the applications that it is best qualified to serve the public interest, and setting all applications for comparative hearing if it is unable to so determine....

The Commission believes that the adoption of this procedure enables it to carry out more adequately the congressional intent that the best qualified person should be licensed for each available frequency....[20]

The chief witness of the broadcast industry testifying against the bill was Justin Miller, former Dean of the University of Minnesota Law School, then president of the NAB. His statement began with an elaborate treatment of the history of the freedom-of-speech amendment, and its application to radio and the press. His testimony was based on a premise that challenged the whole philosophy upon which the existing as well as the proposed communication law was based.

Mr. Miller maintained that the powers of the FCC to regulate radio were limited by the first amendment from

---

[20] Ibid., pp. 49-50. Also see stories in Broadcasting, September 10, 1945, August 5, 1946.

in any way abridging freedom of speech, press, or radio. In addition, it was his opinion that the same reasoning which made broadcasting subject to control under the commerce clause also made it subject to protection under the first amendment. An entire 50-page written statement was directed to a consideration of those sections of the White bill which he claimed abridged the first amendment.

His chief specific objection to the White bill was aimed at the revisions the bill proposed to make in section 326, which would have, in his words,

> give(n) even greater courage to the FCC to expand its administrative interpretation, and further...encroach upon the rights of the broadcaster in the field of free speech by means of radio communication.[21]

In support of this statement he claimed that "poor programming" was not sufficient cause to put a station off the air, and that, "So far as is possible, the analogy between the press and the radio should be kept as close as possible."[22]

Several of the Senators on the committee hearing his testimony demonstrated an unwillingness to accept such a close comparison between the operation of a newspaper and that of a radio station. Senator McFarland stated:

> ...there is a difference between the press and the radio. You can compare them but you cannot assume they are alike. You are granting frequencies in the radio field. Once a license is granted, it is worth a lot of money. That is not true with the press at all. That is where you people get off base, in my opinion.

---

[21] Ibid., testimony of Justin Miller, president, NAB, p. 128.

[22] Ibid., p. 120.

Senator White concurred in the following words:

> A newspaperman, if I may interrupt, starts from the
> ground. He has no special advantages accorded to him
> from the Government except that he is to have the largest
> possible measure of freedom, and he goes on and builds
> a newspaper which takes on the characteristics of a pub-
> lic service. But it seems to me that there is a vast
> amount of difference in principle between the absolute
> right of anyone who wants to go into the newspaper busi-
> ness, and the necessarily limited right to operate a
> broadcasting station.
>
> Now, I never had supposed that there was the slight-
> est question as to the right of the Federal Government
> to grant or to refuse a license, as the circumstances
> might require. I just do not get at all the idea that
> there is a complete analogy between a broadcast license,
> which comes from the Government and is an exercise of
> power by Government, and the right of anybody to start
> a newspaper, anybody who wants to, without a let or per-
> mission or hindrance from the Government....[23]

The Senator declared that in his opinion a definite
relationship existed between the quality of programming and
the public service which a station renders in living up to
its license. Thus, he made this conclusion:

> ...it is pretty difficult, for me to see how a regula-
> tory body can say that a licensee is or is not render-
> ing a public service if it may not take a look and take
> into account the character of the program being broad-
> cast....Why, it seems to me that the quality of the
> program is the outstanding factor in determining whether
> the station is performing a public service or not.[24]

Mr. Miller countered with the argument that it was
not a matter of interpretation but of guarantees written
into the Constitution which could not be applied to any one
group without being applied to all. He charged that the proposed White bill changed the Constitution, giving it special
effect as it applied to radio.[25] The witness attacked both

---

[23]Ibid., p. 120.    [24]Ibid., p. 123.    [25]Ibid., 127.

the "Blue Book" and the FCC's "Chain Rules" as examples of
the exercise by the Commission of power in the regulation of
the businesses of station licensees, and criticized the "Blue
Book" because it undertook "to require broadcasters to
change their program content on the theory that (the industry
was) making too much money and should spend a larger proportion of it for radio programming."[26]

Senator McFarland later countered with the statement:

If it comes to the point of not giving any powers to
the Commission....If we will not even let them look at
a program to see what a station has been doing, to determine whether it has been performing a service in the public interest, I am in favor of wiping them (the Commission)
out.

The following colloquy between the committee and the
witness serves to demonstrate clearly the two major philosophies of broadcasting:

Mr. MILLER.    That may be the best thing to do.

Senator McFARLAND.    I assume that is what the
broadcasters would like.

Mr. MILLER.    No, indeed; far from it.  The broadcasters know as well as anyone the vital importance of
having a commission to regulate the use of these frequencies.  The assignment of frequencies, the licensing
of the operators of the frequencies, that is a vital and
important thing.

Senator McFARLAND.    That is as far as you want them
to go, to give you the monopoly, and after that, let you
do what you want to do with it....When the station comes
up for a new license, it is a relicensing, every time
there is a renewal.

Mr. MILLER.    All right.  If the licensee has failed
to keep on this channel, has failed to use the right
directional antenna, has failed to provide the proper

---

[26]Ibid., p. 129.

engineering standards, if he has failed to observe the
technical and other requirements, which are necessary to
preserve the medium for the most effective use, from that
point on the test should be exactly the same as they are
for any other medium of communication.

Senator McFARLAND.    In other words, you just make
the FCC purely a scientific board to determine whether
the frequencies were being properly used in a scientific
way.

Mr. MILLER.    Properly, yes, from the scientific and
technical point of view.[27]

At a point near the conclusion of his testimony,
Mr. Miller charged that the FCC'S control over broadcasting
"climaxes a long series of steps" toward "star chamber" government.  The phrase "public interest," he asserted, "is used
by administrative crusaders (as) a hook upon which to hang
many strange and devious notions."[28]  Nevertheless, the
industry was "perfectly content to go along with the law as
it now is, rather than have changes made which will expand
(the Commission's) power."[29]  Finally, Mr. Miller argued
that, if left alone and not interfered with by Government
meddling in private business, broadcasters themselves would
"clean up their own house."  However, they should not be
coerced into adopting policies which they did not feel were
in their own best interests, since

>...no self-respecting man can be expected to assume res-
>ponsibilities of the kind called for in professional con-
>trols and self-discipline, when they are being subjected
>constantly to interference, reprisals, and intimidation
>from a Government agency.[30]

---

[27]Ibid., pp. 168-169.      [28]Ibid., p. 174.

[29]Ibid., p. 180.      [30]Ibid., p. 185.

The testimony of Mr. Miller serves as an excellent
illustration of the general attitude of the broadcast industry toward any kind of Government regulation of broadcasting
beyond that of traffic control.  It was followed by several
days of further testimony along the same lines by other
industry and association members, including the NAB's general counsel, executive vice president, director of public
relations, director of broadcast advertising and program
department director, along with a number of individual station owners and program directors.  The most heavily criticized provisions of the new law not previously mentioned
during the balance of the industry testimony were those
which (a) would threaten to change option time agreements
to from three out of five hours to two out of three;
(b) would have limited station ownership by any one interest
to those reaching not more than 25 percent of the population;
and (c) would have made broadcasters subject to license
revocation under the antitrust laws.

In general it may be said that the industry was
strongly opposed to any form of legislation which would give
the FCC new powers, or further define or broaden any of its
old ones; conversely, it was in favor of any clause that
would tend to place a limitation on the Commission's powers.
It preferred maintenance of the status quo, at all costs,
rather than see any changes that might place any limitations
in anyway on the broadcaster's freedom, even though it
believed that the Commission even then exercised more power
than it really possessed.

### 4. Revision of the White-Wolverton Bill (S. 1333) in Senate Committee, Its Final Failure to Come to a Vote in Either Senate or House

The testimony elicited in the hearings did have the effect of convincing the authors of the bill that some revisions were in order. A revised version of the bill, written by the legal staff of the Broadcaster's Association (NAB) was subsequently suggested. In its revised form, section 326 was rewritten in such a way as to eliminate almost half the wordage of the proposed bill and much of the language included in it by Senator White.[31] In doing so, it naturally left the Commission with far less authority over station operation.

In the ensuing period the NAB did draft its much advertised "Code of Practices" for what was termed the "self-regulation of abuses by radio stations." The code did not excite much enthusiasm among the industry, however, which was quoted as giving rise to "intense and widespread mounting criticism and opposition" to the code's provisions. In fact, after the industry convention of 1947, where the code was introduced, charges were made

> ...that commercial limitations in the code (were) unworkable for a majority of the stations...that it never should have been offered in the first place; that it (had been) carelessly drafted without time for proper industry study; that a tight monopoly did the drafting job; that radio (faced) growing competition within

---

[31] See _Broadcasting-Telecasting_, August 18, 1947, p. 18.

itself and from other media, and therefore should work out means of increasing its efficiency to the advertiser rather than diminishing it....[32]

A number of state associations joined the growing list of organized groups demanding changes in the standards that the NAB had adopted. The inevitable occurred when, after a few months of haggling over the various provisions, chiefly those dealing with imposed time limitations on commercial announcements, a sufficiently watered down version of the code was formulated to enable the broadcast association to obtain approval from a majority of its members. Since that time, although frequently revised, the code has been largely ignored by the individual stations, except at those moments when it was felt necessary to exhume it in order to demonstrate what a fine job of "self-regulation" the broadcasters were doing.[33]

---

[32]Broadcasting-Telecasting, November 3, 1947, p. 17.

[33]In its May 15, 1950, issue, for example, Broadcasting had this to say about the efficacy of industry codes:

"If telecasters, in considering the creation of a code for their own programming, paused to study the history of the NAB Standards of Practice for radio, they would be apt to wonder if codes are worth the very great effort it takes to write them.

"In its two years of existence, the NAB code has proved to be a much less controversial issue than it was before it was written. Rereading it today, one is struck by the fact that the code is, in most respects, a painstaking expression of the obvious.

"Excerpts from the NAB code suggest that broadcasters should honor the sanctity of marriage and the home, observe proprieties of civilized society, present news that is factual and without bias, confine children's programs to those that contribute to the healthy development of personality and

En dehors du body

In regard to S. 1333, a new draft of the bill did
emerge from committee. To this draft was added a provision
which forbade any professional employee of the Commission
"to represent in any capacity" for one year after leaving
its employ, "any person within the Commission's jurisdiction."[34] The provision was designed to eliminate what
committee members called "the steppingstone practice" of
using Commission positions as intermediate stopping places
in the process of obtaining more lucrative positions in the
regulated industry.

Other changes in the revised draft produced by the
committee involved the provisions which dealt with (a) the
organization and terms of office of the Commission,

---

and character,' and refrain from airing mystery shows that
'tend to make the commission of crime attractive.'

"Since no broadcaster in his right mind would quar-
rel openly with such precepts (Who would be witless enough
to take a stand publicly against children and dogs?); there
was little disagreement over their inclusion in the document
before it was written and only occasional disregard for them
after the code became 'law.'

"The section of the code over which the greatest controversy raged in the preparatory period was that which fixed
limitations on advertising time. A not inconsiderable number of broadcasters argued that the proposed time standards
were unrealistic. There is no reason to believe that they
changed their minds or their habits in this regard after the
adoption of the code.

"Now, if, on the other hand, the programming principles
contained in the code were in general practice before its
adoption and, on the other hand, the time standards were
the subject of disagreement before and after they were put
into the code, the question arises: What purpose has the
code served?..."

[34]Amendment to subsec. (f) (1) of sec. 4 of the
Communications Act.

(b) limitations on station ownership, (c) identification of news broadcasts, and (d) certain revisions which related to the allocation of equal time to qualified candidates for public office.

Industry spokesmen, although they lauded the revised draft of the White bill as a "vast improvement over the original measure," still were very much opposed to its so-called "censorship section," which the committee refused to omit from the original White bill.[35]

The Commission was reported ready to support the bill except for its section forbidding its members to work for the broadcast industry for a period of one year after leaving.[36] Broadcasting reported that "a virtual wave of resignations from the staff is expected if enactment of the provision becomes imminent."[37] Commissioners themselves were opposed to another provision which would not allow them

---

[35]See Broadcasting-Telecasting, January 12, 1948, p. 13.

[36]Although the "steppingstone" approach to better jobs in industry certainly constitutes a problem in insulation of Commission members from influence from the regulated industry, the fairness of such a provision in a field of specialization so narrow as broadcasting leaves much to be desired. Often ex-employees and Commissioners have, by training, nowhere else to go for work but into the industry itself. A better solution might be to make careers in Government service more of an end than a means by attempting to match more closely the pay scales in the industry supervised.

[37]Broadcasting-Telecasting, January 12, 1948, p. 13.

"to accept employment, during the period for which they were appointed, with persons subject to the Communications Act."[38]

In general, prospects for the Senate passage of the revised draft seemed favorable until the sudden illness of its author made it impossible for him to continue to provide the leadership needed for its passage. In addition, it was an election year and an early June 19 target date for adjournment had been set by the Congress. Finally, Senator Edwin C. Johnson (D. of Colorado) had authored a bill (S. 2231) prohibiting the use of broadcast power over 50 kilowatts by stations. This bill was combined with S. 1333, causing the powerful clear channel broadcast lobby to exert its powers against it. Even though the President, in a surprise move, did reconvene Congress in July of that year to enact his programs on housing, civil rights, Federal aid to education, and other measures, further action on the radio bills was not taken in that session, and the White-Wolverton bill never came to a vote in either House or Senate.

---

[38] At the time S. 1333 was being considered by Congress, salaries for Commissioners in the FCC were $10,000 a year. They had been at that figure since 1934. Soon after the war, there were a series of resignations on the part of Commissioners who claimed they could not afford to remain in that agency. Mr. Denny himself, chairman at this time, was soon to resign from his $10,000 a year job to take one that paid $35,000 as vice president of a network. Congress was beginning to become concerned over this mass exodus...and one of the provisions of the White bill would have raised the pay of the Commissioners to $15,000 annually. In addition to providing more money, however, the White bill envisaged the further assurance of a prohibition against a change of employment during a Commissioner's tenure of office.

### 5. An Assessment of the White-Wolverton Bill

Thus ended the first concerted and only really organized attempt to carry out a systematic revision of the Communications Act. Had the Act passed, it would have left the Commission with considerably less discretion than it possessed in 1934 when "the field of radio was still new... and the Congress felt that there had not been enough regula- tory experience to include in the law detailed standards to limit the Commission's discretion...."[39] The White-Wolverton bill would have made much clearer the principles and policies Congress wanted the Commission to follow in cases involving transfer or sale of a station license. It would have demon- strated in clear and unequivocal terms (a) how Congress felt the Commission should look upon newspaper applicants for a broadcast channel; (b) what kind of treatment it expected the Commission to render to questions involving the program- ming of news, public issues, and broadcast by political candidates; (c) how much power it was willing to give the Commission relative to network regulation; and (d) what limitations were to be placed upon multiple owners and multi- ple ownership itself. It would have bestowed upon the Com- mission the unequivocal right to consider a licensee's past broadcast operation in license renewal procedures to deter- mine whether or not he had satisfied the statutory standards.

---

[39]Bernard Schwartz, The Professor and the Commissions. New York: Alfred A. Knopf, 1959), pp. 37-38.

Finally it would have standardized Commission hearing and rehearing procedures and provided a more comprehensive definition of the jurisdiction of the Court of Appeals in regard to judicial review.

The proposed measure put into firm language what in certain circumstances the Congress felt the "public interest" was. Instead of saying to the Commission: "Here is the regulatory problem, deal with it as you will," the White-Wolverton bill gave the Commission a much clearer idea of what was expected of it while at the same time it was still left with considerable room for maneuver. It was natural to expect in such circumstances that the radio industry would do all it could to defeat its provisions. As long as the Commission's powers were not clearly defined in the law -- the industry would have free room to argue that it did not in actual fact possess many powers that it claimed to have, and the Commission could not assert otherwise without a bitter struggle of the kind it was usually anxious to avoid. Once these powers were to be more clearly defined however, then there could be no denial of their existence. The industry much preferred to deal with a Commission that possessed the kind of "unlimited authority" and "well nigh unfettered discretion" that it was reluctant to employ.[40]

The White-Wolverton bill was the high-water mark of Congressional attempts to lay down the law to the Commission.

---

[40]Schwartz, op. cit., pp. 38-39.

The coming of television and subsequent rush for channels was even then beginning to cloud the issues of broadcast licensing. Soon the frequently used phrases "non-controversial legislation," "emergency measures," and "getting service to the public as quickly as possible" would again emerge to defeat Congress's attempts to provide detailed standards which would both limit and enhance the Commission's discretion.

The White-Wolverton bill was the last real effort on the part of Congress to define its terms relative to broadcast legislation.

# CHAPTER VII

## THE "McFARLAND" BILL

### 1. The Senate Report and the Hoover Study

Early in 1949, the results of two important studies involving radio broadcasting were issued, the first by a congressional committee, the second by the Hoover Commission. These two studies will be briefly analyzed and commented on in the following pages.

#### a. The Senate Report

The _Congressional Record_ of January 27, 1949, carried the text of the "Interim Report by a Subcommittee of the Senate Committee on Interstate and Foreign Commerce, Dealing with a Study of Various Communications Matters."[1] In it were a number of findings in respect to Commission organization, which in a way foreshadowed greater congressional activity in that area.

In commenting on the internal organization of the Commission, the Report stated: "We are of the opinion that (its) administrative faults...are due basically to an archaic and clumsy organization of its administrative machinery." Thus, in spite of the enumerated "weaknesses" of the so-called panel system (which would split the Commission into

---

[1]_Congressional Record_, January 27, 1949, pp. 543-547.

wo or more divisions, as the White-Wolverton Bill proposed
o do in the preceding chapter), the conclusion was that
doption of such a system would improve upon present Commis-
ion organization. However, in commenting on the FCC's own
ecently published plan for organizing itself into panels the
eport admonished:

> Adoption of the panel system without enactment of
> legislation specifically dealing with the subject is not
> contemplated by existing law, which contemplates that all
> decisions must be made by the whole Commission.

The subcommittee Report offered a method which would
expedite" the work of the Commission. It involved "assign-
ent" of contested cases "to a group or subcommittee of the
ommission for writing of the final decision." In perform-
ng this function, "The Commission...should have the legal
id of personnel who are not part of the legal staff who pro-
ecuted or represented the Commission during the hearing or
ehearing procedure." (This perhaps suggested the provision
n the subsequent McFarland bills which provided for the
stablishment of an "Office of Opinion and Review" in the
ommission.)

The Report further recommended that the Commission be
eorganized "along the lines of its workload, i.e., broadcast,
ommon carrier, and safety and special service," and that
the Law, Engineering, and Accounting Departments be made
unctional units of such a divisional setup, with the General
ounsel, the Chief Accountant, and the Chief Engineer dir-
tly under the Commission itself."

The Report blamed FCC for its part in the "FM failure"
by stating that it had followed the words and advice of industry engineers much too readily at a time when important
segments of that industry were opposed to its full development:

> ...The regulatory agency...does...rely on the testi-
> mony and experiences and experiments of engineers who
> are the employees of major commercial interests in the
> industry; that the regulatory agency appears to be over-
> awed and too much impressed by such engineering views
> and does not always balance these views against the
> broad public policy of what is best for the general
> interest of the people of the United States.[2]

Finally, the Subcommittee Report vigorously defended
the FCC against charges of censorship through program review, declaring:

> It is apparent to your subcommittee that a planned
> propaganda effort is being carried on among well meaning
> but uninformed persons to secure congressional revision

---

[2]Senator Tobey (R. of New Hampshire) who was Chairman
of the Subcommittee, had in fact on an earlier occasion, made
the accusation that the FCC and a "certain part" of the
radio industry had "been in cahoots" on the FM settlement.
He claimed that RCA "did its damndest to hamstring FM," and
recommended that FCC "be condemned" for its handling of FM
allocations.

He charged that RCA saw FM was "a good thing," tried
to buy it, and couldn't. Then, he stated, RCA "did everything
they could to hold Armstrong down."

On April 23, 1948, Senator Tobey, then acting chairman
of the Senate Interstate Commerce Committee, ordered an investigation into the subject of radio allocations, regulations,
and patent ownership. Later, when Senator White again re-
sumed the Chair, a new investigation of the Commission was
begun, of which the above report was the result. (See hearings on S. 2231, 80th Cong., 2d sess.; also testimony of
William H. Bauer before the Committee on Legislative Oversight, 1958; also Lawrence Lessing, Man of High Fidelity,
Edwin Howard Armstrong (Philadelphia: Lippincott, 1956),
320 pp.

of the Act with respect to the so-called censorship
questions....To us it appears ridiculous to hold that a
person operating under a Federal license shall not be
answerable to a constituted authority to his performance
under that license.  To hold otherwise would be to set
at naught the license system, to make the licenses in
fact a perpetual grant.  So long as radio frequencies are
scarce national resources, the Government has a right to
expect and demand proper use of them.

No sooner had the Interim Report of the Senate Subcommittee been published then the Hoover Commission's "Report
o Congress on the Organization of the Executive Branch of
he Government" was made public, which included a Report of
ts Special Task Force on the Regulatory Agencies.[3]

. The Hoover Study

In general, the Hoover Task Force Report found what
t called "serious weaknesses" in the performance of the
ommission, "certain deficiencies" in its planning and
olicymaking, "insufficient attention" being given to common-
arrier activities, "repeated departures" from stated FCC
olicies, and "still untapped" staff resources.

The Report concluded that the Commission itself should
e permitted to decide whether a panel system should be
rganized within that agency, but at the same time it recom-
ended that the Commission be organized on a functional basis
n place of the then existing professional units, and that it

_____

[3]See Report of the Commission on Organization of the
xecutive Branch of the Government, Committee on Independent
egulatory Commissions, Staff Report on FCC, prepared for the
ommittee by William W. Tolub, September 15, 1948.  (Released
arch 7, 1949, mimeographed copies of this report are on file
n the National Archives.)

establish a "series of bureaus corresponding to the major areas of responsibility of the Commission." It further recommended that the full Commission divorce itself from administrative problems except for deciding policy questions of the basic moment, such as major organization changes and appointments of top staff personnel.

The Hoover Task Force Report on FCC noted a current trend toward more hearings, and concluded that this situation had resulted in: (1) a consequent strain on the Commission's resources and an increased activity in the courts; and (2) a subsequent and serious backlog of hearing applications. "When a hearing is required, it takes, on the average one-and-one-half to two years from the date of filing of the original application before a final decision of the Commission is rendered." It was expected that consequences of this condition would be felt in the coming rush of television applications, as was, indeed, the case.[4]

The Task Force Report found that the lack of centralized responsibility for staff policymaking contributed greatly to factors which resulted in a less effective policymaking role being taken by the Commission. It complained that there was very little coordination to be found between the Commission's three main bureaus except on an ad hoc basis, and that there was (1) too much diffusion of responsibility at the staff level, (2) a too rapid turnover of staff

---

[4]Ibid., Pt. II, p. 62.

ersonnel, and (3) that the scope of regulatory problems
ad resulted in too much specialization in the agency.[5]
onditions such as this had led to important policy areas
eceiving little or no attention.

Other pertinent findings made in the Hoover Task
orce Report were that the Commission form does not inher-
atly prevent the formulation of long-range policy plans,
at that the chief impediments to the accomplishment of that
arpose have been the rather poor quality of appointments to
ae Commission and the Commission's lack of time for plan-
ing.[6]

Finally, the Report concluded that, in spite of its
aumerated weaknesses, the Commission form should neverthe-
ass be maintained;

> The foregoing discussion indicates that the present
> system of communications regulations has not attained a
> maximum of regulatory effectiveness. The defects in the
> system, however, do not appear to be inherent in the
> Commission form....

> It may be noted that various legislative proposals
> for the alteration of the Commission's organization have
> not included the elimination of the Commission form, nor
> has any serious suggestion been made to Congress along
> those lines. From time to time, students of communica-
> tions have suggested that the Commission's responsibil-
> ities should be divided between two agencies -- one to
> formulate policy, the other to make quasi-judicial
> decisions. This type of arrangement is patently infeas-
> ible.

> For one thing, the development of policies is fre-
> quently an adjunct to the adjudication of cases. It
> consequently would be necessary to provide for a degree
> of coordination between the two agencies which would

---

[5]Ibid., Pt. II, p. 24.    [6]Ibid., Pt. IV, p. 11.

minimize the significance of segregation. In addition,
the creation of another agency would involve problems of
unnecessary duplication of staff personnel and overlap-
ping of functions. Finally, these suggestions all con-
template that the policymaking tasks would be vested in
a commission and not in a single person.[7]

In conclusion, it may be said that the Senate Report
and the Hoover Study came at a time when there was increasing pressure for Congressional revision of broadcast legislation, and, therefore had an important effect on the makeup
of subsequent bills that would be introduced in Congress.
Both the McFarland bill and the Sadowski bill (analyzed in
the following pages) contain provisions similar to those
proposed in these two important studies.

## 2.  The McFarland Bill, S. 1973

In June, 1949, soon after the publication of the
Hoover Task Force Report, an "FCC staff, Commission, and
procedural organization" bill was introduced by Senator
E. W. McFarland, the new chairman of the Senate Communications Subcommittee. It was quickly dubbed by Broadcasting
as being the "radio legislation most likely to succeed" that
year because of its "noncontroversial" nature.[8]

### a.  The Provisions of the Original Version of the McFarland Bill

The bill (S. 1973) envisaged a division of the Commission into two separate panels.  It further provided for

_____

[7]Ibid., Pt. IV, p. 22.

[8]Broadcasting-Telecasting, June 6, 1949, p. 23.

ealinement of the staff on a functional basis and extensive
verhaul of the then current hearing and appellate proced-
res.

According to Broadcasting,

> The bill incorporates less controversial portions of
> the famed White bill of 1947-48, and the cease-and-desist,
> salary, and radio fraud measures introduced earlier this
> year by Senator Ed C. Johnson (Democrat, Colorado),
> chairman of the full Interstate and Foreign Commerce
> Committee.[9]

---

[9]Ibid. Senator Johnson, in a speech against the
lear-channel lobby, had been very critical of the Commission.
e had described it "...as a body exercising vital quasi-
udicial and quasi-legislative functions..." which had
...failed utterly in protecting the people against mono-
olistic exploitation by not blocking the plans of the con-
iving clear-channel lobby, bent on radio domination; by not
oving promptly to correct the Commission's earlier error in
dopting a narrow TV system which insured the control of tele-
ision in a few patent-holding corporations; and by not
ormulating a television plan which would guarantee the
idest and freest competition." Johnson further charged
hat the "Commissioners...are the captives of their own
taff, and that their own staff, in turn, is the captive of
he high and mighty in the very industry the Commission was
reated to regulate."

He complained of the Commission's "hugh backlog of
ases," stating that these delays were "premeditated" and
erving "private interests." He accused "networks and
owerful manufacturing interests" of working "hand in glove"
ith the Commission to "exact their own economic sanctions."

Senator Johnson stated in a somewhat whimsical
ashion that experience showed that "industry lobbyists"
ould always "fly to the rescue" of the Commission when it
as under investigation by Congress, and that, "in the guise
f being anti-Commission, they counsel with the investiga-
ing committee and advise them of leads that turn out to be
ither blind alleys or of little material consequence."
See Congressional Record, 81st Cong., 1st sess., pp. 4781-
783.)

"New" provisions of (S. 1973) not taken from the White bill or pending measures were designed to:

1) Organize the staff along functional lines, setting up a minimum of three "integrated" divisions, with legal, engineering, and accounting personnel in each. Each division would then process the applications in its field.

2) Create a review staff to stand as a kind of "buffer" between the Commission and its regular staff, being responsible directly to it, to draft decisions, orders, and opinions at the Commission's direction.[10]

3) Authorize employment of a $10,000-a-year legal assistant by each Commissioner.

In introducing the bill, Senator McFarland stated that while some difference of opinion existed about the wisdom of panelization of the Commission, the need for horizontal reorganization in the Commission could not be denied:

> I have drafted such a provision after consultation with Commissioners, and my personal opinion is that it must be a part of any bill enacted. Whether panels would be provided is an additional question which I believe our committee can settle with little delay.

The Senator further stated:

> It should be noted that the bill I have introduced today is limited strictly to organization, administration, and appellate provisions. I have included no policy sections simply because the most urgent and pressing problems of the Commission today deal with its internal organization.[11]

---

[10]Four days after the McFarland bill had been introduced, the Commission itself voluntarily adopted a so-called buffer plan.

[11]Congressional Record, 81st Cong., 1st sess., vol. 95, p. 7006.

The first of a line of McFarland bills to amend the
Communications Act of 1934 bears a fairly close relationship
to the McFarland Communications Act Amendments of 1952, and
marks a point of departure in the sequence of events that
was to culminate in their passage.  Its other provisions,
besides those previously mentioned, either taken in whole or
with modifications from the White bill or other pending
broadcast measures, would have:

1) Revised hearing procedures as recommended by the
White bill, meanwhile setting up a 30-day waiting period for
protests against grants without hearing, and making a hearing mandatory upon protest.

2) Forbidden rules which would "effect a discrimination between persons based upon race, religious or political
affiliation, or kind of lawful occupation or business association," (thereby blocking any Commission action which would
exclude or minimize newspaper or motion picture interests in
broadcasting stations.)

3) Sent all appeals to the same court (U. S. Court of
Appeals for the District of Columbia), thus terminating then
existing procedure which sent certain cases to that court
and some to another.  It further would have provided for
appeals to be made directly from the court of appeals to the
Supreme Court on revocations and nonrenewals, but would have
maintained the system of Supreme Court review of other cases
upon writ of certiorari.

4) Raised Commissioner's salaries from $10,000 to
$15,000, as provided for in the then pending Johnson bill
(S. 1626), but without the Johnson bill's $2,500 extra com-
pensation for the chairman.

5) Eliminated that portion of the antitrust provision
(sec. 311) which gave FCC discretionary power to refuse
licenses to firms found guilty of monopoly in radio communications.

6) Eliminated the AVCO competitive bidding procedure
by requiring approval of a transfer if the buyer possesses
the qualifications of an original permittee or licensee.[12]

7) Effective one year after enactment, made it unlawful for bureau heads and Commissioner's legal assistants to
appear before the Commission in behalf of anyone under FCC
jurisdiction for one year after they left FCC.

8) Provided for the issuance of declaratory orders by
the Commission in order "to terminate a controversy or remove
an uncertainty."

---

[12]FCC was already moving toward a repeal of the AVCO
rule on its own motion. On February 23, 1949, the Commission
proposed to repeal the rule (secs. 1.321 (b) through (e) of
its Rules and Regulations), and invited comments on its proposals. See Broadcasting-Telecasting, February 28, 1949,
p. 23. The Commission's plan did not attempt to go as far
as that proposed in S. 1973, however, which called only for
minimum qualifications of the potential purchaser of a station license. What this meant was that the Commission had
to accept his word that he was financially capable of operating the station, was of good character, and would provide
it with an adequate staff for its operation. It would have
denied the Commission all rights to consider whether or not
a second applicant might not be better qualified than the
transferee as purchaser of the station's license.

9) Required issuance of intermediate reports by hearing officers in lieu of proposed decisions by the Commission.

Thus, the McFarland bill of 1949 contained none of the censorship, clear-channel, and similar "policy" provisions which had stirred up such irreconcilable controversy on the White bill. A great deal of the material in the bill echoed recommendations previously made by the Federal Communications Bar Association and individual attorneys over the years.

b.  The Senate Hearings on the McFarland Bill
    Revision of the Measure and
    Its Passage by the Senate

In spite of widespread industry approval of the "non-controversial" bill,[13] the Commission voiced considerable opposition to certain of its provisions in the Senate hearings.[14]  This opposition involved, for the most part, the several major organizational provisions, including rotation of the chairmanship, mandatory division of the Commission into panels, and mandatory reorganization of the staff along functional lines.  The proposed changes in hearing procedures were described as "cumbersome" and "unduly restrictive."[15] Commissioners Hennock and Webster objected to the proposed

---

[13]See Broadcasting-Telecasting, June 20, 1949, p. 25.

[14]See hearings before a subcommittee of the Committee on Interstate and Foreign Commerce, U. S. Senate, on S. 1973, June 16 and 17, 1949, 81st Cong., 1st sess.

[15]Ibid., p. 18.

change in FCC action on renewals, stating that the proposed
amendment would, in effect, permit the holder of a license
to "keep it forever." The other commissioners felt that,
at the very minimum, renewals should be granted according to
findings of public interest.[16]

The Commission was opposed to any amendment of section
311 of the Act, which authorized the Commission to refuse a
station license in cases where there had been a judicial
finding of violation of the antitrust laws, on the grounds
that such an amendment "would undoubtedly lead to the contention that the deletion indicates a congressional intent
that the Commission's authority in this field should be curtailed." And that "extensive and time-consuming litigation
would be inevitable to resolve the point."[17] Unexpected
support for this argument came during an unheralded appearance at the Senate hearing of Justice Department officials
who claimed that these provisions of the bill would weaken
"important" safeguards against monopoly.[18]

Provisions which would require the Commission, when
it considered transfer applications, to determine only if
the transfers possessed the qualifications of an original
licensee were severly criticized by Commission witnesses at
the Senate hearing on the grounds that they would encourage

---

[16]Ibid., p. 17.    [17]Ibid., p. 19.

[18]Ibid. See hearing testimony of David Hume on behalf of the Department of Justice, pp. 119-132.

183

nd permit trafficking in licenses since

> in actual operation, the practice is discovered only
> when a person attempts to sell a station. Under the
> provisions of the bill, if the transferee is qualified,
> the Commission would, presumably, be required to approve
> the transfer and thus condone trafficking in licenses.[19]

Finally, the Commission entered strong objection to
hat it felt was a too strict limitation on the right of
xaminers or Commissioners to confer with staff members,
ven on highly technical points in hearing cases.[20]

After completion of the Senate hearings, the measure
as reported to the floor.[21] In its final form, it contained
number of highly important revisions. For example, as
evised and approved by the committee, the measure contained
section which called for the setting up of a statutory
objective" for final FCC action on nonhearing applications
ithin three months of the date of filing, and on hearing
ases within six months after completion of the hearing.
he Commission was to be required to report "promptly" to
ongress on each case in which it failed to meet the time
imits, and explain its delay.[22]

Additional departures from the text of the original
ill were, it was claimed, adopted in the hope that all
oints of controversy could be eliminated in order that the

---

[19]Ibid., p. 19.    [20]Ibid., p. 22.

[21]S. Rept. 741, to accompany S. 1973, 81st Cong.,
st sess., 20 pages.

[22]Ibid., S. Rept. 741, p. 7.

amendments would pass without delay during that present session of Congress.

These included such changes as the following:

1) The proposal to divide the Commission into two separate panels was abandoned. The plan to require reorganization of the staff along functional lines was retained, with certain modifications of language.

2) The antidiscrimination section was dropped upon the specific understanding that FCC already observed its principles and would continue to do so.

3) The Communications Act of 1934 contained a provision which required action on renewals of broadcast licenses to be governed by the same considerations that applied to original applications. A new provision was added to the McFarland bill which instead would have conditioned renewals upon a finding "that public interest, convenience, or necessity would be served thereby."

4) The ban on "job jumping" was extended to a number of other positions in the Commission. Effective one year after passage of the bill, no Commissioner could resign and accept employment, during the term for which he was appointed, with anyone subject to FCC jurisdiction. Bureau heads and their assistants could not represent such persons before the Commission for one year after leaving its employ.

5) The proposed new cease-and-desist procedure was expanded to make it usable against "any person" under FCC

urisdiction. Formerly, it had applied only to "station
icensees."

6) In renewal proceedings, the burden of proof would
e upon the "appropriate division" of the Commission, or
pon whoever opposed renewal.

The McFarland measure passed the Senate by unanimous
ote on August 9, 1949, and was sent to the House. Broad-
asting reported expectations were that it would breeze
hrough that body with very little hearing opposition.[23]

. Failure of the McFarland Bill to Emerge
   from the House Committee

Opposition, nevertheless, grew during the weeks that
he bill lay in committee in the House. A later issue of
roadcasting reported:

> The McFarland bill passed the Senate, but stumbled
> before the House Commerce Committee, where it encountered
> silent opposition not readily discernible on the Senate
> side. Civil Service objected to the salary provisions
> singling out FCC; FCC interposed certain opposition
> still not disclosed; and House Commerce Committee hinted
> it may wish to delve deeper into the whole communica-
> tions issue. Hearings are indicated.[24]

While House hearings were not held on the bill in
hat session of Congress, some indication of the gravity of
he problems that were of concern to the House Interstate

---

[23]Broadcasting-Telecasting, August 15, 1949, p. 23.

[24]Broadcasting-Telecasting, October 17, 1949, p. 28.

Committee was given by Kurt Borchardt, one of its attorneys,

in a statement released on December 26, 1949:

> The fact that the McFarland measure passed the Senate
> as a noncontroversial bill ignores the feeling of some
> members of the House Commerce Committee and FCC itself.
> There are several controversial issues in this bill --
> in almost every section. There is strong belief, too,
> that the bill already is outdated because of the progress
> of television. This feeling is shared by some congres-
> sional and FCC members alike.
>
> In its comments since the legislation came before the
> House, FCC has strongly emphasized it is not satisfied
> with many provisions as presently written. Furthermore,
> some Commissioners have stressed that the bill almost
> ignores FCC's special services and safety functions;
> that the legislation was written chiefly with broadcast
> provisions in mind; that it does not take into cogni-
> zance the growing importance of television operation.
>
> There is also a time-element factor in problems deal-
> ing with FCC. If the issue is taken up at all, hearings
> would be a necessity. And committee members are very
> interested in the television aspect. Whether the com-
> mittee, or the FCC itself, can find time this next
> session remains to be seen. Television would seem to be
> vital in any consideration of communications at this
> time.[25]

Thus, for the remainder of the first session of the

81st Congress, the McFarland bill languished in the House

Committee. It would be revived, however, in the following

session, and it would finally pass both Houses and become

law two years later.

### 3.  The Sadowski Bill, H. R. 6949

Early in the second session of the 81st Congress,

Representative Sadowski (D. of Michigan), chairman of the

Radio Subcommittee of the House Committee on Interstate and

---

[25]Broadcasting-Telecasting, December 26, 1949, p. 29.

Foreign Commerce, commented on the floor regarding what he called the "pressure tactics" that had been employed by those in favor of the McFarland measure, and announced what the subcommittee's plans were in regard to broadcast legislation:

There has been a great deal of pressure emanating from various quarters, including the radio trade press, that the Interstate and Foreign Commerce Committee... should concentrate on S. 1973, the so-called McFarland bill. There are demands, even, to the effect that the committee should report this bill out without holding any hearings whatsoever.

Mr. Sadowski stated the committee would not act on the bill with such speed; that, in fact, the committee had not had "an opportunity to study (the) substantive problems" of the Communications Act since it had last held hearings on comprehensive amendments in 1942. Therefore, it was his opinion that it would be unable to do "the kind of job which it is accustomed to do unless the committee first gains a clear understanding of the substantive problems involved." He thereupon announced:

...it is my purpose to bring before the committee some of the most important substantive problems connected with radio, and to do that in the most concrete form possible; namely, that of placing before the committee appropriate amendments to the Communications Act in the field of radio. That is the sole reason for my introducing this bill (H. R. 6949) at the present time.[26]

Reaction to the Sadowski bill was immediate in the radio industry; in fact, before the bill had been announced, Broadcasting had labeled it a "Legislative Stiletto" which was "...designed to block House approval of the McFarland

---

[26]Congressional Record, 81st Cong., 2d sess., p. 838.

bill (S. 1973), which unanimously passed the Senate last
August and which had the support of the FCC." The editorial
charged that the bill had been

...drafted in the rough by the Law Bureau of the FCC...
(because)...the lawyers do not want the Commission
reorganized. They do not want to meet deadlines. They
do not want the appellate provisions of the archaic
Communications Act changed.[27]

In the following issue, an editorial stated that the
bill "...shouldn't be taken too seriously as a legislative
threat. It hasn't a chance of passage. It is 'strike
legislation' of the most blatant sort."[28]

An examination of the Sadowski bill would show that
it contained the following major provisions:

1) It proposed to create an independent five-man
frequency-control board to deal with the allocations and
assignment of radio frequencies.

2) It would have given the FCC additional administrative sanctions with respect to radio-station licensees and
holders of construction permits.

3) It would have rendered radio-station licensees
immune to criminal or civil actions for statements made in
the course of political broadcasts, and further clarified
section 315 of the Communications Act relating to such broadcasts.

------------------------

[27]Broadcasting-Telecasting, January 23, 1950, p. 17.

[28]Ibid., January 30, 1950, p. 39.

Each of the major portions of the bill will be examined separately.

## a. Frequency Control

Title I of the Sadowski bill proposed to add an additional section to title III of the Communications Act of 1934 entitled "Frequency Control." The history of the proposal made in this section goes back to a previous congressional investigation. One of the recommendations contained in the report of the Select Committee to Investigate the Federal Communications Commission under House Resolution 21 (78th Congress, 1945) follows:

> The select committee notes that section 305 of the Federal Communications Act of 1934 places personal responsibility on the President to make assignments to governmental radio stations, and it believes, before such power is delegated to a body with an independent rather than an advisory character, the whole problem should be considered by Congress.

This recommendation had been made after the select committee "had gone in great detail into the question of the operation of the Interdepartmental Radio Advisory Committee (IRAC).[29]

It found that --

> This Committee had been created on a voluntary basis by the Government agencies that were using radio. The President, thereupon, had formally delegated to that Committee his functions of assigning frequencies to Government stations. Members of the IRAC were, therefore, Army, Navy, Air Force, Commerce, Treasury, Agriculture, Interior, Justice, State Maritime Commission, and, finally, the Federal Communications Commission. The Committee had been in existence since 1922, but its membership and organization had never been formalized by Executive order or in any other manner.

---

[29]See H. Rept. 2095, 78th Cong., 2d sess.

Representative Sadowski said he believed that the
IRAC had done its work well over the years, but added the
following words to his appraisal:

> ...in a democracy it is poor business to leave the
> apportionment of an important natural resource like the
> radio spectrum...to a planless system of compromises
> between two public bodies, each sovereign in its own
> field, neither of which is responsible to the people for
> the apportionment that results from their respective
> actions. And yet, under the Communications Act as it
> now stands, this procedure is the only possible one.
>
> It is my belief that, under our system of government,
> the apportionment of the radio spectrum as between Fed-
> eral Government and nongovernment uses must be entrusted
> to public officials responsible to the President and the
> Congress and, through them, to the people.[30]

For the enumerated reasons, and because it was the opinion
of its author that such a provision would "lighten the workload" of the Commission so that its "backlog of applications
for the assignment of frequencies and hearings" could be
dealt with  more quickly, the frequency-control provisions
of H. R. 6949 were created.

If the bill had passed, there would have been created
a five-man board whose members would have had the authority
to --

1) Allocate frequencies and cancel or modify any such
allocation.

2) Assign frequencies to Government stations and cancel or modify any such assignments.

3) Prescribe regulations to govern the assignment by
the FCC of frequencies to nongovernmental stations.

---

[30]Congressional Record, 81st Cong., 2d sess., p. 839.

The Board would be directed to disapprove proposed assignments or renewal of assignments of any frequencies by FCC to nongovernmental stations, if such assignment (a) would cause harmful interference to any Government use of radio; (b) would violate any regulation prescribed by the Board with respect to assignments by the FCC.[31]

---

[31] During 1958, the problem of frequency allocation was again revived by the introduction of S. J. Res. 106, which proposed to establish a special commission to investigate Government use of the spectrum. The proposal at the outset had the enthusiastic approval and support of the broadcast industry, which for some time had been making the charge that the military was not effectively using the substantial space allotted to it. (See editorial in Broadcasting, August 18, 1958, p. 110.)

The resolution was approved in committee on July 9, and unanimously approved in the Senate on July 21 and sent to the House Commerce Committee. In that committee, amendments were added which would have permitted the proposed Commission to investigate and study the overall use of the entire spectrum, by military and civilian bodies alike, and, additionally, to investigate the FCC's administration of the Communications Act.

This was something the broadcast industry had not called for, and, in the words of Broadcasting: "Tremendous opposition to the measure arose...and it was never considered by the House...consequently, the bill has been effectively killed for the session..." (Ibid., p. 34.)

In its editorial, the magazine stated: "The...bill was killed because broadcasters felt, in their battle for self-preservation, that they had no alternative....More had to be known about the reason for shift in emphasis from military to broadcast use of the spectrum...."

If it is true, as Broadcasting seems to claim in its statement, that the bill was killed because "broadcasters felt...they had no alternative...." this circumstance would seem to furnish another indication of the disproportionate strength of the broadcast lobby in Congress.

#### b. Administration Sanctions

Since the very inception of broadcast legislation, revocation of a license had been the only sanction given to the Commission to enforce the provisions of the Act as well as its own rules and regulations. Along with numerous other bills that had been offered in the past, H. R. 6949 proposed to provide additional sanctions to the Commission, less drastic than that of license revocation. In pointing out the need for new and less stringent ways of obtaining compliance from owners of stations, Mr. Sadowski quoted from a recent decision of the Commission in a case of license renewal. In this decision, the Commission had cited its own apparent powerlessness to invoke an appropriate sanction upon an operator who had violated Commission rules:

> We find ourselves in a difficult situation in deciding this case. This is not due to any deficiency in the record, for we are convinced that the attitude which responsible Don Lee officers displayed in this record with respect to the Commission's chain-broadcast regulations -- an attitude which can best be characterized as one of indifference -- warrants critical examination of the qualifications of the applicant to be a broadcast licensee. We are, however, faced with important practical difficulties in this case which arise from the fact that the only sanction we have the authority to apply is denial of license -- an action which will put the licensee out of business. Except in an aggravated case, the Commission is reluctant to impose a sentence on a licensee which not only terminated his existing operations but would preclude him from holding any other radio licenses. Had we the authority to order a suspension, assess a penalty, or impose some other sanction less than a "death sentence," we should have no hesitancy whatsoever in doing so in this case.[32]

---

[32]Decision of Commission in re Don Lee Broadcasting System, cited in Congressional Record, 81st Cong., 2d sess., p. 839.

The Sadowski bill would, therefore, have amended section 312 of the Act in order to (1) give the Commission power to suspend a license for a period not to exceed 90 days; (2) issue cease-and-desist orders; (3) order a forfeiture to the United States of a fine not to exceed $500 for each day of violation. The Commission was to have power to suspend a station license for 90 days, or to revoke, but not suspend, any construction permit for any of the following:

a) False statements.

b) Conduct of a type which would warrant the Commission's refusal of a grant of a license or permit under an original application.

c) For willful and repeated failure to operate substantially as set forth in the license.

d) For willful and repeated violations of, or failure to observe, any provision of the Act or any rule or regulation of the Commission authorized by the Act or by a treaty ratified by the United States.

e) For conduct designed to persuade, induce, or coerce any other station licensee, (i) to violate, (ii) to disregard any measure of the Communications Act or rule of the Commission.

f) For violation of, or failure to observe, cease-and-desist orders.

Cease-and-desist orders themselves could be issued by the Commission in any case where the licensee had failed to operate substantially as set forth in his license; had violated or failed to observe any provisions of the Act, or any rule of the Commission.

c.  Political Broadcasts

Section 315 of the Communications Act of 1934, while
it left station licensees free to determine whether they
should allow time for the broadcast of speeches by candidates for public office, required a licensee, once he had
permitted a legally qualified candidate to broadcast, to
allot equal time to all other qualified candidates for that
same office.  The section further provided that licensees
could not censor any statements made in the course of such
political broadcasts.  The problem that arose, consequently,
was what should be done to protect the licensee from actions
for libel and slander brought because of statements made by
a political candidate -- over which the licensee by law had
no control?

The Sadowski bill proposed to leave unchanged the
provision that a licensee might not censor, alter, or in any
way change material broadcast by a political candidate, provided that in any of these instances the licensee could not
be held liable in any civil or criminal action which might
result.  Additionally, the amendment would have broadened the
provision for allowance of equal time to include not only
political candidates themselves, but also "any person or persons designated by such candidate" to speak for them.

d.  Reaction to the Sadowski Bill

The trade press voiced the general industry opposition to the bill by calling it nothing more than a "delaying
action," designed to prevent passage of the McFarland measure.

ts proposed new "Frequency Control Board" was written off
s a "super FCC...and this when Congress and the administra-
ion talk economy in Government and relief for the taxpayer!"

The proposed new FCC "sanctions" were equally criti-
ized. It was stated that "to suspend a station for even 30
ays is tantamount to revocation. The station will lose
isteners and its business. The provision is unrealistic
nd ludicrous."

Finally, the station fine proposal was considered
perhaps less onerous, if legal," although the language was
dded:

> Can you imagine what would happen to a station that
> might violate a simple rule such as station identifica-
> tion? At $500 per day it could run itself into bank-
> ruptcy before the FCC's legal mills ground out the
> necessary citations to serve on the perhaps innocent
> offender.

The political broadcast section was considered to be
the "sugar-coating that would make the bill palatable to
many a harried broadcaster." However, although the provision, when contained in previous bills, had enjoyed the support and acclamation of the broadcast industry, the subsequent sentence stated: "...we shall have to leave to the
Congress and the courts the delicate question whether Congress can so legislate."[33]

---

[33]_Broadcasting-Telecasting_ editorial, January 30, 1950,
p. 38.

**e.** The Views of the Commission Regarding
   the McFarland Bill (S. 1973)

At the request of Chairman Sadowski, the Communications Commission later submitted its own views regarding certain measures contained in S. 1973. This memorandum disclosed that (1) a majority of five of the Commissioners were in favor of staff reorganization into functional units, but felt that the time limit for such reorganization should be lengthened from 60 days to twelve months; (2) the Commission was equally in favor of the creation of a special review or "buffer" staff -- but in addition, felt it should be permitted to advise the Commission -- a power that was expressly withheld in S. 1973; (3) the Commission was opposed to the statutory setting up of any deadlines for Commission action on applications, and to the provision that the filing of a protest against a grant would automatically stay the grant; (4) the Commission felt that portion of the antitrust bill proposed for deletion by S. 1973 should be retained; (5) the Commission was of the opinion that the prohibition against "job-jumping" by commissioners and senior staff members should be deleted; (6) the Commission felt that the present language of the law involving transfer and sale of a station should be retained, and (7) that the new provision under which renewals were to be granted should be eliminated from the bill because it might be interpreted so as to prevent competing applications for a station's facilities. A very strongly worded objection was made to the provision which would

rohibit Commissioners from consulting with staff "after
ormal hearing in any adjudication within the meaning of...
he Administrative Procedure Act." The Commissioners
Commissioner Jones excepted) felt they should be permitted
o talk to staff members concerning questions relating to

whether applications, complaints, petitions, or other
matters should be designated for hearing, the issues to
be considered at such a hearing, requests for changes in
hearing issues...and similar matters not involving decisions on the merits of the hearing record.

The majority of the Commission contended that any ban
n such staff assistance was tantamount to charging that Com-
issioners "are incapable of carrying out their oaths of
ffice and of fairly administering the duties assigned to
hem."

In a move which may have been designed to head off
ny drastic reorganization of the Commission by Congress or
he President, a staffwide reorganization of FCC, which "had
een under study for some time," was soon afterward
nitiated.[34] While this procedure was underway, however, a
ew reorganization plan, which concentrated the Commission's
xecutive and administrative functions in the Commission
hairman was sent to Congress by President Truman. The Presi-
ent's proposal was one of 21 affecting Government agencies
nd stemmed from the work and recommendations of the Hoover
ommission on the Organization of the Executive Branch.

---

[34]Broadcasting-Telecasting, March 13, 1950, p. 25.

Hearings were held on the President's proposal which,
according to the Reorganization Act of 1949, would become
law unless the plan was rejected by one or both Houses of
Congress.[35]   The plan was favorably reported out by the Senate Committee on Interstate and Foreign Commerce,[36] but was
"vetoed" in the Senate on May 17 by a vote of 50 to 23.[37]
Grounds for Senate disapproval centered in the main around
the objection that placement of such broad powers in the
hands of the Chairman, who is appointed to his position by
the President, would jeopardize the independence of the Commission, and possibly subject it to too great a degree of
executive control.

### 4.   The Revival of the McFarland Bill (S. 658)

#### a.   The Senate Version of S. 658

On July 26, 1950, the Senate passed a slightly modified version of the McFarland bill of 1949 as an amendment to
another House-approved bill, which had been designed to
permit the FCC to acquire land for radio monitoring purposes.
The McFarland measure (because it had been tacked on as an
amendment to a bill already approved by the House) was thereby earmarked for a joint House-Senate conference.

---

[35]See hearings on S. Res. 253, 81st Cong., 2d sess.,
April 24-26, 1950.

[36]S. Rept. 81 to accompany S. Res. 256.  (The majority was an unfavorable report on a resolution of disapproval.)

[37]Congressional Record, 81st Cong., 2d sess., p. 7173.

Modifications involved only minor changes, which included
elimination of the salary provisions for FCC Commissioners
(they had already received pay raises through passage of
another bill), readjusted salary limits for certain key personnel, and permitted Commissioners to receive payment from
publications for technical or professional assistance. So-
called "job jumping" bans were also changed to the degree
that a Commissioner upon his resignation from office before
his appointed term had expired, could not represent any
interest within FCC jurisdiction for one year instead of the
remainder of his term, as had been previously provided.

Subsequent to the bill's Senate passage, however, the
House elected not to appoint conferees, but instead announced
that hearings would be held by the House Commerce Committee.
Hearings were begun and completed in August, in which the
various positions of industry, the Commission, and the Justice Department were again reiterated, but due to the urgency
of other legislation in the committee, and the approaching
adjournment of Congress, no further action was taken in that
session.

Very early in the following session (82d Congress,
1st sess., 1951), the McFarland bill was again revived. Except for its new number (S. 658), the bill was virtually
identical to its predecessor, S. 1973. It was introduced in

the Senate and referred to Senate committee on January 23, 1951;[38] approved and reported back on January 25;[39] and amended and passed by the Senate on February 5.[40]

Four amendments were offered from the floor by Senator Case of South Dakota, and included in the Senate-passed measure, none of which affected any radical change in the bill:

1) Each commissioner was given the opportunity to fix the salary of his legal assistant, which, under the bill, he would be permitted to appoint, as long as the annual salary was not in excess of $10,000.

2) A new group was added to those bureau heads and their assistants and the Commissioner's personal legal assistants who were affected by the bill's clause that barred practice before the Commission for one year after leaving its employ. The new group was to be designated as "the chief of each integrated division and his assistants."

3) A commissioner's right to present his own or minority views on all legislative matters affecting the Commission was clearly defined. Thus, an individual commissioner would be accorded the right to appear before congressional hearings and present an independent report or statement to augment FCC testimony, customarily presented by the FCC chairman.

---

[38]Congressional Record, 82d Cong., 1st sess., p. 549.
[39]Ibid., p. 658.    [40]Ibid., p. 960.

4) The Commission's rights in a national emergency, i.e., one proclaimed by Congress or the President as affecting national security were defined.[41]

After passage in the Senate of the McFarland bill with the Case amendments added, the bill was again submitted to the House Committee on Interstate and Foreign Commerce. In the House hearings, the Commission voiced repeated opposition to the bill. Recommendations were made by the Commission looking toward changes in the measure to conform it to its own "model" bill.[42]

b. The House Version of S. 658

Senate pressure for the bill's passage was made apparent once again on February 28, 1951, when that body attached the provisions of the McFarland bill as a "rider" to a House-approved measure (H. R. 1730) permitting the FCC to construct additional monitoring stations. Yet, in spite of great pressure both from industry and the Senate, the House committee was not to be rushed into giving its approval to the McFarland bill until it had the opportunity to make a full examination of its content. Hearings on S. 658 were held in April, 1951,[43] and once more gave ample evidence that the bill

---

[41]Ibid., pp. 960-961.

[42]Broadcasting-Telecasting, February 29, 1951, p. 26.

[43]Hearings before the Committee on Interstate and Foreign Commerce, House of Representatives (82d Cong., 1st sess.), on S. 658.

was not as uncontroversial as it was claimed, although
there could be no doubt that the broadcast industry was overwhelmingly for it.

At the request of Representative Lindley Beckworth
(D. of Texas), Commissioner Coy summed up the principal
points of the bill which were of utmost concern to the Commission: (1) Separation of Commissioners from staff in adjudicatory proceedings, (2) Renewal provisions, which put
the burden of proof that the applicant had or had not operated in the public interest upon the Commission rather than
the applicant himself, (3) Provisions that would permit station protests on the grounds of economic injury, (4) Provisions on transfers, which limited the proceeding to a
determination as to whether the new licensee was qualified
as such, requiring Commission approval if it was the finding
that he possessed minimum qualifications. (This, it was
feared, would relieve the Commission of any right to decide
whether the transfer would be in the public interest.)
(5) The antitrust provisions of the proposed amendment which,
it was stated, would tend to "throw doubt upon the Commission's jurisdiction with respect to the antitrust laws."[44]

---

[44]Ibid., pp. 107-108.  Industry support for the bill,
while overwhelmingly in favor, was by no means unanimous in
regard to all its provisions.  The testimony of Joseph H.
Ream, executive vice president of CBS, was in substantial
agreement with that of Commissioner Coy in opposition to
points (1) and (3) above (Ibid., pp. 299-328).

In answer to the oft-stated charge that the Commission was too often guided in its decisions by its staff, Mr. Coy stated:

> I do not think it has any validity. I wish I could use the kind of language that I could use in a private conversation in referring to those people who have spread such stories, both by word of mouth and in publications. They spread those stories because parties in interest to proceedings have not got what they wanted out of the Commission, and they preferred not to attack the Commission but to attack its staff. It is a lie....[45]

Later in the hearing, Mr. Coy stated:

> I think the worst thing that can happen to the Commission would be to make eunuchs of all these people, where they would have no right to express an opinion at all any time, but merely to come up with some research and say, "Well, here are all of the arguments on this side, and here are all of the arguments on the other side," but have no views about the matter. They are no help to the Commission unless, in reviewing, they are able to come up and suggest to the Commission that here is a course of action that is dictated, and that is the experience of every administrator. He does not want eunuchs on his staff, and he does not want yes men. He wants people that will speak their own minds....I am talking now about where the encouragement I have given to people to speak up is given to people who have not been involved in the investigation or the prosecution of the case.[46]

This opinion, however, was not widely held outside of the Commission itself, and both the Communications Bar Association and witnesses from industry for the most part held directly opposite views.

House hearings on the McFarland measure were completed April 30, 1951. The full committee of the House began its consideration of the bill in September, but the conclusion

---

[45]Ibid., p. 108.  [46]Ibid., pp. 155-156.

was reached that in view of the impending adjournment there
could be no opportunity for passage in that session of Congress. Later, however, after the House committee had "worked
for two months" that fall on the bill "and for two months
more upon resumption of the session of Congress on January 3
(1952)," the bill emerged from committee and was presented
to the House.[47]

The House report amended the McFarland bill by striking out all that followed after the enacting clause of the
Senate bill, thereupon substituting its own provisions which
in many respects were not unlike those in the original Senate version. Several important differences as well as the
principal similarities are noted:

1) The provisions of the Senate version relating to
the reorganization of the Commission were retained substantially intact.

2) The provisions of the Communications Act authorizing the Commission to divide itself into panels, which
would have been eliminated by the Senate version, were
retained in the House version. The so-called "job jumping"
clause was eliminated from the House version for the reason
that "similar agencies" did not have such a bar.

3) As revised in the House committee, the bill retained
the Senate provision requiring the Commission to report to

_____

[47]H. Rept. No. 1750, 82d Cong., 2d sess., to accompany
S. 658.

Congress any case where an original application for a broadcast license, or renewal or transfer thereof had not been
decided by the Commission within three months after the
application had been filed, or within six months wherever a
hearing was required.

4) The House version provided, before the Commission
might formally designate a license application for hearing
(and this included applications for renewals or for construction permits), that it must notify the applicant and all
other known parties in interest of the grounds and reasons
for its inability to grant the license without a hearing.
The applicant was then to be given an opportunity to reply,
and the case could be scheduled for hearing only after the
Commission had considered the reply.

5) Regarding renewal of broadcast licenses -- the
House version required that a grant be made if the Commission
found that the public interest, convenience, and necessity
would be served thereby. (The burden of proof of performance
thereby remained with the applicant. The Senate version
placed such burden of proof upon the Commission, and did not
require the licensee to prove he had operated in the public
interest when applying for renewal.)

6) The House version modified the transfer provisions
of the Communications Act by providing that the Commission
should, in all such cases, proceed as if the transferee were
the only applicant for an original license or permit. The
Commission was required to approve the transfer if it

determined that the public interest would be served thereby.

7) The House version did not change section 311 of the Act, which authorized the Commission to refuse a license to persons who had been finally adjudged guilty by a Federal court of unlawfully monopolizing radio communications. (The Senate version would have eliminated this language from the law.)

8) The House version gave the Commission power to issue cease-and-desist orders, to suspend licenses for a period not to exceed 90 days, and to levy fines up to $500 a day for violations of the Communications Act, Commission regulations, or treaties. The Commission's power to revoke licenses was limited so that it could be exercised only in cases of violations which were willful and repeated. (The Senate version of S. 658 provided for issuance of cease-and-desist orders, but did not contain the additional powers of suspending licenses and levying fines.)

9) With respect to Supreme Court review in cases of license revocation or failure to renew, the House version retained then present law that stated such review was discretionary with the court. (The Senate version granted such appeals as a matter of right.)

10) The House version restored the so-called newspaper provision, which had been left out of the Senate bill, and which dealt with "discrimination" against persons "primarily engaged in the gathering and dissemination of information." No application for a construction permit, license, or

icense renewal could be denied "solely" because of any such
nterest.

11) An entirely new provision was included in the
ouse bill, which permitted an unsuccessful applicant for
icense renewal to request FCC to condition its grant to the
uccessful applicant with the right of purchase of physical
acilities (plant and equipment) owned by the unsuccessful
pplicant.

Industry reaction to the House version, which in most
espects was by no means as lenient and favorable toward
roadcasters as the Senate bill had been, was, as might be
xpected, mostly unfavorable.

An editorial in Broadcasting stated:   "...that House
ersion would subject broadcast licensees to the kind of
ress that could reduce radio and television licensees to
rfdom, subject to the whim and caprice of the FCC."

Chief objections of the trade journal were to the
ll's license suspension and fine provisions, and the res-
ration of the "iniquitous 'double jeopardy' antitrust pro-
sion."   The reader was told ominously that "some folks are
aying fast and loose with the House Committee, with the
tter informed Senate, and with broadcasters."[48]

On June 17, 1952, the House version of S. 658 passed
e House with only one major amendment introduced by
presentative Horan (R. of Washington) having been adopted
the floor (a provision which exempted radio stations for

---

[48]Broadcasting-Telecasting, March 24, 1952, p. 50.

libelous utterances by political candidates or their authorized spokesmen). The Horan amendment was adopted after
the House defeated an amendment offered by Representative
Joseph P. O'Hara (R. of Minnesota) which would have permitted station operators to censor candidates' speeches for
defamation and obscenity.[49] The House also defeated an
amendment to strike the provision that forbade the Commission to discriminate against newspaper applicants "solely"
because of newspaper ownership.[50]

It should be remarked that (1) while both Senate and
House versions of the McFarland bill forbade Commission
staff from consulting with or making recommendations to
Commissioners in regard to decisions on cases before them,
and (2) while both versions set up a review staff the sole
function of which was to digest evidence for Commissioners,
the House version was somewhat more rigid in that regard
than that of the Senate.

As explained by Representative Oren Harris (D. of
Arkansas), chairman of the House subcommittee which considered the bill, it was the intention of its authors that

> ...the review staff shall perform no duties or functions
> other than to assist the Commission, in cases of adjudi-
> cation which have been designated for hearing, by prepar-
> ing, without recommendations, a summary of the evidence
> presented at any such hearing; by preparing without
> recommendations, after an initial decision but prior to
> oral argument, a compilation of the facts material to

---

[49]Congressional Record, 82d Cong., 2d sess.,
pp. 7412-7416.

[50]Ibid., pp. 7417-7418.

the exceptions and replies thereto filed by the parties;
and by preparing for the Commission or any member or
members, without recommendations and in accordance with
specific directions from the Commission or its members,
opinions, decisions, memoranda, and orders.[51]

In the matter of quasi-judicial proceedings, it was
stated that

the bill contains prohibitions against consultation by
the examiner with any other person on any fact or question
of law in issue unless upon notice and opportunity for
all parties to participate...and it also prohibits consultation between the examiner and any member or employee
of the Commission with respect to the examiner's initial
decision or any exception taken to it....

Similar prohibitions against consultation, except to
the extent required for the disposition of ex parte
matters, are imposed upon the Commissioners themselves....
Of course, there is no prohibition against consultation
among Commissioners or between a Commissioner and his
professional assistant.[52]

Passage of the McFarland Bill (S. 658) Following
Joint Senate-House Conference Committee Hearings

After its passage in the House, the bill was referred
a joint Senate-House conference committee, where "objec-
ons by broadcasters to some provisions of the Senate and
use passed McFarland bill...were enumerated...."[53]

According to the testimony, broadcasters wanted
) repeal of the equipment purchase section of the House
rsion, which put the FCC into the position of being "a con-
mation appraisal agency," and (2) repeal of the suspension
l fine provisions of the House version; (3) reinstatement of

---

[51]Ibid., p. 7392.    [52]Ibid., p. 7394.

[53]Broadcasting-Telecasting, June 30, 1952, p. 28.

the Senate version removing the "double jeopardy" clause in
the Communications Act, (4) reinstatement of the provision
in the Senate version which provided the Commission might
only issue declaratory orders upon request; and finally,
(5) deletion of the word "minimum" from the amount the broadcaster could charge a political candidate for time on the
air, and its replacement with the following language:  "For
the purpose of this subsection, charges shall include base
rates and all other terms and conditions affecting charges."[54]

The conference report on the McFarland bill was
issued July 1, 1952.[55]  It contained the following compromises between the two Houses:

Former commissioners.  The Senate proposal forbidding commissioners who resigned to practice before the FCC
for one year from the date of their resignation was accepted
by the House.  Representation of persons before the Commission was taken to include "appearance as a matter of record
on applications, briefs, and other matters, as well as personal appearances."[56]

Preparation or delivery of papers or publications
by commissioners.  Both versions contained amendments to
section 4 (b) of the Communications Act to allow members of
the Commission (who, while in office could not "engage in

---

[54]Ibid., p. 28.
[55]H. Rept. No. 2426, 82d Cong., 2d sess., to
accompany S. 658.
[56]Ibid., p. 16.

any other business or employment") to accept payment for
"preparation of technical or professional publications for
which reasonable honorarium or compensation may be paid."
In conference the provision was "somewhat modified to clarify
its purpose and meaning." It was "deemed advisable to permit not only the preparation of publications but also their
delivery or presentation at, for example, public meetings."

Appointment of personnel. The conference bill permitted each commissioner to hire both a legal and an engineering assistant. (The Senate version specified "legal assistant" while the House version specified "professional assistant.") In addition, the chairman was given authority to
appoint an "administrative assistant."

Organization of the Commission. (1) The Senate version would have amended section 5 of the Communications Act
so as to include, among other things, a provision requiring
the Commission, within 60 days after the enactment of the
legislation, to organize its legal, engineering, and accounting staff into integrated divisions to function on the basis
of the Commission's principal workload operations. Identical
amendments were included in the House version, and in the conference report the House version was retained "except that
certain language specifying in detail the function of divisional organizations had been omitted as surplusage."
2) The Senate version called for the establishment of a
review staff. It was stated in the report that the "provisions relating to the establishment of a review staff were

considerably modified in the House version, but the modifications had to do primarily with details rather than changing the basic purposes intended to be accomplished by the Senate bill." Therefore, in the conference substitute the provision was modified only by the elimination of the words "without recommendations" in that part of the House provision which dealt with the preparation of a summary of the evidence, and in that part which dealt with the preparation of a compilation of the facts material to the exceptions and replies submitted.

Purchase of plant and equipment of unsuccessful applicant. The equipment purchase provision of the House version which would have required a successful applicant to purchase the equipment of the unsuccessful applicant for license renewal was dropped because the Senate members of the conference felt "this was too important and far reaching a provision to enact into law unless interested persons were given the opportunity to present their views on it in a public hearing." They pointed out that the matter had not been brought up in the Senate hearings or during Senate consideration of the legislation.

The newspaper amendment. The anti-discrimination amendment contained in the House version, which would have forbidden the FCC to discriminate against newspaper applicants "solely" because they were newspapers, was omitted from the conference bill "because the committee of conference felt that it was unnecessary." It was the view of the conference

committee that under the present law the Commission was not
authorized to make such a rule or regulation, and that the
Commission "could not arbitrarily deny any application solely
because of any such interest or association."[57]

The antitrust provision. That portion of the Communications Act which permitted the FCC to revoke the license
of anyone found guilty in Federal court of antitrust violations, which the House version retained, was deleted in conference because

> ...the committee of conference does not feel that this is
> of any legal significance. It is the view of the mem-
> bers of the conference committee that the last sentence
> of the present section 311 is surplusage and that by
> omitting it from the present law the power of the United
> States or of any private person to proceed under the
> antitrust laws would not be curtailed or affected in any
> way....
>
> ...The Commission's existing authority under law to
> examine into the character of a licensee or permittee in
> granting a license or a renewal is in no way impaired or
> modified by the change here recommended in section 311....[58]

Administrative sanctions. The House version's suspension and fine authority was dropped from the compromise
measure:

> It is believed that the authority to issue cease-and-
> desist orders will give the Commission a means by which
> it can secure compliance with the law and regulations by
> licensees. As an alternative to revoking the license in
> case of failure to obey a cease-and-desist order, the
> Commission will be able to invoke the aid of the courts,
> under section 401 (b) of the Act, to secure compliance.
> The courts will be able to enforce compliance through their
> power to punish for contempt.[59]

---

[57]Ibid., p. 19.    [58]Ibid., p. 20.    [59]Ibid., p. 21.

Facilities for candidates for public office. The
Horan amendment to the House version of the McFarland bill
(which would have exempted radio stations for libelous utterances by political candidates), was dropped from the conference bill because: "The proposal involves many difficult
problems and it is the judgment of the committee of conference that it should be acted upon only after full hearings
have been held." The House provision which prohibited
broadcasters from charging political candidates more than
the "charges made for comparable use of such station for
other purposes" was retained, after the word "minimum"
preceding "charges" was omitted.

Separation of functions. The Senate version provided that the Commission could not employ attorneys or
other persons for the purpose of reviewing transcripts or
preparing intermediate reports of final decisions, except
for review staff and legal assistants assigned separately to
Commission members. The House version provided that in any
case of adjudication (as defined in the Administrative Procedure Act) which has been designated for a hearing, no
commissioner, and no professional assistant appointed by a
commissioner,

> ...shall (except to the extent required for the disposi-
> tion of ex parte matters authorized by law) consult on
> any fact or question of law in issue, or receive any
> recommendations from, any other person, unless upon notice
> and opportunity for all parties to participate.

The House version provided further that the provision
should not restrict consultation, or the making of

recommendations, "between a commissioner and another commissioner or between a commissioner and a professional assistant
appointed by him." The House version also specified that
this provision should not restrict commissioners in obtaining from members of the review staff the limited assistance
authorized by the other provisions of the House amendment.

The conference substitute omitted the provisions of
both Senate and House versions of the McFarland bill and included in their place the following:

(2) In any case of adjudication (as defined in the
Administrative Procedure Act) which has been designated
for a hearing by the Commission, no person who has parti-
cipated in the presentation or preparation for presentation of such case before an examiner or examiners of the
Commission, and no member of the Office of the General
Counsel, the Office of the Chief Engineer, or the Office
of the Chief Accountant shall (except to the extent
required for the disposition of ex parte matters as
authorized by law) directly or indirectly make any
additional presentations respecting such case, unless
upon notice and opportunity for all parties to participate.

It was stated:

This provision is included in the conference substitute because the members of the committee of conference are of the definite opinion that all parties should
have a knowledge of, and an opportunity to refute, any
matter or argument presented to the Commission.[60]

Once the McFarland bill had been agreed to in the conference committee, there were no further bars to its passage.
It was approved in both Houses on July 2, 1952, and was
signed into law July 16, 1952.[61]

[60]Ibid., p. 22.
[61]Public Law 554, 82d Congress.

Thus, the McFarland amendments to the Communications
Act of 1934 (S. 658) were the result of ten years of congressional effort to improve upon the Communications Act.
They were to a very large degree procedural in character.
They did very little to narrow down the meaning and intent of
Congress in respect to the Commission's broadcast licensing
functions. While throwing out all the so-called "controversial issues" (usually controversial in the sense that the
broadcast industry did not want them passed), the amendments
at the same time gave the industry a great deal of what it
was after in the way of changes in the law to benefit them.
The power to issue cease-and-desist orders was the only
change in the law which posed any kind of threat to the
broadcaster, and this a mild one. In contrast, the changes
brought about which resulted in the complete separation of
the Commission from its staff in adjudicatory proceedings as
well as those affecting the transfer provisions were to
complicate needlessly the already vacilliating and inconsistent licensing procedures, and contribute their share to
making a mockery of the entire hearing process.

In spite of this, however, many of the provisions
supplied by the passage of the McFarland bill were necessary
changes, and we should by no means draw the conclusion that
it was a wholly bad job of reconstruction of the Act. What
it can be criticized for is that it dodged the more important
issues involving fundamental weaknesses in the administration

of the law by the Commission, and needlessly hampered the
Commission (as will be pointed out more fully in subsequent
chapters) in the performance of certain of its functions.

## CHAPTER VIII

## AN ANALYSIS OF CERTAIN McFARLAND AMENDMENTS --
## THEIR INFLUENCE ON THE ADMINISTRATIVE FORMULATION OF
## POLICY IN THE COMMISSION

Having examined in the preceeding chapter the issues
involved in the passage of the McFarland Amendments of 1952,
it is appropriate to analyse and examine certain of these
amendments in the light of their relationship to the subsequent formulation of administrative policy in the Commission.
Our analysis will be limited to amendments which, directly
or indirectly, have affected such policy formulation. Those
amendments included in the McFarland Acts which are merely
procedural in character and, in addition, have not affected
policy formulation, will not be included. The amendments
will first be enumerated, and later discussed.

### 1. An Analysis of Certain McFarland Amendments

### a. Provisions Relating to the Commission

Section 4 (b) of the Communications Act of 1934, prior
to the enactment of the McFarland bill, read: "Such commissioners may not engage in any other business, vocation, or
employment. Not more than four commissioners shall be members
of the same political party."

In the Act of 1934 as modified by the McFarland bill
the original language was kept, except that "business,

ocation, or employment" was not meant to apply to "the
resentation or delivery of publications or papers for which
reasonable honorarium or compensation may be accepted."

In addition, language was added which prohibited any
ommissioner who resigned before his term of office had
xpired from representing any person before the Commission
n a professional capacity, for a period of one year, follow-
ng the termination of his services.

## . Provisions Relating to the Organization and Function of the Commission

The 1952 McFarland amendments specifically stated the
uties of the chairman of the Commission, who is designated
y the President. Section 5 (a) made him "Chief Executive
fficer of the Commission," whose duty was "to preside at
ll meetings and sessions," and "to represent the Commission
n all matters relating to legislation and legislative
eports, except that any Commissioner may present his own or
inority views or supplemented reports." (Emphasis supplied.)
n case of vacancy of the office of chairman or temporary
neligibility to serve, the Commission was given authority to
ppoint one of its members to be temporary chairman.

Paragraph (b) of section 5 as amended required that
the Commission staff be reorganized into "integrated bureaus,
to function on the basis of the Commission's principal workload operations."

Paragraph (c) as amended called for the setting up of

a "review staff," directly responsible to the Commission
alone, which was to perform --

> No duties or functions other than to assist the Com-
> mission in cases of adjudication...by preparing a summary
> of the evidence presented at any...hearing, by preparing,
> after an initial decision but prior to oral argument, a
> compilation of the facts material to the exceptions and
> replies thereto filed by the parties, and by preparing
> for the Commission or any member or members thereof,
> without recommendations (emphasis supplied), and in
> accordance with specific directions from the Commission
> or such member or members, memoranda, opinions, decisions,
> and orders.

Except for personal assistants to the Commissioners,
no Commission employee "who is not a member of the review
staff," could "perform the duties and functions which are
to be performed by the review staff."

Section 5 (d) (1) as amended provided that, except in
adjudicatory proceedings, the Commission could refer or
assign any portion of its work "to an individual Commissioner
or to a board composed of one or more employees of the Commission," but that any order, decision, or report made by
such person or group could be appealed to the entire Commission by "any person aggrieved," and that "every such
application shall be passed upon by the Commission," which
could "affirm, modify, or set aside such order, decision,
report, or action," and could order a rehearing.[1]

---

[1] The Communications Act of 1934 authorized the Commission (sec. 5 (a)) to divide its members into not more than
three divisions, "each to consist of not less than three members," and "each division shall choose its own chairman."
Each division so constituted was to have the power and authority to make its own decisions, subject to appeal and rehearing
to the full Commission. This authority, which had seldom

Finally, paragraph (c) contained language intended to speed up the processing of applications before the Commission:

(1) within three months from the date of filing in all original application, renewal, and transfer cases in which it will not be necessary to hold a hearing, and (2) within six months from the final date of the hearing in all cases...the Commission shall promptly report to the Congress each case which has been pending before it more than such three or six month period, respectively, stating the reasons therefore.

## Provisions Relating to Action upon License Applications and the Term of Licenses

1) Section 307 (a) of the Communications Act was amended. Where formerly the 1934 Act had stipulated that no license for a broadcast station could be granted for a period longer than three years, now, after passage of the McFarland amendments, upon license expiration, renewals could be granted for a period not to exceed three years, "if the Commission finds that public interest, convenience, and necessity would be solved thereby." In addition, the amendment stated that in order to

expedite actions on applications for renewal...and...to avoid needless expense to applicants for such renewals, the Commission shall not require any such applicant to file any information which previously has been furnished to the Commission, or which is not directly material to the considerations that offset the granting or denial of such application, but the Commission may require any new or additional facts it deems necessary to make its findings.[2]

---

been put into effect in the Commission's history, was removed in the 1952 amendments.

[2]Prior to 1952, subsec. (d) required that "action of the Commission with reference to the granting of such application for the renewal of a license shall be limited to and governed by the same considerations and practice which offset

2) Section 309 (b) was amended in order to furnish much more explicit detail regarding the methods and procedures whereby license applications were processed. As the 1934 Act had provided, the law required the Commission to grant the application whenever it found that "public interest, convenience, and necessity would be served," but in cases where the Commission was unable to make such a finding, it now had to send what has since become known as a "McFarland Letter" to

> ...forthwith notify the applicant and other known parties in interest of the grounds and reasons for its inability to make such a finding. Such notice, which shall preceed formal designation for a hearing, shall advise the applicant and all other known parties in interest of all objections made to the application as well as the source and nature of such objections. Following such notice, the applicant shall be given an opportunity to reply. If the Commission, after considering such reply, shall be unable to make the finding...it shall formally designate the application for hearing on the grounds or reasons then obtaining and shall notify the applicant and all other known parties in interest of such action, and the grounds and reasons therefore, specifying with particularity the matters and things in issue, but not including issues or requirements phrased generally....

Parties in interest not notified by the Commission of its action could acquire the status of a party in the proceeding by "filing a petition for intervention showing the basis for their interest at any time, not less than ten days prior to the date of hearing." Any hearing held afterwards was required under the McFarland amendments to be a

---

the granting of original applications." Thus, while previously burden of proof in renewal cases had fallen upon the applicant, under the 1952 amendments, the burden of proof became the task of the Commission.

full hearing in which the applicant and all other parties in interest would be permitted to participate. Burden of proof on all issues specified by the Commission was to be upon the applicant.

3) Subsection 309 (c) of the McFarland amendments, an entirely new provision, required that a grant should remain subject to protest for a period of 30 days when any instrument of authorization had been granted without hearing by the Commission.

During this time, any "party in interest" could protest under oath and request a hearing on the application that had been granted. The Commission was thereupon required to enter findings on the protested matter within 15 days, and to set a time for hearing on the untested application, if it found the issues set forth in the protest conformed with requirements of law. Pending hearing and decision, the effective date of the Commission's action, to which protest had been made, was to be postponed

> unless the authorization involved is necessary to the maintenance or conduct of an existing service, in which event the Commission shall authorize the applicant to utilize the facilities or authorization in question pending the Commission's decision after hearing.[3]

---

[3]This amendment was revised on January 20, 1956, Public No. 391, 84th Cong., 2d sess. (70 Stat. 3).

After the 1956 revision the Commission was allowed 30 days to enter findings on the "sufficiency of the protest," instead of the original 15, and thereupon designate the application for hearing.

Effective date of the grant, while it still could be postponed, or, conversely, could be authorized pending final decision in the case because the authorization was "necessary

4) A very significant change in subsection (b) of
section 310 of the 1934 Act was made in 1952 as the result
of the passage of the McFarland Acts. This amendment required that the Commission, in all cases of transfer of a
station construction permit or license, dispose of the application

> ...as if the proposed transferee or assignee were making
> application under section 308 (the licensing section) for
> the permit or license in question, but, in acting thereon,
> the Commission may not consider whether the public inter-
> est, convenience, and necessity might be served by the
> transfer, assignment, or disposal of the permit or
> license to a person other than the proposed transferee
> or assignee.4 (Emphasis supplied.)

---

to the maintenance or conduct of an existing service," could
also, under the new amendment, be authorized pending final
disposal by the Commission if it found that the public interest required "that the grant remains in effect."

The so-called protest rule has been the subject of
strong attack on several occasions by FCC Chairman John C.
Doerfer. According to a story in Broadcasting (Oct. 28,
1957, p. 72), Mr. Doerfer stated that employment of sec. 309
(c) had led to "extortionate" practices.

In a strong plea to have the section repealed, the
Chairman stated that the manner in which sec. 309 (c) has
worked would be a "fit subject for congressional investigation."

In his speech, delivered at a luncheon meeting of the
Federal Communications Bar Association, Mr. Doerfer stated
that, since January 20, 1956, the rule had involved 72 cases
at a total cost to the Government of $72,000. Mr. Doerfer
maintained that the 1952 amendments, particularly the protest
rule, gave precedence to private rights over that of the
public, and that these had also had the result of delaying
service to the public.

4Formerly, this section had read, "The station license...
and the rights therein granted shall not be transferred,
assigned, or in any manner either voluntarily or involuntarily
disposed of...to any person, unless the Commission shall,
after securing full information, decide that said transfer is
in the public interest, and shall give its consent in writing."

**d. Provisions Relating to Administrative Sanctions**

Section 312 of the Act of 1934 was extensively
revised, and several new subsections were added. The following quotation delineates the exact terminology used in the
amending legislation. Italicized words were added to the
language of the Communications Act by passage of the McFarland Acts:

1) Subsection 312 (a) as amended states that any
station license or construction permit may be revoked

a) for false statements knowingly made either in
the application or in any statement of fact which may
be required pursuant to section 308;

b) because of conditions coming to the attention
of the Commission which would warrant it in refusing
to grant a license or permit on an original application;[5]

c) for willful or repeated failure to operate substantially as set forth in the license;

d) for willful or repeated violation of, or willful
and repeated failure to observe any provision[6] of this
Act or any rule or regulation of the Commission authorized by this Act or by a treaty ratified by the United
States; and

e) for violation of or failure to observe any
cease-and-desist order issued by the Commission under
this section.

2) Subsection (b) as amended gave new power to the
Commission to issue cease-and-desist orders --

Where any person (1) has failed to operate substantially as set forth in the license or (2) has violated
or failed to observe any of the provisions of this Act or

---

[5]Former language: "Conditions revealed by such statements of fact as may be required from time to time."

[6]Former language: "Any of the restrictions and
conditions...."

(3) has violated or failed to observe any rule or regulation of the Commission authorized by this Act or by a treaty ratified by the United States....[7]

3) Subsection (c) of section 312 outlined procedures to be followed in cases of license or permit revocation for such causes as those outlined in subsection (a), or for issuance of any cease-and-desist orders as those which might be involved under subsection (b). In all cases, the Commission was required to serve upon the licensee, permittee, or person involved "an order to show cause why an order of revocation or a cease-and-desist order should not be issued." Any such order was to contain a statement relative to the matters in respect to which the Commission was inquiring, and was to call upon the witness to appear before the Commission. After hearing, the Commission could, if it so determined, issue a cease-and-desist order.

4) Subsection (d) as amended put the burden of the proceeding, introduction of evidence, and burden of proof in such hearing upon the Commission.

5) Subsection (e) as amended stated the provisions of section 9 (b) of the Administrative Procedure Act would be applicable to this section.

---

[7]Former language in the Act permitted the Commission to "modify...for a limited time or for the duration of the term thereof..." any license or permit if the Commission believed such action would benefit the public interest, or was required by the Act or any ratified treaty, provided, however, that no such order could become final until the holder of the license or permit had been notified in writing and had "been given reasonable opportunities to show cause why such an order of modification should not issue."

**.** Provisions Relating to Action on Appeals from
Commission Decisions and Conduct of Hearings

1) The so-called "appeals section" (sec. 402) of the
Communications Act was substantially revised by the 1952
amendments.

As was the case under the Communications Act of 1934,
appeals could be brought to the United States Court of
Appeals for the District of Columbia by any applicant whose
application for a construction permit, station license,
license renewal or modification had been turned down by the
Commission.

2) However, the 1952 amendments added several new
categories where appeal could be brought:

a) Sec. 402 (b) (3) By any party to an application for authority to transfer, assign, or dispose of
any such instrument of authorization, or any rights
thereunder, whose application is denied by the Commission.

b) Sec. 402 (b) (4) By any applicant for the permit required by section 325 of this Act whose application has been denied by the Commission, or by any permittee under said section whose permit has been revoked
by the Commission.

c) Sec. 402 (b) (5) By the holder of any construction permit or station license which has been modified
or revoked by the Commission.

d) Sec. 402 (b) (6) By any other person who is
aggrieved or whose interests are adversely affected by
any order of the Commission granting or denying any
application described in paragraphs (1), (2), (3), and
(4) hereof.

e) Sec. 402 (b) (7) By any person upon whom an
order to cease and desist has been served under section
312 of this Act.

f) Sec. 402 (b) (8) By any radio operator whose
license has been suspended by the Commission.

3) Subsection 402 (c) provided all appeals should be filed with the court within 30 days "from the date upon which public notice is given of the decision or order complained of."[8]

The 1952 amendment provided, where the Communications Act of 1934 had not, that --

> Upon filing of such notice, the court shall have jurisdiction of the proceedings and of the questions determined therein and shall have power, by order, directed to the Commission or any other party to the appeal, to grant such temporary relief as it may deem just and proper. (Emphasis supplied.)

## 2. The Influence of the Aforementioned McFarland Amendments on the Administrative Formulation of Policies in the Commission

### a. Provisions Relating to the Commission

The previously mentioned McFarland Amendments to the Communications Act of 1934 have had considerable influence on the formulation of administrative policy in the Commission since 1952. As a somewhat indirect example of this influence the amendment to section 4 (b) of the Communications Act of 1934 (to permit the payment of "honorariums" and "compensations" to commissioners) has contributed to the practice of attempting to "buy favors" from the Commission. There have been frequent instances of various commissioners receiving

---

[8] Former language had provided a limit of 20 days "after the decision complained of is effective....Unless a later date is specified by the Commission as part of its decision, the decision complained of shall be considered to be effective as of the date on which public announcement of the decision is made at the office of the Commission in the city of Washington."

payment for speeches and public appearances from applicants
and "parties in interest" to rule making proceedings or
cases in an adjudicatory posture. One case occurred in which
(after having been invited by an applicant for a TV channel
to speak before a group of broadcasters) a commissioner
spent a week's vacation at the summer home of that applicant
(whose case was then before the Commission). That same commissioner later voted for the applicant.[9]

b. Provisions Relating to the Organization and
   Function of the Commission

Similarly, those provisions in the McFarland Amendments, dealing with the "organization and function of the
Commission," have had important subsequent effects on the
formulation of its administrative policy, in particular the
amended section 5 (c) (involving the establishment of a
Review Staff to write the Commission's adjudicatory decisions). This amendment has brought on a complete separation
of the Commission from its professional staff at times when
it must decide on the winning applicant in a comparative
hearing case. Under the present system, the Commission is
presented with a hearing docket of several thousand pages,

---

[9]Because of evidence of abuses of this provision, and
because no such similar provision is contained in the legislation affecting other independent regulatory agencies, a bill
(H. R. 11886), which would enact its repeal, was introduced
by the Honorable Oren Harris, Chairman of the House Committee
on Interstate and Foreign Commerce, and the Subcommittee on
Legislative Oversight, after hearings on the matter had been
held by the Oversight Committee.

along with a one hundred to three hundred page summary of
the case compiled by the hearing examiner and containing his
initial decision. The Commission is not required by law to
read the record before it decides upon a winning applicant,
nor is any commissioner required to attend the hearings
themselves. All the law requires the Commission to do is
make a decision awarding the channel. The Commission may,
following its own oral hearing, choose to accept the initial
decision of the hearing examiner or it may choose to award
the channel to a different applicant. (According to testimony elicited in hearings before the Subcommittee on Legislative Oversight, the Commission has reversed its hearing
examiners in one-third of its comparative television hearing
cases conducted since 1952.)[10] After it has rendered its
decision the Commission issues instructions to the Review
Staff to write an opinion looking toward award of the channel to applicant "X." The Review Staff is thus given the
task of rationalizing the Commission's decision by writing
an opinion, which is already based on a "fait accompli."
Under this system, opinions have been written by the Review
Staff -- and later, upon remand or reconsideration, revised,
with a different conclusion based upon the same set of facts.
It is not surprising under such conditions, where commissioners bear no individual responsibility for the writing of

---

[10] See the testimony of Chief FCC Hearing Examiner
Herbert L. Sharfman before the Subcommittee on Legislative
Oversight.

decisions, that the outcome of similar types of comparative
television hearing cases since 1952 has been so varied.[11]
In view of the fact that Congress delegated powers to the
Commission based on the theory that these powers would be
personally exercised by the appropriate administrative
experts, it would seem that for these same experts then to
further delegate the job of explaining their decisions to
others would in effect defeat the whole theory of agency
expertise.

c. Provisions Relating to Action upon Applications
   and the Term of Licenses

1) Amendments to section 309 of the Communications
Act of 1934 (governing action upon license applications, in
particular the amendment of section 309 (c), relative to
"parties in interest" to proceedings) have added greatly to
the length of time required to obtain Commission action on
certain types of license applications. To cite a certain
type of example, let us examine the Commission's policies as
they relate to questions of economic injury in the granting
of licenses.

Certain vital Commission procedures underwent a subtle
but enervating shift as a result of passage of section 309 (c).[12]

---

[11]For a compilation of FCC decisions and bases for
awards in 14 representative comparative hearing cases decided
since 1952, see Appendix I.

[12]Section 309 (c) was enacted in 1952. It grew out of
the Supreme Court's decision in the Saunders case which held
that "Congress had some purpose in enacting section 402 (b)
(2). It may have been of opinion that one likely to be

This so-called "protest provision" was enacted in order to
provide parties with a legitimate interest an opportunity to
raise substantial questions as to the validity of authoriza-
tions granted by the Commission.[13]   The decisions of the various Courts of Appeal in protest cases have taken an extremely broad view of the classes of persons entitled to protest.

The term "party in interest" has been frequently interpreted by the courts, not only in connection with the Communications Act, but also as it is used in other statutes.
It is apparent, from court decisions, that the term has been
taken to include licensees and permittees of radio or television stations who might be adversely affected economically
by the particular grant. This economic effect can be applied
even when it allegedly stems from the loss of a minute percentage of the station's potential listening audience hundreds of miles away.

Persons wholly outside the field of radio or television have been awarded standing as parties in interest
under this provision. In one of its decisions, the Court of

---

financially injured by the issue of a license would be the
only person having sufficient interest to bring to the attention of the appellate court errors of law in the action of
the Commission in granting the license. It is within the
power of Congress to confer such standing to prosecute an
appeal." (Saunders v. FCC, 309 U. S. 470, 60 S. C. 693,
1940.)

[13] The Act does not define or indicate the qualifications of a party in interest. Nor does it indicate in what
way, if at all, the protester must be affected by the action
he protests, in order for him to have the necessary interest.

Appeals stated that it agreed that a newspaper in Clarksburg,
West Virginia, had standing as a party in interest (alleging
economic injury) to file a protest against the grant of a
new television station in that city. This illustrates quite
clearly the broad interpretation that has been given the
party in interest concept.[14]

---

[14]The reported cases decide that a protester is a
party in interest where there is likelihood that he will suf-
fer economic injury or competitive injury from the protested
action. They do not, however, limit "parties in interest" to
those who are so affected. (Saunders v. FCC, 309 U. S. 470,
60 S. C. 693.) Except in two instances, the cases deal with
protests made by station licensees against grants by the Commission of licenses for new stations or changing the privileges of other stations, on the ground that the new or
changed grants affect the existing licensee-protester economically or electrically.

Important cases decided since the amendment of section
309 (c) in 1952 are:

Elm City Broadcasting Co. v. U. S., 235 F. 2d 811,
1956.

Granick and Cook v. FCC, 234 F. 2d 682, 1956.

Clarksburg Publishing Co. v. FCC, 225 F. 2d 511, 1955.

Federal Broadcasting System v. FCC, 225 F. 2d 560,
1955.

Greenville Television Co. v. FCC, 221 F. 2d 870, 1955.

Metropolitan Television Co. v. U. S., 221 F. 2d 879,
1955.

Camden Radio Inc. v. FCC, 220 F. 2d 191, 1955.

Each case has been decided on its own facts, with little or no reference to preceeding cases; and they afford little guidance for future cases. The Granick and Clarksburg
Publishing Company cases dealt with protests made by non-
broadcasters. In Granick the protester was the holder of an
option for the assignment of a station and license. In
Clarksburg the protest was made by a newspaper publishing
company not engaged in broadcasting. In both cases decisions
that the protesters were not parties in interest were reversed by the Court of Appeals.

In the Federal Broadcasting case the court of appeals
made a clear statement of what is required of a protest under
sec. 309 (c): "What is required is merely an articulated
statement of some fact or situation which would tend to show,

2) Hearings of the Committee on Legislative Oversight developed considerable testimony which attested to the unfortunate effects the amendment of section 310 (b) of the Act has had on TV station transfers.[15] (Section 310 (b) stated that, in all cases of transfer of a station construction permit or license, the Commission might not consider whether any person other than the proposed licensee might be better qualified to operate the station.)

A recent United States court of appeals ruling suggested that Congress may want to reconsider its amending of sec. 310 (b). In its August 28, 1958, dismissal of the appeal of St. Louis Amusement Company v. FCC appellee, CBS, KWK, Inc., 220 Television, Inc., Broadcast House Inc., intervenors, the District of Columbia Court of Appeals ruling stated:

> The Commission, relying on the legislative history, contends that, under sec. 310 (b), as amended in 1952, when a construction permittee seeks to assign its permit, the Commission is empowered to consider only whether the assignee selected by the permittee is qualified, and that

---

if established at a hearing, that the grant of the license contravened public interest, convenience and necessity, or that the licensee was technically or financially unqualified, contrary to the Commission's initial finding. (Fed. Broad. Systems v. FCC, 225 F 2d 560, 563 (1956))

In the Clarksburg Publishing Company case the court severly criticized the Commission for its failure to follow the letter and the spirit of the protest section 309 (c), calling attention to the fact that in appropriate instances the statute contemplates that the Commission's inquiry may extend even beyond matters alleged in a protest. (See Clarksburg Pub. Co. v. FCC, 225 F 2d 511, 515 (1955))

[15]See testimony made at hearings during the last two weeks of May 1958. A more detailed examination of the effect of the amendment on FCC policy regarding station transfers is given in the following chapter.

the Commission has no power to consider the comparative
qualifications of prior unsuccessful applicants, even
when, as in this case, the assignment follows close on
the heels of a comparative hearing. If the Commission's
present interpretation is correct, the 1952 amendment
operates to allow a private entity to decide who shall
receive the permit, without regard to which one of these
applicants the Commission has selected on a comparative
basis.

Whether Congress intended this result, or even anti-
cipated the possibility, is not clear from the legislative history. This interpretation of the 1952 amendment could, conceivably, open the door to something not
unlike the "trafficking in licenses" long since disapproved. If this interpretation is correct, there may
be a serious gap in the statutory scheme to which congressional attention should be directed. (Emphasis
supplied.)

Equally as important as the question of comparative

qualifications, however, is whether, in effect, as maintained

in the Commission's brief, it "is empowered to consider only

whether the assignee selected by the permittee is qualified...."

Certainly, the Commission today, as at any time, has express

authority to consider the public interest aspects of any case,

including that of transfer. The question may be asked

whether or not the Commission has all too readily relinquished

its desire to do so.

3) As has been pointed out in this chapter, when Con-

gress amended section 311 of the Communications Act of 1934,

it deleted language which empowered the Commission, at its

own discretion, to refuse a license to anyone adjudged guilty

by a Federal court of unlawfully monopolizing or attempting

to monopolize radio communications. Because of the deletion

from the Act of the aforementioned language, the FCC, which

has seldom been eager to prosecute antitrust matters,

concluded that primary jurisdiction in such instances as affected broadcast licensing was the prerogative of the Department of Justice, rather than the Commission.

In <u>United States</u> <u>v</u>. <u>Radio Corporation of America and National Broadcasting Company</u>,[16] the Commission claimed that no action it had taken (in previously approving the transfer and sale of a station by the Westinghouse Corp. to NBC) could foreclose the Government from proceeding under the antitrust laws. It also stated that, in its opinion, there was no requirement that the Justice Department participate in FCC proceedings before filing suit in a court.

The Commission brief stated:

> ...The Commission has made clear that it does not believe it can effectively enforce the antitrust laws in cases such as this one, but, rather, must leave the enforcement of those laws to the Department of Justice and other governmental agencies. The Commission has, therefore, examined transfers such as the subject one from the viewpoint of its own expertise in the communications field and the general standard of public interest. And, while the question of possible violation of the antitrust laws may, of course, be pertinent to the Commission's determination under the public-interest standard, the Commission has normally left the determination of possible antitrust cases such as the instant one to agencies and courts having the statutory responsibility and expertise to properly deal with it....

The court disagreed with this stand, however, and, in a ruling handed down January 10, 1958, stated that the Government could not sue RCA-NBC on antitrust charges after the FCC had approved the acquisition of a Philadelphia station

---

[16] U. S. District Court, E. D. Pa., January 10, 1958 (16 R. R. at 2020).

from the Westinghouse Broadcasting Co. In essence, it held that since the FCC had approved the transaction, the Justice Department's only recourse would have been to appeal to the FCC, and, failing that appeal, to the circuit court of appeals. Judge Kirkpatrick, in the ruling, also held that, when Congress struck out the former wording of sec. 311, which permitted the Justice Department to move against broadcast licenses even after the FCC had acted in a case, it "estopped" exactly that action. Recently, however, the Supreme Court in its review of this case overruled this opinion, ruling that FCC approval of a particular transaction in the broadcast field does not block the Justice Department from attacking the transaction on antitrust charges.

Now that this has happened, an article in the Wall Street Journal indicates that the FCC may once again have changed its mind regarding its powers to enforce the antitrust laws. Since Supreme Court reversal of the previously mentioned case, antitrust officials have been acting on the theory that the regulatory agencies are failing to preserve competition in the industry. It is felt that certain industry practices may not necessarily be antitrust-exempt, even if approved by a regulatory agency, and that FCC approval of a broadcasting transaction does not preclude antitrust action against it. According to the newspaper article, John C. Doerfer, FCC Commission Chairman, recently reacted to this idea by saying:

> I wish the Justice Department would stay in its own back-
> yard....Sure, they should alert us to obvious antitrust

violations, but that's all. They should not try to make
everybody else shape policies the way the Department of
Justice thinks they should be shaped. They don't understand the broadcasting industry or why the FCC was
created.

Equally vehement according to the Journal article

was the reply to this statement of Mr. Doerfer by "a veteran

Government trustbuster" (unnamed): "These agencies started

out as simple administrative agencies to look after the

public interest...then the industries took over, and now

the agencies look after the industry interest...."[17]   Thus,

if any conclusion at all were to be drawn by the writer

relative to the frequently changing attitude of the Commis-

sion regarding its antitrust obligations, it would be that

the Commission, whether it has the power or not, definitely

does not want to tangle with such a powerful adversary as

the RCA and its subsidiary, NBC.

d.  Provisions Relating to Administrative Sanctions

According to complaints voiced by the Commission,

revision by Congress of section 312 of the Act of 1934 by

the McFarland Amendments (permitting issuance of cease-and-

desist orders in cases of violation of Commission rules and

regulations) has not greatly aided it in the enforcement of

its rules and regulations.  Once the so-called "cease-and-

desist order" has been issued, it is appealable to the courts,

thus greatly delaying the time when such orders become

---

[17]Monroe W. Karmin, "Battling Bureaucrats, Antitrust
Crusades Set Off Inter-Agency Row Over Business Controls"
Wall Street Journal, Wednesday, July 8, 1959.

effective. In addition, according to Commission spokesmen,
the cease-and-desist order has proven particularly in-
effective and unwieldy in cases of minor violations of Commission regulations by nonbroadcast operators (who employ
broadcast equipment in the conduct of their business.) It
has therefore been the suggestion of the Commission that
Congress allow it to assess small fines, rather than being
required to resort to the lengthy process of contempt of
court action. Thus, passage of this provision, intended to
aid the Commission in securing compliance from the regulated
industry, has not greatly aided it in this regard.

e.  Provisions Relating to Action on Appeals from
    Commission Decisions and Conduct of Hearings

Although the Communications Bar Association has never
complained about the much broadened provisions for appeal
and rehearing allowed by the McFarland Amendments of 1952
(perhaps not without reason -- since these amendments have
provided a lucrative means of employment), the Commission
itself has often voiced its objections. It has charged that
the total effect of these provisions taken together with
those supplied by the Administrative Procedure Act of 1946[18]
has greatly added to the volume of testimony, length of hearings, incidence of court appeals, and duration of adjudicatory
matters.[19] Comments have been made to the writer both by

---

[18]60 Stat. 237, 5 U. S. C., secs. 1001-1011.

[19]In comparative hearings in the Miami Channel 10 case,
for example, there were 23 volumes of dockets, comprising

Commission staff and by Commissioners themselves that, in their opinion, the greatly broadened appeal provisions have constituted a form of "legal blackmail" to afford delay of Commission decisions and harassment of applicants. In his appearance before the Subcommittee on Legislative Oversight (March 28, 1958), Commissioner Robert T. Bartley expressed himself in a manner that perhaps illustrates this point of view:

> There has been a gradual chiseling away of the end of these commissions over a period of ten years or more from the organizational concept. I doubt if we would have had the commissions if the courts could have handled a lot of these matters in an expeditious manner, but they could not, and so commissions were set up to expedite matters so that, by the time you decided a case, why, it would be timely, not five years later.
>
> But gradually, when people start losing cases, they start looking for reasons other than the real reason; that is, they didn't have the best case, and they want to drag it out a little longer, get another chance at it; maybe somebody will die in the process, and knock some applicant out.
>
> We just go around and around on these things, and I heard it said by very reputable lawyers that a fellow being denied an application before the FCC gets more due process than a murderer would, and I believe it.
>
> A contributing factor for delay is the recent increase in the laws providing for more "due process."[20]

---

seven feet of shelf space. (See testimony of Commissioner Lee before the Subcommittee on Legislative Oversight, March 28, 1958, vol. 27, p. 3932 of Reporter's transcript of hearing.) For a compilation of the volume of testimony, length of hearings, and duration of adjudicatory matters in 14 representative cases decided since 1952, see Appendix II.

[20] Reporter's transcript of hearing, March 28, 1958, vol. 27, p. 3834.

Commissioner Hyde in his testimony made similar
reference to the problem:

>...the various procedures which have been adopted by Con-
gress which we must observe do make (decisionmaking) an
inherently long and tedious process. I am sure that
these conditions were designed to assure due process. I
think, however, that they go to extremes, and might very
well be reexamined.[21]

In addition, Commissioner Hyde underlined the effect
that certain provisions of this legislation have had on court
decisions, which in recent years have been calling for ever
greater documentation in the handling of adjudicatory
matters:

>We are required by decisions of the court to be most
careful (in opinion and decision writing) in dealing with
every point of contest in them, and, try as well as we
will, there doesn't seem to be any shortcut under the
present status of the law....

>If you will include compliance with these various
statutory requirements, legal interpretations which apply
to the writing up of a judgment in an administrative
case, I would like to suggest to you that a trial court
has a very simple task in making his judgment compared
to what we have....The process of arriving at an administrative decision under the requirements of law and in
the light of court decisions is inherently a very tremendous job.[22]

Whether or not we accept the thesis that these Commission's complaints are justified, there can be no doubt of
the fact that the previously cited amendments have had a
considerable effect on the formulation of Commission policy.

---

[21]Testimony of Rosel Hyde before the Committee on
Legislative Oversight, March 26, 1958, vol. 25, p. 3677, of
reporter's transcript of hearing.

[22]Ibid., pp. 3687-3690.

From our study of the legislative history of the McFarland
Act and those proposed but unenacted bills, such as White-
Wolverton, which preceeded its passage, it is clear that the
McFarland bill (1) gave the least of any of them in the way
of added power to the Commission, and (2) gave the most of
any of the previously proposed reorganization bills in the
way of concessions to the industry. It was a prime example
of legislation which took so long to pass the Congress, that
by the time passage was obtained, industry pressures had
almost completely had their way in removing those provisions
which they did not favor. In a way, it was also a perfect
example of one of the major weaknesses of our democratic system -- in that true democracy is based upon a compromise
between two strong forces which counterbalance one another.
Here, there was no counterbalancing of the forces of "public
interest" vs. "private interest" -- since the Commission was
unable to fulfill adequately its obligation to the former.

# CHAPTER IX

## THE COMMISSION AS A LICENSING BODY

In the preceding chapters of this study, an examination of the birth, development, and philosophy behind the communications Act has been made. Since the main purpose of his Act was the creation of an independent governmental commission to function as a licensing body -- it now remains the ask of the writer to assess how effectively, fairly, and ith what degree of consistency the Commission has succeeded n carrying out this purpose. This can be done only by an xamination of actual instances where the Commission has een called upon to perform its licensing duties.

It must be noted that a statute such as the Communications Act poses a very real problem to the Agency created by t. On the one hand, the Agency is endowed with very wide reas of discretion and very broad powers of regulation -- owers which in effect give it life and death force over the roadcast industry -- yet on the other hand, the Agency was ot furnished by Congress with any real guide to assist it in etermining the exercise of its powers in specific licensing nd renewal cases.

In the case of the Federal Communications Commission, ae only standard contained in the enabling statute is that f "public interest, convenience, and necessity." Such a tandard is in actuality so vague as to be all but meaningess. It gives the Commission almost complete latitude

to decide individual cases as it wishes -- not even subject
to the need for maintaining the corpus of its law consistent.

How then is such an Agency to deal with the specific
cases that come before it? There is only one answer; it
must itself supply the missing directions of the Communications Act. This it can do only by developing its own administrative standards which will guide it in making specific
decisions under the Act. Such a development of administrative standards is one of the primary justifications for wide
delegations of power to the administrative process.

Paul Clifton Fowler's comments are very well put in
regard to FCC policies as they are employed in cases of
initial licensing as well as those of license renewal.
He states:

> Discretionary authority has been extensively used by
> the Commission in two general areas of regulation: licen-
> sing and the review of a station's operating policies.
> In licensing, the Commission has produced a broad and
> comprehensive program of regulatory policies with almost
> no restraint imposed from Congress and the Courts. When
> reviewing broadcast activities of stations, the Commis-
> sion has been alternately bold and cautious, but it is
> in this area that the Commission's discretion has been
> most severely criticized and condemned....In licensing...
> as long as a decision is based upon substantial evidence,
> the Commission has almost complete freedom to determine
> the merits of license applications.[1]

Mr. Fowler further observes that prior to World War II,
in its processing of single applications the Commission had
fixed rather definite standards of judgment.[2] In regard to
the handing down of its decisions in its comparative hearings

---

[1]Fowler, op. cit., pp. 390-391.     [2]Ibid., p. 397.

n television cases since that time, however, Mr. Fowler

tates with equal correctness:

> The record of the Commission decisions in comparative
> hearings in television is another story.  The Commission
> has been inconsistent in the value it has attached to
> each value considered.  A factor which may be judged as
> favorable toward a license grant in one case may be
> treated unfavorably in another.  The Commission has made
> exceptions to the general standards which has led to
> opinions granting licenses in different cases for almost
> exactly opposite reasons.[3]

Mr. Fowler's conclusions are that this type of "flexi-

ility" is manifestly undesirable because it places an

pplicant in a totally unpredictable position.  He therefore

ecommends that the Commission establish its own "relatively

flexible standards" to be employed in comparative cases,

nich would indicate how the Commission views each factor

nd would clearly state whether such a factor would aid or

rt an applicant's case.[4]

Since the licensing of television channels has by

ar outweighed in importance the assignment of radio frequen-

es in recent years, our examination of the development of

dministrative standards by the FCC will be confined exclus-

vely to the licensing of television channels.  Additionally,

nce the scarcity of as yet unassigned television channels

as resulted in an increasing degree of purchase and sale of

elevision stations on the open market, thus further invol-

ng the Commission in important licensing functions, it

ecomes necessary to examine also the methods by which the

---

[3]Ibid., pp. 398-399.    [4]Ibid., p. 399.

Commission approves the transfer of a television station
license.

## 1. Licensing Standards as Applied
in Comparative Television Cases

The manner in which the Federal Communications Commission has developed and applied its own standards in
administering the Communications Act can best be seen from
an analysis of certain of the comparative television hearing
cases that have been decided by the Commission. As the
recent Barrow Report on Network Broadcasting states:

> It is in the comparative hearing context that the
> Commission is afforded an appropriate forum for an
> exploration of the full range of factors which may con-
> tribute to or detract from the ability of a given appli-
> cant to serve the public interest. This proceeding
> permits the Commission to consider in the fullest degree
> the qualitative elements entering into service to the
> public.[5]

Such comparative television hearing cases occur when
there are two or more competing applicants in the same
community for the same television channel. Since these
applications are by their nature mutually exclusive, the
burden falls upon the Commission to determine which of the
applicants is best qualified to serve the public interest.
This principle was previously enunciated by the Supreme Court
in a leading case in which it stated that the Commission's

---

[5]Network Broadcasting, Report of the Network Study
Staff to the Network Study Committee, III-II (Federal Communications Commission 1957).

icensing function is not limited to determining that there

re no technological objections to the granting of a license:

If the criterion of "public interest" were limited to
such matters, how could the Commission choose between
two applicants for the same facilities, each of whom is
financially and technically qualified to operate a
station?  Since the very inception of federal regulation
of radio, comparative considerations as to the services
to be rendered have governed the application of "public
interest, convenience, or necessity."[6]

The Federal Communications Commission itself has

ecognized the necessity for such comparative standards.  In

letter dated August 30, 1956, from the then Chairman

Connaughey to the Hon. Warren G. Magnuson, Chairman of the

enate Interstate and Foreign Commerce Committee, Commis-

ioner McConnaughey stated:

Congress in the Communications Act of 1934 or its
several amendments refrained from laying down definite
criteria to guide the Commission in selecting the best
qualified applicant among several competing applicants
for a particular channel or facility.  Instead, it has
left that task to the Commission to work out under the
applicable standard, the public interest, convenience,
and necessity.[7]

This same letter states some of these criteria:

Proposed programming and policies, local ownership
and management, participation in civic activities, record
of past performance, broadcast experience, relative
likelihood of effectuation of proposals as shown by the
contacts made with local groups and similar efforts,
carefulness of operational planning for television,
staffing, diversification of the background of the persons controlling, diversification of control of the
mediums of mass communications.[8]

---

[6]NBC v. U. S., 319 U. S. 190, 216-17 (1943).

[7]Hearings on S. Res. 13 and 163, 84th Congress,
l sess., p. 979 (1956).

[8]Loc. cit.

It is important to bear in mind that not all the comparative criteria listed by the chairman have the same relative importance. Thus, in the words of Mr. McConnaughey in the same letter, "We could say that three factors on the list, diversification of the background of the persons controlling, participation in civic activities, or carefulness of operational planning for television, do not carry the same weight as the others."[9]

While we can agree, "It is true that a precise delineation of the relative importance of the criteria is both inappropriate and, as a practical matter, impossible,"[10] an analysis of Federal Communications Commission decisions can, all the same, enable an approximate delineation to be made. Such an analysis was made in 1958 and reported to the Subcommittee on Legislative Oversight by its then Chief Counsel, Dr. Bernard Schwartz, and placed in the Subcommittee files. This analysis demonstrated that the following criteria tended to be determinating in the vast majority of comparative television cases.[11]

a) Local ownership

b) Integration of ownership and management

c) Past performance

d) Broadcast experience

---

[9]Ibid., p. 980.     [10]Ibid.

[11]Confidential Memorandum (now released) to the Honorable Morgan M. Moulder, Chairman, Special Subcommittee on Legislative Oversight, from Bernard Schwartz, January 4, 1958, p. 16.

e) Proposed programming policies

f) Diversification of control of the media of mass ommunications.

Examination by the staff of the outcome of some sixty elevision cases which involved comparative hearings held by he Federal Communications indicated --

> A most disturbing inconsistency on the part of the Commission in its application of the standards developed by it in particular cases....At times, in truth, the Commission appears to have made decisions which are dia- metrically opposed both to the standards which it itself has developed and to its own decisions in other contem- poraneous cases.[12]

It was further noted in the study and reported by r. Schwartz that there had been a tendency in the Commission n recent years to modify the weight given to the different riteria developed by it. This modification was made in the irection of diminishing the importance of criteria such as ocal ownership, integration of ownership and management, nd diversification of control of the media of mass communi- ations (all of which tended to favor the small newcomer, ithout established broadcasting interests) and the magni- ication of the weight given to the criterion of broadcast xperience (which tended to favor the large established ompany, with extensive existing broadcast interests). The tudy reported that in a number of recent cases the exper- ence factor has tended to be all but conclusive with the esult that there has been a growing number of decisions that

---

[12]Ibid., p. 16.

have tended to favor the already pronounced tendency toward concentration of ownership in the broadcast field.[13]

In addition, the study noted, the Commission did not even begin to be consistent in the application of its modified criteria, so that along with decisions which appeared unduly to favor the large applicant were cases in which the Commission continued to give preponderant weight to standards such as local ownership, integration of ownership and management, and diversification, which favored the small local applicant without extensive interests in radio and television.[14]

A number of disturbing factors were noted by the subcommittee staff in its analysis of the Federal Communications Commission's application of its own criteria. For example, the criteria of "local ownership" in the past was considered to be one of fundamental import because of the basic congressional intent to have broadcast stations owned as far as possible by local residents who presumably would be more cognizant and responsive to the needs of the local community. In a number of recent cases however such as Indianapolis Channel 13 and St. Louis Channel 4, the Commission has decided against local owners and preferred applicants wholly owned by outside interests.[15]

---

[13]Ibid., p. 17.     [14]Ibid.

[15]In re Indianapolis Broadcasting Inc., et al., 12 RR 883 (1957). In re application of St. Louis Telecast Inc. et al., 22 FCC 625, 12 RR 1289 (1957).

In other recent cases which involved corporate applicants the Commission looked to the residence not of the
owners (i.e., the stockholders) of the corporation, but to
that of its principal officers.[16]  On the other hand, with a
complete lack of consistency, the Commission has in other
recent cases continued to look to the residence of stockholders in analagous situations.

In addition, there have been instances where the
Commission arrived at diametrically opposite conclusions
based on very similar sets of facts so that, in the Omaha,
Nebraska, Channel 7 case an individual domiciled in Nebraska
but resident in Washington was treated as a Nebraska resident for purposes of local ownership while in the Miami,
Florida, Channel 7 (Biscayne TV) decision an individual
domiciled in Ohio but resident in Florida was treated as a
Florida resident.[17]

Likewise, the criterion of "integration of ownership
and management" has been applied in recent years in highly
inconsistent fashion.  The philosophy behind this criterion
lies in the assumption that there will be a closer relationship between the promise and performance aspects of a broadcast applicant's programming proposals if the applicant is

---

[16]See, for example, the Commission's decision in the
Miami Channel 10 case, In re WKAT, Inc. et al., 12 RR 1
(1957).

[17]In re KFAB Broadcasting Co., 12 RR 317 (1956).
In re application of Biscayne Television Corporation, et al.,
11 RR 1113 (1955).

both owner and manager of the new facility. This criterion
has been largely rationalized out of existence in such cases
as Miami Channel 10. Here equal weight as to integration of
ownership and management was given to a promise made by the
president of National Airlines that he would devote seventy-
five percent of his time to the management of the station,
and the promise of a competing application wholly owned and
operated by one man (who not only was to own the station,
but also proposed to manage it). Similarly in the Hartford
Channel 3 decision the Commission equated the owner-
management qualities of the largest block of insurance
companies in the nation with an application submitted by a
number of local citizens who themselves promised to operate
and manage their station.[18]

In the matter of "diversification of control of media
of mass communications" as opposed to "broadcast experience"
the Commission has on occasions preferred to give conclusive
weight to the diversification factor, while in others, although the facts are similar, it has preferred to emphasize
broadcast experience. Thus while in the Madison, Wisconsin,
Channel 3 (Radio Wisconsin) and the Sacramento, California,
Channel 10 (McClatchy) cases awards were made to an applicant solely on the basis of the need for diversification of
the mediums of mass communication in the area, in the Miami
Channel 7 (Biscayne TV) case an applicant with an even greater

_____

[18]In re Traveler's Broadcasting Service Corp., 12 RR
689 (1956).

concentration of communications ownership was preferred over three others with no affiliations with any mass media facilities on the basis of its greater broadcast experience.[19] (As a further indication of how the Commission manipulates its criteria mention should be made of the fact that the broadcast experience of McClatchy was far greater than that of the successful applicant.) The Court of Appeals for the District of Columbia subsequently stated in regard to the Miami Channel 7 case:

> The comparative qualifications of the competing appli-
> cants made the choice between them a close one. This is
> emphasized by the decided advantage of the other appli-
> cants with respect to diversification of media of mass
> communication, long considered important because of the
> public interest in non-concentration of control over,
> and of the sources of, media of communication. The Com-
> mission held "there can be no question that each of the
> other three applicants is entitled to a preference over
> Biscayne in this factor." The importance of this pre-
> ference given to the appellants over Biscayne is intrin-
> sically obvious. But the importance of Biscayne's own
> preferences based on broadcast experience and past
> records of its principals is not so obvious. In consid-
> erable part these preferences appear to have arisen from
> Biscayne's concentration of media of mass communication,
> which is itself an adverse rather than a preferential
> factor.[20]

In other words, the Court of Appeals drew attention to the fact that the criteria of experience and that of diversification are in actual fact inversely related: experience in broadcasting can be achieved only through ownership of or

---

[19] In re application of Radio Wisconsin et al., 10 RR 1224 (1955). In re application of McClatchy Broadcasting Co. 9 RR 1190 (1953). In re application of Biscayne Television Corporation et al., 11 RR 1113 (1955).

[20] Sunbeam Television Corporation v. Federal Communications Commission (D. C. Cir. 1957).

affiliation with existing radio-television facilities. The
large concentrated broadcast owner must inevitably be preferred if experience becomes the primary consideration --
to the inevitable detriment of the diversification policy.
Then, too, it should be noted that, as one commentator
stated: "While lack of experience is cured with time, lack
of diversification is not."[21]

With such examples outstanding, it is no wonder
that a witness in hearings before the Legislative Oversight Committee was able to state in regard to the comparative criteria of the FCC:

> It is apparent from the 14 representative cases
> examined and summarized...that the FCC decisions are not
> governed by the rule of stare decisis.
>
> In each case it would have been impossible to predict
> in advance the degree of weight which would be given to
> each of the foregoing criteria.
>
> In some cases the diversification of control of media
> of mass communication is given decisive weight; in some
> it is subordinate to other factors.
>
> In certain cases past experience of the applicant is
> made decisive and in others this factor is subordinated
> to that of local interest considerations.[22]

This lack of consistency in the decision making process has been frequently mentioned by writers and observers

---

[21]66 Yale Law Journal 365, 377 (1957).

[22]Testimony of James P. Radigan, Jr., Senior Specialist, American Public Law, Legislative Reference Service,
Library of Congress, relative to a staff study entitled "FCC
Standards or Comparative Criteria as Applied in 14 Representative Comparative TV Proceedings." Reporter's transcript of
hearings, Subcommittee on Legislative Oversight, House of
Representatives, May 15, 1958, p. 264. For an analysis of
these 14 representative cases, see Appendix I.

of Commission function, and by no means has this occurred
only in recent publications. H. P. Warner, in 1946 in the
Southern California Law Review, made the following observations:

> The Commission, through its published decisions, has
> exhibited a vacillating and inconsistent process; there
> has been no adherence to previously established policies.
> The administrative interpretation of the standard of
> public interest, convenience, and necessity, has resulted
> in the exercise of untrammeled discretion, with vagrant
> policy and expediency as its touchstone....It is possible
> to find decisions both affirmative and negative on prac-
> tically every topic discussed....There is no administra-
> tive pattern; it is like a patchwork quilt, with policies
> emerging, disappearing, and reappearing with no consis-
> tent design.[23]

In addition the 1948 Hoover Commission staff report on
the FCC made the following similar observation:

> Not a single person at the Commission who is con-
> cerned with broadcast work will even pretend to demon-
> strate that the Commission's decisions in its broadcast
> cases have followed a consistent policy, or for that
> matter, any policy other than the desire to dispose of
> cases and, if possible, to do so by making grants.[24]

In September 1957 two articles appeared in popular
publications, one by Louis L. Jaffe, Professor of Administrative Law at Harvard Law School, the other by Robert Bendiner,
a contributing editor to Reporter Magazine.   In referring

---

[23]H. P. Warner, "Administrative Process of the Federal
Communications Commission," Southern California Law Review,
vol. 19 (July 1946), pp. 346-347.

[24]Op. cit., Commission on Organization of the Executive Branch of the Government, staff report on the Federal
Communications Commission, 1948, Pt. II, p. 40.

to the Commission's comparative criteria Professor Jaffe

stated they are

> ...unfortunately extremely imprecise, and they are
> capable of infinite manipulation. They can become --
> and, in my opinion, the record shows they have become --
> spurious criteria, used to justify results otherwise
> arrived at.[25]

Professor Jaffe later states he believes that the

Commission's standards "...are announced only to be ignored,

ingeniously explained away, or so occasionally applied that

their very application seems a mockery of justice."[26]

Mr. Bendiner, in much the same vein concluded:

> ...the field is wide open to subjective judgment. The
> weighing of qualifications is often highly personal....
> And the criteria are so easily juggled that the Commis-
> sion can reach almost any decision and then order the
> staff to draw up the reasons for it...the stakes have
> been far higher, and the pressures on the FCC accordingly
> much greater, since 1952, because comparatively few tele-
> vision licenses were issued before that year.

> Instead of sharpening its criteria and increasing its
> vigilance however, the FCC seems to have fallen into
> such a morass of inconsistency and ad hoc judgments that
> there now seems to be almost no rule of law in parceling
> out these fabulously valuable public assets. As one
> former commissioner puts it, they are being handed out
> like door prizes.[27]

Most recently of all the 1958 "Bowles Report" makes

the charge that

> ...indecision, lack of affirmative policy, and in-
> consistency in the bases for decisions are manifest. The
> Commission's pattern of behavior in comparative hearings,

---

[25]Louis L. Jaffe, "The Scandal in TV Licensing,"
Harper's Magazine (September, 1957), p. 79.

[26]Ibid., p. 84.

[27]Robert Bendiner, "The FCC - Who Will Regulate the
Regulators?" The Reporter (September 19, 1957), p. 27.

where so much is at stake for the competing applicants, makes the going really rugged....

Comparative cases are resolved through an arbitrary set of criteria whose application, if one judges from history, is shaped to suit the cases of the moment.[28]

It would seem logical to assume when comparative cases reach solution through the application of such arbitrarily applied criteria, the opportunities for the successful exertion of _ex parte_ pressures upon the Commissioners who are entrusted with the power to give licenses and franchises worth millions of dollars are much more numerous. The investigations of the Special Subcommittee on Legislative Oversight did in fact disclose that extra record representations to members of the Commission were a common occurrence. Specific instances of improper _ex parte_ pressures in television cases, several of which have since been remanded by the court, are set forth in the hearings held on May 20, 21, 22, 26 and 28 and June 2, 1958.[29]

Quite frequently these pressures are built along political lines, as was the case for instance in the previously cited _Radio Wisconsin_ decision, where letters opposing the grant to the _Capital Times_ were received at the

---

[28]Op. cit., Report of the Ad Hoc Advisory Committee on Allocations to the Committee on Interstate and Foreign Commerce, United States Senate, March 14, 1958, p. 9.

[29]See Reporter's transcript of hearing for these dates.

Commission. These letters were sent by Senator McCarthy, to whom this Madison paper had been antagonistic.[30]

---

[30]Senator McCarthy's letter to Mr. Paul A. Walker, Chairman, Federal Communications Commission, Washington 25, D. C., dated January 8, 1953.

Dear Mr. Walker:

I understand that Badger Television, Inc., has applied for a television license for a station to be operated in Madison, Wisconsin. I also understand that the President of the corporation is William T. Evjue.

I understand that Mr. Cedric Parker, the city editor of the Capital Times of Madison, Wisconsin, will play an important part in the operation of this television station after the license has been granted.

I would like to bring evidence to the Commission showing that it would be against the public interest to have either Mr. Evjue or Mr. Parker exercising any control over a television station. May I hear from you as to whether you are interested in evidence along the above lines and if so, when you would care to receive it.

A copy of this letter is being forwarded to Mr. Evjue and Mr. Parker for their information.

With kindest regards, I am

Sincerely yours,

Joe McCarthy

McC:lb
cc: Mr. William T. Evjue
Mr. Cedric Parker

---

Senator McCarthy's letter to Honorable Rosel H. Hyde, Chairman, Federal Communications Commission, Washington 25, D. C., dated November 25, 1953.

Dear Mr. Hyde:

As indicated in prior correspondence with the Commission, the people of the City of Madison and of the entire State of Wisconsin are vitally interested in the forthcoming hearing to be held concerning the licensing of a new television station in Madison, Wisconsin. That interest stems from the fact that Mr. William Evjue, the leading principal of Badger Television Company, Inc., one of several television applicants at Madison, has proved himself in my estimation to be totally unfit to own and control a television station with the result that Badger Television Company, Inc. should be

At that time both Commissioners Doerfer and Lee owed their appointments to the Commission to Senator McCarthy, and both Commissioners followed the McCarthy line in voting against the Madison newspaper.

---

disqualified from being the licensee of such a station.

We all appreciate the fact that the qualifications of television licensees, and thus television applicants, are of critical concern to the proper development of our television system. It is commonplace that that system cannot be better than the persons and organizations primarily responsible for operating the stations which compose it. For these reasons I consider it both my duty and responsibility to bring certain information concerning Mr. William Evjue to the Commission's attention for its consideration in connection with the application of Badger Television Company, Inc. It is our mutual concern, as indeed it is of all who will be affected by the operation of the station involved, that those persons and organizations who are not qualified from the standpoint of reputation, character and record of past activities should not be permitted control over so powerful a medium of mass communication as a television station.

Many of Evjue's activities have gone to the extreme of being inimical to the best interests of this country. Thus, in many broadcasts and editorials, as well as in the general policy that he has implanted in his station and paper, he has fought, ridiculed and generally obstructed effective action on the State and National level to expose and destroy Communism and the Communist conspiracy in this country. He has persistently used the media at his command to attack the work of legislative committees investigating un-American activities. He opposed the passage of the Smith Act, the Mundt-Nixon Bill and has gone to the length of defending Communist leaders accused of perjury even after their conviction in a court of law. His broadcasts and editorials have derided fundamental American institutions, such as our general administration of justice and the activities of the American Legion. He has hired, retained and promoted to the important position of City Editor of his paper, one Cedric Parker, whom Evjue himself has called the "leading Communist in Madison" and who has never publicly repudiated his membership in the Communist Party. On many instances he has pleased the cause of Communist leaders in this country and followed a position closely collateral and similar to that advocated by the DAILY WORKER, the Comintern's echo in the United States. He sought the release of Communist Chief Earl Browder from prison and

In other cases, such as Biscayne and Boston there was
evidence of direct political intervention by Republican
leaders.[31] Although it is not the intention of the writer

defended Harry Dexter White against "harassment." The in-
numerable instances of such activities is long, too long to
relate here, but it is almost common knowledge and easily
provided.

It is then clear that whatever his personal
political beliefs and allegiance are, Mr. Evjue through his
station and paper has pursued a policy of affording aid and
support to those who follow the case of Communism while at
the same time opposing those persons and organizations who
have been fighting that insidious cause. Whatever the reason for Evjue's policies, be it ignorance, blindness or
incredible naivete, it speaks ill of his qualifications to
be the licensee of a television station.

All of the above information makes it clear that
Mr. Evjue and the Badger Television Company, Inc., in my
opinion should not be granted a license for Channel 3 at
Madison, Wisconsin.

In accordance with an earlier Commission letter to
me, I anticipate being informed as to the date, time and
place for the hearing involving the application of Badger
Television Company. In the meantime I would appreciate your
comments and a statement of the Commission's position as to
what use in general it will make of the information contained in this letter and the exhibits attached hereto.

Sincerely yours,<br>Joe McCarthy

McC:oc
Enclosures:
1. Daily Worker, March 23, 1949
2. Daily Worker, March 9, 1948
3. Letter dated November 10, 1949 from WLRB
   to Senator McCarthy
4. Daily Worker, May 8, 1942
5. Times-Herald, Washington, D. C., November 15, 1953
6. Capitol Times Editorial, March 14, 1941
7. Press Release By Senator McCarthy Re
   Capitol Times

[31] In re application of Biscayne Television Corporation, et al., 11 RR 1113 (1956). In re application WKDH
Inc., 13 RR 507 (1957). Both cases have since been remanded
by the Court.

to indicate that the influence of political considerations
in the grant of broadcast channels has been only a phenomena
of recent years and a Republican Administration (for there
is adequate evidence to indicate otherwise), nevertheless as
Dr. Schwartz has stated, it is unfortunately true that --

> The vast majority of TV licenses has been awarded by
> the present Eisenhower-appointed FCC, and in making
> these awards the Commission appears definitely to have
> been influenced by the political affiliations of the
> applicants. What was sauce for the Republican goose in
> Boston was not necessarily sauce for the Democratic
> gander in Madison. But the same has been true, in over-
> whelming degree, in the FCC's other comparative TV
> decisions involving newspaper applicants.
>
> Under the present Commission some eight outspokenly
> Republican newspapers have received TV licenses and ten
> Democratic papers have been denied same. More revealing,
> perhaps, is the fact that no Republican papers have lost
> comparative TV applications except in cases where they
> were opposed by powerful Republican interests. On the
> other side, no important newspaper that supported Adlai
> Stevenson has won a comparative TV case before the
> present FCC. No loyal Democratic (as distinguished from
> Eisenhower Democratic) paper of consequence has received
> a comparative award except when it has been a joint
> applicant with a Republican paper, as in the Miami
> Channel 7 case.[32]

Dr. Schwartz concludes from these observations that
in the award of channels the Commission has frequently been
swayed by motives other than the "public interest":

> The results in these TV cases involving newspaper
> applicants are most suggestive. They indicate that per-
> haps the last things influencing actual FCC decisions
> are the comparative criteria that the Commission still
> ostensibly professes to follow. Nor are the FCC's
> actions dominated purely by chance. The Commission has,
> on the contrary, been motivated by extremely rational

---

[32]Bernard Schwartz, The Professor and the Commissions
(New York: Alfred A. Knopf, 1959), pp. 163-64.

considerations -- but they are surely not the factors
that Congress intended to govern the grant of TV
awards.[33]

Thus there is much evidence which indicates the Commission
has proved itself unable or unwilling to develop definite
standards or policies of its own.

The Hoover staff report concludes that this lack of
policy has been directly responsible for much of the guess-
work and delay in adjudicatory and rulemaking proceedings.
It may explain why hearing examiners so often arrive at widely
varying conclusions based on the same or similar sets of facts,
and why Commissioners have shown so little hesitance in over-
throwing the decisions of their hearing examiners. It
accounts for the fact that the decisions of the examiners
show no consistency whatever in emphasis given the various
criteria. In fact, it is stated that the Commissioners
themselves have remarked: "...over and over again how easy
it would be to decide cases if there were only governing
policies."[34]

Such confusion has not gone without attention by the
courts. Recently, Circuit Judge Bazelon in a dissenting
opinion commented:

I vote to grant the petition for rehearing en banc in
order to reconsider this court's recent rulings which
appeared to render us powerless to restrain the Commission

---

[33]Loc. cit.

[34]Op. cit., Commission on Organization of the Execu-
Branch of the Government, staff report on the Federal Communications Commission, 1948, Pt. II, p. 43.

from employing shifting emphasis of comparative criteria obliterating any predictable pattern of decision.[35]

The Commission's attitude toward its policies has had the natural consequence of diminishing the public's confidence in its own integrity. Lawyers and broadcasting entrepreneurs must have some basis for predictability in regard to the Commission's decisions. If these bases do not exist because of the lack of an announced and continuously applied policy, some are naturally tempted to endeavor in some manner or form to buy their way into the Commission's favor.[36] Such conditions as these have contributed to a general lessening of public confidence and respect for the hearing process, and indeed, of the Commission system itself. The situation has been further complicated because

> ...there is no appeal from an administrative decision of the Commission where the decision has been adjudged by the Federal courts to meet the legal tenets of the statutes and the Constitution.

> Courts, in reviewing appeals from Commission action, can only pass on points of law. They are by statute powerless to pass on the wisdom of the Commission's administrative decisions. They must credit the Commission with the expertise imputed to it by law. They have no power to pass on the existence or nonexistence of this quality in that official body. They have a long, consistent record of supporting scrupulously the Commission's rights to make administrative judgments, however good or bad these judgments may appear. The court of appeals has been quick to add that whatever

---

[35] Beachview Broadcasting Corporation v. FCC, U. S. D. C. Court of Appeals, September term 1958, filed October 22, 1958.

[36] Certainly there has been adequate testimony developed in hearings of the Special House Subcommittee on Legislative Oversight (85th Cong.,) to bear out this statement.

the ultimate results from the Commission's policies and
actions, good or bad, the responsibility must lie with
the Commission.[37]

Even while their hands are tied, however, the courts
in recent decisions have drawn attention to the vagrant
nature of the Commission's discretionary power. Recently
the District Circuit Court of Appeals affirmed a decision of
the Federal Communication Commission, doing so only after
wondering whether Congress had given the Commission too much
discretion. The FCC decision involved the grant of a television license where the original recommendation of the
hearing examiner was overruled. Indications were clear from
the court's opinion that the judges were far from convinced
that the Commission had been right in overruling the
decision of its hearing examiner. However, in view of the
asserted vagueness of the statutory provisions involved, the
court refrained from reversing the Commission.[38]

The above circumstances lead us to a consideration of
an extremely anomalous situation which exists in the Commission today, resulting from the 1952 amendments to the
Communications Act. One of the most disturbing discoveries

---

[37]Op. cit., Report of the Ad Hoc Advisory Committee on
Allocations to the Committee on Interstate and Foreign
Commerce, United States Senate, March 14, 1958, p. 13.

[38]The Beachview Broadcast Corporation v. FCC, D. D.
Circuit Court of Appeals, Sept. 18, 1958; See also St. Louis
Amusement Co. v. FCC, D. C. Circuit Court of Appeals, August
28, 1958 (affirmed by Supreme Court, October term 1958), in
which the court of appeals expressed its reluctance to approve
the transactions of Columbia Broadcasting System complained
of by St. Louis Amusement Co., but did so on the theory that
existing law required approval.

to one who analyzes the FCC's decisions in its comparative
licensing cases is the process of decision-making within the
Commission itself. The Commissioners do not hear the
evidence at hearings. They are not required to read the
record. They do hear oral argument but even that has not
been deemed an essential prerequisite for a Commissioner to
cast his vote in a case.[39] They do not write opinions
explaining their decisions. They are not permitted to seek
information, clarification, or advice from members of the
Commission staff, yet they are given the full responsibility
for the making of decisions in each case. Hearing examiners
preside at the taking of testimony during hearing and on the

---

[39]Recently, the United States Court of Appeals set
aside the FCC's award of Channel 13 in Indianapolis. (WIBC,
Inc. v. FCC, appellee, and Crosley Broadcasting Corporation,
intervenor.) On September 25, 1958, Judge Wilbur K. Miller,
in an opinion on intervenor's petition for rehearing en banc,
explained why the court had held in its decision of July 16,
that Commissioner Craven's participation in oral argument had
not been "clearly waived":

"Objection to Craven's participation was based on two
grounds: (a) that he had not heard oral argument which was
held before he became a Commissioner, and (b) that he had
been previously employed by one of the parties. As to the
second basis, we said in the order complained of, '...the
court does not reach the decision whether Commissioner
Craven is disqualified, to vote in this case, and expresses
no opinion on the subject.' So the order was based, as it
said, solely on the fact that the decisive vote was cast by
one who had not heard oral argument. It was not claimed in
argument that Craven's possibly disqualifying previous employment had been waived. It was said that his participation
in oral argument had been waived; and the basis for saying so
was the announcement that any absent Commissioner might take
part, to which there was no objection. But Craven was not
then an 'absent Commissioner' -- he was not a Commissioner
at all. That is the reason we said in the order that oral
argument before him had not been clearly waived.'"

basis of such make initial decisions. The hearing examiners themselves are equally cut off from others of the staff. Similarly, unlike any other independent agency, the Commission's own General Counsel is barred by statute from consulting with the Commission once the case has been presented to the Commission for its decision.

Recently, attention has been called to this condition:

Fancy the Federal branch operating as a judicial body in such a bifurcated environment. No wonder, according to report, the Commission almost never examines the record. In appeals from the hearing examiner's initial decision, it relies for the most part on staff summaries. It is as if in a trial one judge heard the testimony and studied the witness, whereas another judge wrote the decision. Because of their manifold burdens, no wonder, according to report, the Commissioners do not write their own opinions, but simply vote, depending on a followup by a group of opinion writers who, it would appear, now rationalize the majority-type decision. The procedure appears to relieve the judge (Commissioner) from responsibility of justifying his decision and signing it in token. The opportunity for arbitrariness and capriciousness is relatively great.[40]

This so-called "separation of functions" required by the Communications Act precludes both commissioners and hearing examiners from the use of Commission personnel for advice and consultation when problems arise. Yet, the Commission is expected to perform the function of providing the final decision in each case, based on a massive body of evidence which it does not have time to read, summaries of evidence provided by the "review staff," with whom they are equally unable to consult, and upon whatever further information in the way of proposed findings and conclusions,

---

[40]Op. cit., Report of the Ad Hoc Advisory Committee on allocations, p. 13.

xceptions and supporting reasons they receive from the
leadings of the interested parties. As a result of this
rovision, the Commission is furnished with a staff of
xperts with whom it cannot consult without reopening the
ecord, allowing the interested parties to be present, giv-
ng opportunity for reply, and needlessly adding to the size
nd volume of testimony which, in all probability, already
xtends to thousands of pages. The judicial imputation of
xpertise to Commission decisions under these circumstances
s in effect a legal fiction.

## 2. Licensing Standards as Applied
## in TV Station Transfers

While the situation in initial licensing cases where
the Commission is required to choose between two or more competing applicants is one which seriously detracts from its
reputation for fairness and impartiality, this alone does
not adequately describe the extent to which it has failed to
create or sustain its policies in licensing cases. Even
more important today than initial licensing procedures are
instances of station transfer, in which a licensee decides
to sell his facilities and the Commission is called upon to
approve transfer of the channel or frequency.

During the year the writer was a member of the staff
of the Subcommittee on Legislative Oversight, he made a
detailed investigation into the nature and frequency of television station mergers, sales and transfers. He thereupon
selected a number of representative cases, illustrative of

the Commission's lack of positive policy.[41] The results of
this investigation indicated that the grant of licenses
through the "back door" of transfer stands out as the most
significant means today whereby license grants are made,
particularly in the field of television.

Almost all the VHF channels (those most in demand and
of greatest financial value in the television field) are
already in use. Thus to obtain a desirable channel under
present circumstances a potential operator must purchase a
station already on the air or under construction. These
circumstances in part explain why prices commanded by VHF
television stations are frequently so far in excess of the
physical value of the property transferred to the new owner.
The lack of available new channels creates a strong demand
for the acquisition of those in existence, and inflates the
price of existing stations. This demand and inflation have
been encouraged by the knowledge that a transfer proceeding
before the FCC is a mere formality. With few exceptions
Commission transfer approvals since 1952 have been pro forma,
and it has been since this time that most of the buying and
selling of television stations has occurred.

---

[41]See testimony of Robert S. McMahon before the Subcommittee on Legislative Oversight, House of Representatives,
May 15, 20, 21, 1958.

a.  The Background of the Transfer Situation[42]

While the history of radio regulation traces back to
1910, the first regulation controlling transfers was the
Radio Act of 1927 which required "the consent in writing of
the licensing authority." The Communications Act of 1934 re-
enacted this provision and added the "public interest"
criterion as a basis for judging transfers. Under this
statutory mandate, the FCC has emphasized a number of factors
in approving or disapproving transfer applications. Primary
attention was given the relation of sale price to the value
of the station, qualifications of the transferee, benefits
to the public from transfers, and prevention of trafficking
in licenses.

In a series of proposals to amend the Communications
Act beginning in 1942, it was advocated that the FCC be
limited to a consideration of a transferee's qualifications.
These proposals aroused objections from the FCC which maintained that such limited inquiry would permit trafficking
and auctioning of licenses and would eliminate controls over
marginal licensees. When the Act was amended in 1952, the
"public interest" test was maintained, with the added provision that transfer applications should be "disposed of as
if the proposed transferee or assignee were making application under section 308 (the licensing provision) for the

---

[42]For a more complete treatment see Indiana Law
Journal, 30:351-65 (Spring 1955), and Journal of Broadcasting, Vol. 1, No. 2 (Spring 1957).

permit or license in question." This reference to the licensing section requires the FCC to determine whether the proposed transferee possesses the qualifications of an original licensee. Since the Commission has in the past considered the qualifications of a transferee under the "public interest" test, it may be questioned why the statutory amendment was added.

It might be contended that the only possible significance of the inclusion of this criterion is that it was intended to be the sole consideration in judging transfers. Such an interpretation is unjustified, since before a transfer can be approved the statute requires a finding that the "public interest, convenience and necessity will be served thereby." The only stated restriction on the FCC's evaluation is that it may not consider whether a third party would be more qualified than the intended transferee.[43]

## b. Factors Previously Considered by FCC in Transfers

An understanding of the present status of transfer law must be based on an evaluation of various factors considered under the test of public interest.

1) Sale price. The sale price of the station was at one time a salient consideration in transfers. Although legislation to eliminate profits made from transfers has been proposed, there has never been a direct enactment imposing

---

[43]Section 310 (b) of the Communications Act of 1934 as amended.

such restrictions. Congress has specifically provided that
a license is for the use of the airwaves alone; a license
does not confer ownership. Consequently, to prevent the
licensee from obtaining a profit from the sale of his license,
the FCC at one time required a reasonable relationship
between the value of station assets and price. The parties
were often allowed to justify discrepancies between price
and cost, however, by including as assets the capitalized
earning power, expenses and a wide range of intangible
assets. Nevertheless, an unreasonable relationship between
price and value was never held sufficient in and of itself
as a ground for disapproving a transfer. Frequently, the
price factor was completely ignored.

In 1945 the Commission admitted to Congress its
inability adequately to consider price, except in limited
circumstances, and requested Congressional direction. Guid-
ing legislation did not ensue and the Commission continued
to exclude consideration of price as an element in transfers.
Recently a four million dollar sale was consummated with no
consideration being given to price.[44] Commissioner Lee in a
concurring opinion pointed out that a seventy-five percent
profit was made in the sale but concluded that he did not,
"...complain at the fact that the licensee is making a very
substantial profit."

———————

[44]Wrather-Alvarez, Inc., 10 RR, 539, 540 (1953).

Permitting unlimited prices for stations appears to
be inimical to public interest even though the public has no
direct financial stake in broadcasting. The public interest
in receiving efficient radio and television service is
undoubted. In order to further this interest, Congress preserved competition in the field of broadcasting. The freedom
of an entrepreneur to develop his business and sell it for a
profit is fundamental to an effective competitive system.
While there are advantages derived from competition, it must
be remembered that, in the broadcasting field, frequencies
are limited and licenses are a prerequisite to operation.
The grantee's license, conferring upon him a natural monopoly, should not be permitted to be bartered at will.
Exorbitant prices are demanded for stations with a substantial premium being paid for the license itself. Such payment
is not a compensation for developing a successful station,
but reward for merely acquiring a license. It has been
indicated that excessive prices for stations intensifies the
pressure to make a profit thereby fostering "over-commercial-
ization." Program quality is often sacrificed for less
expensive methods of operation. Under this system, potential
transferees who are the highest bidders are invariably preferred by the seller. It is obvious that there is no necessary relationship between the person willing to make the
largest investment and the most competent operator.[45]

---

[45]C. B. Rose, A National Policy for Radio Broadcasting (New York: Harper Bros., 1940), p. 108 ff.

2) **Trafficking.** A further outgrowth of excessive
price is stimulation of trafficking in licenses. (The pro-
curement of licenses for the purposes of selling them for a
profit is usually preferred to as trafficking.) A recent
decision in which a second license was awarded to a party
two years after he had sold one for a $100,000 profit
indicates the FCC's indifference toward this practice.[46] The
competitor for the license was foreclosed from raising the
issue of trafficking, the Commission stating that re-entry
into broadcasting within two years indicated only "...a
possible attachment to that area."

Trafficking raises a serious threat of inferior and
mediocre standards of broadcasting. Applicant R may compete
for a license with the intent to transfer it to S if he wins.
In a close decision, he defeats applicant T and transfers
immediately to S who may have only minimum qualifications,
perhaps much less than T. There is a grave inconsistency in
providing elaborate procedures for licensing to determine
the best qualified applicant only to have the basis for the
decision shattered by a transfer.[47] The seriousness of the
problem was recognized by the FCC in 1945 in its adoption of

---

[46]Versluis Radio and Television, Inc., 9 RR, 1123,
1141 (1953).

[47]Commissioner Lee recently stated: "...I am concerned because the transfer processing does not answer for
me the question as to how the prospective purchaser would
have fared in a comparative hearing..." Concurring opinion
in Wrather-Alvarez, Inc., 10 RR, 539, 540 (1954). Similar
expressions are found in Commissioner Lee's dissenting
opinion in Aladdin Radio and Television, Inc., 10 RR, 773,
776 (1954).

the AVCO rule. This rule in essence required transferors to advertise their proposed transfers in order to enable interested parties to compete for the station. The rule was abandoned by the Commission in 1949, and the possibility of comparative regulation as of this time seems precluded by the 1952 amendments.

3) Public benefit. An earlier method used by the Commission to control transfers hinged on the requirement of a resulting public benefit as justification for a sale. Unless improved service, which encompassed an extensive group of factors, was indicated, applications for transfer were generally denied. For the period of the past ten years at least the FCC seems to have departed from such policy. Abandonment of this practice may deprive the public of additional improvements it formerly might have received from such transactions.

c. Current Factors Considered by FCC in Transfers

Except for requiring minimum qualifications in transferees, there are currently few substantial restrictions on transfers. Limitations developed by the Commission under the "public interest" criterion have lost their effectiveness. This permits a lowering of the competitive level and may result in mediocrity in the industry. The current volume of transfers which receive only pro forma treatment intensifies these possibilities. The Commission's announced purpose of securing the best possible service for the public is thus thwarted.

Even without additional legislative guidance and standards, the FCC could considerably strengthen its regulation of transfers. A showing of some public benefit to be derived from each transfer could be required. The Commission could impose its own discretionary limitation on excessive sale prices without doing violence to legislative authority. In addition, the Commission could and should be more willing to consider evidences of trafficking. Yet testimony received by the subcommittee on May 15-21, 1958,[48] revealed extensive trafficking in broadcast licenses at prices greatly in excess of the actual investment in the enterprise. Stations whose operation had barely begun had been sold for large sums of money such a short time after grant of license as to bring into question the good faith of the applicant in seeking the license. In one case brought to the subcommittee's attention, a construction permit was sold to one of the unsuccessful applicants two months after it was granted.

In recent years the Federal Communications Commission has usually approved proposed transfers without a hearing. The effect has been to nullify the results of the long and complicated comparative hearings to select the most qualified applicant. For example, in Aladdin Radio & Television, Inc.,[49] a comparative hearing was held in which one applicant was preferred on the basis of its superior local ownership,

---

[48]See Reporter's transcript of hearing, pp. 300-458.

[49]See Reporter's transcript of hearing, May 15, 1958, pp. 317-327.

superior integration of ownership and operation, greater
participation in local community affairs and greater broadcasting experience. Less than one year later the winning
applicant filed petition for transfer of the license to LTF
Broadcasting Corp. (a subsidiary wholly owned by TIME Magazine), an entity lacking in the aforementioned qualifications by which the winning applicant was preferred. As a
result of this transaction the transferor realized a profit
all out of proportion to his investment in the station,
which had been in operation for only four months time. The
costly and protracted comparative hearing as well as the
Commission standards announced in its decision were rendered
meaningless in a proceeding where the grantee was permitted
to voluntarily assign its license to a concern which, in the
first proceeding, could not have measured up to the standards
applied in making the grant, and, in the second, was enabled
to acquire the channel without any hearing or consideration
of the merits.

In the St. Louis Channel 11 hearing[50] the Commission
permitted the winning applicant (within two months after the
grant) to settle the judicial appeals of the three unsuccessful applicants who were appealing the decision. This settlement was arranged by assignment of the channel, "without
consideration" to one of the losing applicants, which then

---

[50]See Reporter's transcript of hearing, May 15, 1958,
pp. 328-347. See St. Louis Telecast Inc. et al., 22 FCC 625,
12 RR 1289 (1957) and St. Louis Amusement Company v. CBS
et al., D.C. App. August 28, 1958.

undertook to issue $200,000 worth of its three percent
convertible debentures to each of the two other unsuccessful
applicants which had appeals pending.  Thus, the three judicial appeals from the grant were withdrawn, and the winning
applicant was enabled to purchase another existing channel
in that same city (which was unencumbered by the pressure of
pending court appeals).  It would appear from the testimony
presented in this case that the Commission voluntarily
abdicated its functions to the winning applicant (the
Columbia Broadcasting System) and that the power of the FCC
was invoked and used to assist a grantee in settling its
judicial appeals.  Such maneuvers circumvented the FCC
decision and encouraged the questionable use of the judicial
process to accomplish such circumvention.  In addition,
where the award had originally been made on the basis of the
winning applicant's "superior broadcast experience," the
final result after the transfer was in complete contradiction
of that standard, since the transferee had never done any
television broadcasting and had no experience in the television field.

In the case of WINT (now WANE), Fort Wayne, Ind.,[51]
the Commission approved the sale of a station which had been
acquired by the then owner only four months before.  The sale
had the effect of consolidating two TV stations in Fort Wayne

---

[51] See Reporter's transcript of hearing, May 21, 1958,
pp. 408-415.

and of eliminating a TV station in Angola, Ind., 39 miles away. Acquisition and sale within a few months raised serious questions as to the then owner's good faith with respect to the public interest. The acquisition certainly does not appear to have been made for the purpose of operating the station as a public service -- yet the Commission failed to investigate the matter, preferring instead to allow the transaction to take place after pro forma approval (one Commissioner dissenting).

In WVUE, Channel 12, Wilmington, Delaware,[52] the Commission permitted the Storer Broadcasting Co. (a corporation with a reputation for buying and selling stations), to purchase Channel 12, the State of Delaware's sole TV channel. The Commission then permitted Storer to move his transmitter site to a location nearer to Philadelphia, after he promised that the station would be maintained and developed as a local Wilmington station providing service to both cities. In effect thereafter Channel 12 for all intents and purposes became a Philadelphia station, and later, when Storer entered upon negotiations to purchase a station in another community, the defunct channel was returned to the Commission with the result that in the entire State of Delaware no TV station is in operation today. This case illustrates another instance of the Commission's failure to observe to the full extent its

------

[52]See Reporter's transcript of hearing, May 21, 1958, pp. 415-421.

duties and obligations in regard to the public interest
aspects of the licensing process.

In the KMGM case, Minneapolis, Minnesota,[53] the
Commission (by its attitude of approving all transfers if the
transferee possess "minimum" qualifications) gave further
impetus to an increasing tendency toward vertical integration in the communications industry and its component distributors, producers, and exhibitors of programs, thus
raising at this point the question as to whether Congress or
the Commission should place some restrictions on vertical
integration within the industry.  In this case, as in others,
the transferers were in and out of the station within a few
months, without any showing required to be made of the
effect on the prime criterion for the award of a grant --
the public interest.

The Commission itself in its 22nd Annual Report
called attention to the fact that "There has been increasing
activity in the broadcast industry in acquiring stations by
purchase...."  Further,

> a review of these applications indicates a trend in
> the types of purchasers.  For example, there appears to
> be a tendency on the part of large investment and other
> interests to acquire stations....Also there have been
> cases of applicants who were unsuccessful in competitive
> hearings being able to later purchase the desired facil-
> ities without going through another hearing process.[54]

---

[53]Ibid., pp. 421-429.

[54]See 22nd Annual Report of the Federal Communications
Commission (1956), p. 113.

Annual figures for 1956 did in fact show that there were
1085 applications for broadcast license transfer amounting
to transactions in excess of $100 million for that year.
An examination of the extent of television station sales
shows that approximately 10% of operating stations change
hands each year, and that 25% of all stations on the air
before 1952 have been sold at least once.

### 3. Licensing Standards as Applied in "Payoff" and Merger Agreements

Worst of all, however, have been those instances
where competing applicants for mutually exclusive grants
have with the Commission consent "bought off" one another in
order to avoid the necessity of going through the process of
a hearing.

A flagrant example of this occurred with respect to
Channel 12, VHF, Providence, R. I.[55] There, two of three
applicants consented to dismissal of their applications,
receiving in return an interest in a new corporation to which
the construction permit to be issued to the third applicant
would be transferred. Thereafter, an option for stock which
had been issued to the parties to one of the withdrawn applications (whose original investment was nominal), was
canceled upon the payment of more than $200,000. Thus,
adequate appraisal after public hearing of the merits or

---

[55]In re application of Cherry and Webb Broadcasting
Co. et al., FCC File No. BPCT-223.

demerits of the applicants was foreclosed.

This case involved an apparent profit of $200,000, on almost no investment, to two individuals who had nothing to sell other than the uncertain possibility of the grant of a television channel. In previous cases of instances of "trafficking" in station licenses the seller frequently had nothing more to sell than a construction permit and a partially completed station. In the present case not even these "assets" were in existence at the time of "sale," since the Commission had not acted in awarding the channel. Only the knowledge that, according to the Commission practices in effect at the time, the channel would be quickly granted as an uncontested application (two of the three competing applicants having withdrawn pursuant to merger agreement with the successful applicant) afforded any real basis for the payment of $200,000.

A corollary question to the question of "payoff" is whether the Commission, in granting an application only two days after request for dismissal of competing applications were filed, fulfilled its duty as Congress intended in the writing of the Federal Communications Act? Did a Commission rule which permitted applications to be dismissed as a matter of right prior to the designation of hearing date serve the public interest (insofar as it allowed the award of a channel to an applicant which was perhaps the most financially able but not necessarily the best qualified license holder)? Such a policy appears to give undue advantage to applicants

having the means to "buy off" other competing applicants.
At the same time it would appear to be conducive to the filing of "strike applications" by persons interested only in
a quick windfall profit. The apparent profit in excess of
$200,000 (plus potential additional payment up to $62,500
for unspecified services for which they may be engaged)
obtained by two individuals having an original investment
of about $1,800 appears on its face to be a "purchase" of a
grant by buying off the competing applicants in order to
assure an uncontested proceeding. Out of this arrangement,
sanctioned by the FCC, a comparative hearing was avoided,
which would at least have weighed the individual qualifications of the competing applicants.

If this case correctly reflects the FCC philosophy in
the awarding of VHF TV channels in the years 1952 to date,
it would appear that many channels have been awarded with
little or no investigation of the real qualifications of the
grantee. Commercial transactions among competing applicants - which may or may not have any relation to service of
the public interest - apparently have been permitted by the
Commission, thus foreclosing adequate appraisal at public
hearing of the merits or demerits of particular applicants.
The FCC rule which permitted the dismissal as a matter of
right of an application prior to its designation for hearing
appears to have been conducive to "strike applications,"
"quickie grants" and "payoffs." This rule, section 1.366,
was recently revised to no longer allow this practice.

Shrewd operators and not the public appear to have benefited from this type of administration.

### 4. Summary and Conclusions Based on an Examination of FCC Standards as Applied in Comparative TV Cases, TV Station Transfers, and "Payoff" and Merger Agreements

In summary in regard to the Commission's policies in transfer and merger proceedings, the author reached the following conclusions (which appear in his testimony before the Oversight Committee) based on his investigations:

a) There have been occasions when, after long and complicated comparative hearings have been held to choose the best applicant for a TV channel, the winning applicant has, soon after receiving the grant, transferred his permit for construction and dissipated the very grounds for the Commission's decision.

b) Stations have been sold for large sums of money where actual operation has barely begun, and where indications were that buyer was basically purchasing a channel allocation since seller had little else to sell.

c) Stations have been sold such a short time after original grants have been made as to question the applicant's good faith in applying.

d) Stations have frequently been sold repeatedly before they have done any actual broadcasting; and on other occasions, before station licenses have been granted.

e) In one substantial case, a successful applicant in a comparative hearing soon afterwards entered into an agreement with some of the unsuccessful applicants with the result that an applicant which the Commission decided originally was less qualified to receive the grant was given the channel and the original grantee purchased an existing outlet in the same community.

f) There are instances where transferee realized a profit all out of proportion to the actual value of the assets sold.

g) There are instances of an increasing tendency toward vertical integration in the communications industry and its component distributors, producers, and exhibitors of programs.

h) There are numerous instances of increasing concentrations of ownership of broadcast facilities in major markets.

i) There is a growing tendency on the part of major corporate interests to "diversify" their corporate activities by an expansion into the so-called "growth industries." Of late the broadcast industry has been a major target of this "diversification."

j) There is "trafficking" in licenses. (One instance involves a transfer acquired by purchase as recently as July 17, 1956, which was sold only two months later.)

k) The Commission's responsibility to decide which applicant is the most "qualified" among applications for mutually exclusive grants has on a number of occasions been taken out of its hands by various "deals" among competing applicants. In some cases one is "bought off" by the other, or makes certain promises and arrangements for the other's withdrawal. Often these deals are made in the name of "getting television service more quickly to the public."

l) In order to get an application for a TV license approved by the Commission as quickly as possible, an applicant in one case (with Commission sanction), promised to pay two of the parties involved in a competing application over $200,000 in order to get their agreement to a merger.

m) Multiple owners, to an ever increasing degree, are taking over the television field.

It would seem that if such conditions as those listed above exist that they do so either because it is the Commission's policy and these conditions are to be permitted; or one must conclude that the Commission has been unable or unwilling to form policy respecting such situations. If such policies are indeed those of the Commission, then these must be matched up with the broad measure of what is considered to be in the "public interest"; if such conditions are the result of lack of policy in the Commission, then one can only conclude that the Commission has failed in its task of expanding its "broad mandate" into understandable, clear, and equitable practices.

# CHAPTER X

CONCLUSIONS AND RECOMMENDATIONS BASED ON AN
EXAMINATION OF 50 YEARS OF GOVERNMENTAL
REGULATION OF BROADCASTING

### 1. By the Communications Act of 1934 the Commission Was Vested with Broad Discretionary Powers

From our study of the legislative history of the Communications Act of 1934 it is clear that the Federal Communications Commission was vested with very broad discretionary authority. All that was provided by way of a standard for the licensing of stations was the phrase "public interest, convenience, or necessity." Thus, throughout the Act with minor variations the broad standard is repeated that a broadcast license shall be awarded to an applicant if "public interest, convenience, or necessity will be served thereby."[1] Plainly this standard is not mechanical or self-defining. On the contrary it implies the widest area of administrative judgment and, therefore, of discretion. According to the Supreme Court's definition it "serves as a subtle instrument for the exercise of discretion by the expert body which Congress has charged to carry out its legislative policy."[2]

---

[1] Supra, Chapters II, III, IV.

[2] FCC y. Pottsville Broadcasting Company, 309 U. S. 134, 135 (1940).

Recent occurrences have raised the critical questions whether the broad standard in the Communications Act furnishes an effective guide to administrative action. From our study of the legislative history it is clear that Congress intended that the Commission, over a period of time, should develop its own administrative standards to guide it in making specific decisions under the Act. Indeed, the Supreme Court in the Pottsville case referred to the fact that underlying the whole law of the Communications Act was the recognition by Congress --

> ...of the rapidly fluctuating factors characteristic of the evolution of broadcasting and of the corresponding requirement that the administrative process possess sufficient flexibility to adjust itself to these factors.

The Court stated that as of that time the statutory standard of "public interest, convenience, and necessity" is "as concrete as the factors for judgment in such a field of delegated authority permit."[3]   Thus, one might assume that while it remained the power alone of Congress to exercise a primary legislative function, the administrative agency was given authority to exercise a secondary one, limited by the terms of the enabling statute. The justification for "skeleton" legislation of the type contained in the Communications Act was not so much legal as it was practical. In the 1934 law, Congress sought to regulate a newly created industry. In this instance, with no legislative or administrative experience to guide it, the Congress of necessity was obliged

---

[3]Loc. cit., 135.

to leave the details of regulation to the Commission it
established.  This it did by vesting in the agency wide discretion to deal with specific regulatory matters as they
might arise.

### 2.  When It Vested the Commission with Such Broad Powers, Congress Expected That the Commission Would Utilize Those Powers to Develop Its Own Adequate Standards

Inherent in the philosophy underlying the Communications Act is the notion that Congress fully expected that
the Commission, in the natural course of events, through
accumulated expertise, would develop standards to guide it in
specific cases.  It was also clearly stated during the period
of formulation of the Communications Act of 1934 that the
Commission was fully expected, from time to time, to make
recommendations to Congress.  Indeed, it was expected that the
Commission would "make recommendations to the Congress in the
next session."  For that reason it was decided that the more
controversial subjects should be omitted from the bill so
that they might be left open to the new Commission to study
with the view to further legislation.  The Commission unfortunately was never anxious to come to grips with such items of
controversy and such "studies" were seldom pursued.[4]

As the Hoover Commission's staff report so aptly
stated following its own study of the FCC, the Commission on
the whole has behaved in a manner that has been described as

---

[4]*Supra*, Chapters III and IV.

"essentially passive." Instead of utilizing the wide powers delegated to it, it has preferred to undertake only those tasks which were "thrust upon it." Indeed, it has often used the admitted latitude of the term "public interest, convenience, and necessity" as an excuse for its own inability to formulate definite policies.[5]

### 3. Up to the Present Time the Commission Has Failed to Establish Definite Standards in Its Licensing Cases upon Which the Nation and the Industry Can Rely

Evidence from all sides indicates the Commission has proved itself unable or unwilling to develop definite standards or policies of its own. As the recently published Bowles report states:

> ...indecision, lack of affirmative policy, and inconsistency in the bases for decisions are manifest. The Commission's pattern of behavior in comparative hearings, where so much is at stake for the competing applicants, makes the going really rugged. After the hearing examiner's initial decision, after the usual appeal to the Commission, the final decision may bear little resemblance to the examiner's conclusion.

> Comparative cases are resolved through an arbitrary set of criteria whose application, if one judges from history, is shaped to suit the cases of the moment....

A national authority on administrative law had this to say:

> "Standards are announced (by the Commission) only to be ignored, ingeniously explained away, or so occasionally applied that their very application seems a mockery of justice."[6]

---

[5]Commission on Organization of the Executive Branch of the Government, "Staff Report on the FCC," 1948. Pt. IV, pp. 30-31.

[6]Report of the Ad Hoc Advisory Committee on Allocations to the Committee on Interstate and Foreign Commerce, United States Senate, March 14, 1958, p. 9.

Again, in the Hoover Commission "staff report" on
FCC the statement is made:

> Not a single person at the Commission who is con-
> cerned with broadcast work will even pretend to demon-
> strate that the Commission's decisions in its broadcast
> cases have followed a consistent policy, or for that
> matter, any policy other than the desire to dispose of
> cases and, if possible, to do so by making grants.[7]

### 4. The Commission Criteria Must Be Redefined or Replaced

The present criteria or standards that have been
developed by the Commission in its adjudicatory proceedings
should be better defined, or new standards should be provided. The word "diversification," for instance, has no
meaning whatsoever under present case policy in the Commission. (Compare the manner in which this criterion was
employed in, for example, the following cases: The Enterprise
Company, 9 RR 816; Radio Fort Wayne, Inc., 9 RR 1221;
McClatchy Broadcasting Company, 9 RR 1190; St. Louis Telecast
Inc., 12 RR 1289; Indianapolis Broadcasting, Inc., 12 RR 883;
Biscayne Television Corporation, 11 RR 1113.) Likewise, the
criterion of "integration of ownership and management" has no
more meaning than that of "diversification." (Compare, Radio
Wisconsin, 10 RR 1224, Beachview Broadcasting Corporation,
11 RR 939, Biscayne Television Corporation, supra. See also

---

[7]Op. cit., "Staff Report on the Federal Communications
Commission," 1948, Pt. II, p. 40.

comment in the <u>Yale Law Journal</u>, vol. 66, January 1957,
p. 365, re: "Diversification and the Public Interest: Administrative Responsibility of the FCC.") Similar findings can
be made in regard to several other of the Commission's
criteria. The observation has, in fact, been made:

> The qualitative nature of these criteria, the freedom
> at the disposal of the Commission in electing emphasis
> of one or another of these arbitrary factors, and the
> fact that none is affirmative make for a randomness of
> decision disconcerting for the seeming lack of judicial
> precision and systematic determination.[8]

Still other considerations point toward the need for
the provision of more precise standards in the enabling
statute of the Commission. In testimony in hearings before
a special subcommittee of the Committee on Rules, Dr. Bernard
Schwartz stated that where there are no precise standards in
enabling statutes to delineate delegations of power, judicial
control under the doctrine of <u>ultra vires</u> can have no practical effect. Statutes which contain no real standards to
limit administrative authority and which are aptly characterized as "skeleton" legislation can afford no adequate basis
for judicial review since their limits become so broad as to
cover almost all executive action.

Dr. Schwartz further stated that while it is true that
the Supreme Court has said there are no constitutional prohibitions against "skeleton" legislation, this decision on
the constitutional question does not relieve Congress of its

---

[8] <u>Op. cit.</u>, Ad Hoc Advisory Committee on Allocations
Report, p. 213.

responsibility to insure that delegations of power made by it are limited ones. If anything, the legislative responsibility -- based in part on the basic principle of our Constitution that no one may be deprived of his personal property or rights without due process of law -- is greater "now that the Supreme Court has all but removed itself as a controlling factor in this field."[9]

### 5. Since the Commission Has Been Unable to Formulate Consistent Standards and Policies on Its Own, Congress Should Provide Further Guides Looking Toward Their Formulation

In view of the fact that the history of the Commission's attempts to formulate its standards and policies has been one of general failure, it is desirable that Congress should itself provide workable standards to govern the exercise of Commission discretion. Apart from the revelations by the Oversight Committee, one of the strongest arguments in favor of such a step is an historical one -- Congress, in 1934, gave the Commission broad powers to establish its own standards because it was expected that an "expert" body would be much more able to cope with the problems of the new media. The Commission has, after more than 20 years of operation, by itself been unable or unwilling to develop a dependable set of standards.[10]

---

[9] Testimony of Dr. Bernard Schwartz, at hearings before a special subcommittee of the Committee on Rules, 84th Cong., 2d sess., under authority of H. Res. 462, pp. 54, 55.

[10] Supra, Chapter IX.

This is not to suggest that Congress should perform
an A to Z function of establishing the regulatory objectives
and policy determinations of the Commission. But Congress
should heed the lessons of history and provide definite and
constructive guidance and support, looking toward the development of a well rounded regulatory program. Such a move
should come as a relief to both regulators and regulated,
since only by the more definite action of Congress would it
appear that firm policy can be created.

### 6. Both Congress and the Commission Bear a Share of the Responsibility for Its Failure to Function Effectively as a Regulatory Agency

Although the previously cited factors lead to the
conclusions that (a) the Commission has made no careful,
intelligent or persistent effort to achieve its regulatory
objectives "in the public interest," (b) it has failed to
define its primary objectives with clarity, (c) it has been
unduly responsive to outside pressures in its choice of
regulatory projects, and (d) it has failed to develop a
tradition of enforcement of its policies, we must observe
the fault has not always been that of the Commission alone.
The evidence resulting from an examination of broadcasting's
legislative history indicates that the scope of the Commission's problems has not been entirely appreciated by the
President, Congress, or the members of the bar who have day-
to-day dealings with the Commission. Their attitudes toward
such matters as appointments and appropriations requests

as well as the advantage taken of existing weaknesses in the
Commission setup provide further evidences of this fact.
Moreover, individual members of Congress have frequently
shown a ready disposition to disapprove the actions of the
Commission on occasions when it has attempted through rule-
making proceedings to formulate more specific policy.

During congressional hearings on the 1952 amendments,
for example, a proposed amendment which would have prohibited
the Commission from "discriminating" against newspaper owners
in the award of broadcast licenses was dropped from the bill
upon assurance from the Commission that it did not and would
not ever practice such "discrimination." This amendment was
added to the bill as a product of a long chain of events
which began when the Commission, in a rule-making proceeding
some years before, had attempted to formulate a policy
regarding newspaper ownership of broadcast media.[11]  A second
proposed amendment (to sec. 310 (b) of the Act) was actually
included in the amendments passed by Congress in 1952 which
prohibited the Commission from taking into account whether
the public interest might be better served by the award of
the license to a person other than the proposed transferee.[12]
This amendment resulted from industry opposition to an
earlier attempt (the AVCO procedure) of the Commission to
arrive at a workable solution to the problem of station
transfers.[13]  This action on the part of Congress, in

_____

[11]Supra, Chapter VII.    [12]Supra, Chapters VI and VII.
[13]Supra, Chapter IX.

addition to giving the Commission much less maneuverability
in its attempts to arrive at solutions to its policy problems, is generally accepted as a deterrent to any attempt to
find a definitive solution to the problem of transfers.

The broadcast industry is almost invariably opposed to
more active regulation on the part of the Commission in any
respect. Experience shows that the Commission is fully
aware that Congress is more responsive to industry pressure
for less firmness in regulatory actions than it is to the
Commission's recommendations in the opposite direction.
Thus it has been made too obviously apparent that the best
way for the Commission to stay out of trouble is for it to
remain quiescent.

Actions on the part of the broadcasting industry
and its defenders in the Congress have, to a large extent,
discouraged the Commission from formulating firm policies.
Even when victories have been won by the Commission, as was
the case when the Supreme Court sustained the validity of the
Commission's chain-broadcasting regulations, little if any
effort was put forth by the Commission to take full advantage of its victory. Thus the Supreme Court victory in the
Chain Rules case has been characterized as one where "the
Commission won the battle but lost the war."[14]

---

[14]Op. cit., Staff Report, Commission on Organization
of the Executive Branch etc., Pt. III, p. 45.

## 7. Flexibility Versus Predictability and the Need for Continuing Congressional Review of Policy Problems

The basic difficulty, indeed, the dilemma the Congress must face in the enactment of regulatory legislation involves the need for flexibility as well as predictability in the setting up of standards. Standards themselves are useful only as long as they have a present meaning -- and are consistently applied in harmony with the spirit in which they were established.

Once the Congress has provided the Commission with basic and explicit guides for it to follow, it must stand ready to provide continual oversight to determine that the spirit and intent in which they were passed is maintained.

In hearings before a special subcommittee of the Committee on Rules this extremely important point was brought out in eloquent fashion by a witness who began that portion of his testimony by quoting as follows:

George B. Galloway, senior specialist in American Government, Library of Congress, stated in a recently published pamphlet that --

One of the most important functions of a legislature is to inspect and review the administration of the laws and the exercise of delegated powers by the executive branch of the Government. Political thought in English-speaking countries has long assigned this function of oversight to the elected representatives of the people (Congress and Parliament, p. 67).

In recent years a few legislative committees have developed the practice of holding periodic or sporadic question-and-review sessions with heads of executive agencies under their jurisdiction. These meetings afford an opportunity for the review of administrative action, the discussion of constituent complaints, and the reaching of informal understandings concerning administrative policies.

The need for a legislative process to determine whether agency action comports with congressional policy is heightened by the fact that the courts are showing more and more reluctance to review fully questions involving the statutory authority of administrative agencies....it should first be noted that government by administrative agency has resulted in a loss to the Congress of a substantial part of its constitutional function of determining legislative policy. In many statutes, which delegate legislative authority to administrative agencies, standards are vague, indefinite, or completely lacking. Where this occurs, an unnecessarily broad range of discretionary authority is conferred upon the administrative officials entrusted to carry out the legislation.

The results are (a) inability of the citizen to understand the laws with which he is expected to comply; (b) difficulty on the part of the administrative agency to formulate policy in the public interest; (c) determination by the agency of the limits of its own power -- frequently unreviewable; and (d) inability of the courts to provide satisfactory redress.

Congress frequently lacks the time or knowledge to formulate precise standards of delegation when legislative action is taken in emergency situations.

With respect to some legislation, definite standards may not be desirable or feasible except in the light of administrative experience. In other legislation, even where precise standards have been supplied, "unusual and unexpected" powers are sometimes exercised. If Congress is to perform its constitutional function of determining legislative policy, there should be:

Periodic examination...of the standards of delegation and the manner in which statutory language has been interpreted in its administrative application. This could take the form of legislative studies of specific fields of law enforced by administrative agencies.[15]

---

[15]Hearings before a special subcommittee of the Committee on Rules, under authority of H. R. 462, H. R. 8412, May 22, 23, 24, 1956, pp. 7-8. Statement of Rufus G. Poole, chairman of administrative law, American Bar Association.

### 8. General Recommendations Looking Toward a More Satisfactory Relationship Between Congress and the Commission

In view of the foregoing comments and observations, it is the writer's opinion that standing committees should make full use of their authority under the Reorganization Act to study the overall operations of the Commission rather than merely giving attention to emergency situations as they arise. In addition, regular meetings should be arranged between the chairman of the Commission and members of the interested congressional committees for the purpose of discussing important developments. The periodic reviews of Commission activities held at the beginning of each Congress are a step in the right direction. These reviews could be further implemented if the Commission was called upon to give attention to a development of its current problem. If this were required on a continuing basis, attention could be directed to top policy problems rather than simply those of an emergency nature. The opportunity to go well beyond the scope of the current briefing sessions that are held at the beginning of each session of Congress would also be presented.

There is a need further for coordination among the several congressional committees which are concerned with Commission matters, especially between those committees charged with the appropriation of funds and those which enact legislation affecting Commission activities. On numerous occasions these legislative committees have found themselves, so to speak, "legislating in a vacuum," because the enactment of legislation which is not self-executing requires staff, and arrangements for supply of the requisite funds looking toward the implementation of newly authorized activities are frequently neglected. For this reason it would seem advisable for members of the legislative committees on occasion to make appropriate representations to members of the Appropriations Committee looking toward the implementation of activities required of the Commission, which, as an example, would involve additions to its staff.

### 9. Specific Legislative Proposals for Congress to Consider and Rules and Regulations for the Commission to Adopt

Since it is fairly obvious that in many cases comparative licensing procedures can only be resolved by the Commission's function of choice between relatively equal applicants, what seems to be required as a solution to the problem of licensing procedure, where ultimate choice is made "in the public interest," is to see that the likelihood the public interest will be served is as great as it can be made. Among the corrective steps that might be taken by Congress and the Commission to better assure that the goal of fulfillment of the public interest is achieved are the following:

a) Congress should reexamine certain provisions of the Communications Act Amendments of 1952 which deal with the separation of functions within the Commission.

b) Congress should instruct the Commission to require the grantee to own and operate the station for which he applies for a specific minimum period of time before the station can be sold.

c) Congress should instruct the Commission to hold compulsory hearings in all cases involving television station grants and transfers.

d) Congress should instruct the Commission that no payoffs and mergers be condoned until after hearing and decision that such solutions are in the public interest.

### a) Congress Should Reexamine Certain Provisions of the Communications Act Amendments of 1952 Which Deal with the Separation of Functions Within the Commission

In the testimony given in hearings on S. 658 (the 1952 amendments to the Communications Act) Joseph H. Ream, executive vice president of CBS, warned Congress of the damage that might be done by any wholesale cutting off of the Commission from its staff:

> We have endorsed the concept that there should be a clear-cut distinction between those persons who engage in investigation or the trying of adjudicated cases, and those who have decision-making functions. In other words, no one person should perform the duties of prosecutor, judge, and jury. This concept is spelled out in S. 658, and is accepted by the Commission.
>
> The only substantial difference between the provisions of S. 658 and the recommendations of the Commission in this respect are the designations of the persons whom the Commissioners may consult in their decision-making functions in adjudicatory cases. In Chairman Coy's statement before this committee last August, he made a very strong and persuasive argument that the Commission should not be precluded from consulting with its General Counsel, Chief Engineer, and Chief Accountant, and their staffs

for advice and information in making decisions in
adjudicating cases, provided that these persons were
completely divorced from prosecutory or investigatory
functions.  This bill would limit this consultation by
members of the Commission to their own legal assistant
and to a special review staff, and the bill would
obviously not allow the Commissioners to seek advice of
other members of the staff, even though they were not
engaged in investigation or adjudicatory proceedings.

In view of the fact that the Commission has so strongly embraced the principle of separation of prosecutor
from judge, we know of no reason why this committee
should not accept the recommendation of the Commission
with respect to the need and desirability of the Commissioners to consult with appropriate members of the staff
who are not engaged, directly or indirectly, in prosecu-
tion or investigation.  We can see that such wider latitude in consultation would contribute to the efficient
and expeditious handling of cases, and we believe that
the essential purposes of section 5 would be accomplished[16]
without this more rigid limitation of the Commissioners.

In addition to Congress' amending section 5 (c) of

the Communications Act in order to bring its provisions

respecting separation of staff from the Commission in line

with similar statutory provisions applicable to the other

five commissions, it should recommend to the Commission that

one of its  members be responsible for the writing of its

decision in each adjudicatory case, thereby restoring once

again to the Commission itself the responsibility of justi-

fying its decision and signing it in token.[17]

Since in each instance the appointed commissioner

would have the aid of his own legal assistant as well as the

-----

[16]Testimony of Joseph H. Ream, executive vice president, Columbia Broadcasting System, in hearings of the Senate
Committee on Interstate and Foreign Commerce on S. 658,
82d Cong., 1st sess.

[17]Supra, Chapter IX.

members of the Office of Opinion and Review, the major
effect of such a policy would be a result whereby the responsibility for the justification of a decision would become
that of the Commission rather than that of its staff, and
the opportunity for arbitrariness and capriciousness would
be lessened. (Provided that, the types of cases should be
rotated among the members of the Commission so that no one
Commissioner would be required to handle all cases falling
within a single category.)

b.  Congress Should Instruct the Commission to Require
    the Grantee to Own and Operate the Station for Which
    He Applies for a Specific Minimum Period of Time
    Before the Station Can Be Sold

The Commission should insist upon the prior commit-
ment of the grantee to own and operate the station for which
he is applying.  One of the greatest abuses of the licensing
privilege today has been the rather considerable amount of
"horse trading" of  channels among applicants, and the frequent sale of television stations where the license grant
has been in effect for only a short period of time.   Frequently stations have been sold so soon after the comparative television grant as to make a mockery of the entire
hearing procedure and basis for award of the channel.  Television channels have been held assignable by grantee with
the Commission taking no action whatever in the matter except
that of giving its tacit approval.[18]

---

[18]_Supra_, Chapter IX.

In some instances purchasers have been of the type who would not have had the slightest chance of an award in the comparative hearing. In spite of the public-interest considerations clearly called for in sections 303, 308, 309, and 310 as well as elsewhere in the Act, the Commission claims that section 310 (b), as amended, limits its authority in transfer cases and in effect makes its approval essentially a rubber-stamp affair. While it is clear that the amended section does limit Commission authority to the extent that it states it may not consider the merits of a third party in transfers, that authority is not in any way limited for the Commission to find that "the public interest, convenience and necessity will be served by the granting of such application." The Commission not only has the power but the duty to inquire into the public interest aspect of transfer cases and to construe the Act as a whole rather than giving undue emphasis to any of its single parts.

More specifically, in order to overcome this unhappy situation, the Commission should prohibit a newly authorized grantee from engaging in a voluntary sale of his station for a period of five to six years after the grant is made, unless it be shown affirmatively that the proposed transfer is in the public interest (the Commission being required to hold hearings on this issue). Such showing could be made, for example, on the basis that the licensee no longer has the necessary operating capital to continue operations or that principal parties involved in the operation have died or

have become incapacitated to continue operations. Adoption
of such policy with respect to transfers would result in
discouraging those individuals from applying for licenses
who are interested in making a capital gain at the earliest
possible opportunity and who are actually not interested in
operating the station in the public interest.

### c. Congress Should Instruct the Commission to Hold Compulsory Hearings in All Cases Involving Television Station Grants and Transfers

Next, steps should be taken to tighten up the methods
by which broadcast licenses themselves are awarded. Frequent
complaint has been made regarding the delays which have been
encountered by parties interested in securing decisions from
the Commission. Much importance has been attached to the
fact that one of the reasons for the creation of commissions
was to avoid the long delays experienced in court. Certain
members of the Commission have complained frequently that the
various appeals sections now provided in the law have contributed greatly to the unreasonable decisional delays experienced in Commission function. In particular, complaint
has been lodged against section 309 (c) of the Act, as
amended (relative to "parties in interest" to proceedings).[19]

By far the greater majority of 309 (c) questions have
arisen subsequent to complaint by interested parties who
have been unable to voice their objections to a particular

---

[19]_Supra_, Chapter VIII.

applicant or to Commission action in open hearings. This
brings up the point whether it would not be in the long run
a better practice for the Commission to hold hearings in all
cases involving station grants and transfers. It would seem
to follow that if all "interested parties" were given an
opportunity to come forth and state their views, there would
be, as a natural consequence, no 309 (c) question.

The greatest objection to this requirement would come
from the Commission itself, which would in all likelihood
maintain that such a practice would add immeasurably to the
workload of the Commission. However, in the light of present-
day events which seem to indicate that both the Commission
and the courts have, by construction, transferred the function of determining what is in the "public interest" from
the regulatory body to the persons whom the Commission is
required to regulate, it would seem that the time has arrived
for the Commission to reassume some of the responsibility
that it has, by its own inactivity, relegated to the regulated industry.[20] Although compulsory hearings would add to
the burden of the Commission in one respect, they would
decrease its burden in another to perhaps an even greater
degree since they would very largely eliminate the unpleasant
"after effects" of Commission decisions which so often never
become final until they have progressed to the courts.

---

[20]Supra, Chapter IX.

Finally, it should be realized that the "gold rush" days of 1952 to 1956, when highly desirable television frequencies were available and when great numbers of television applications were consequently being filed, are gone. Now that these frequencies have been assigned, economic considerations make it apparent that there will be no great rush for additional channels even if reallocation should open them up. It does not seem likely that the channel application situation will again get very much out of hand.

Instead of new applications for frequencies, there will be an increasing amount of "horse trading" among channel owners, and it is through the "back door" of transfer that the major part of future television license change seems to lie. Hearings in all such instances should be scheduled, with the Commission required, in the public interest, to examine the qualifications of the assignee alongside those of the present owner. In particular, when multiple owners seek to buy additional facilities, hearings should be held in order to develop full information.

The right of the station licensee to sell his property is unquestioned; his right to dispose of the channel on which he broadcasts is a much more limited one, however, tempered at all times by the needs and requirements of the particular community which it serves.

**1. Congress Should Instruct the Commission That No Pay-offs and Mergers Be Condoned Until After Hearing And Decision That Such Solutions Are in the Public Interest**

Likewise Congress should require that no payoff or merger be condoned by the Commission in such initial license grants until a public hearing on the question has been held and the decision rendered that such a payoff or merger is in the public interest. Additionally, the Commission should be instructed not to permit any so-called "payoff" in any amount that exceeds the proved out-of-pocket expenses of the party whose authorized withdrawal from the proceeding is sought. This amendment should apply only to payoffs and withdrawals subsequent to the date on which license applications have been designated for comparative hearing. In addition, when only one applicant for a facility remains after such merger or payoff takes place, the Commission should, after giving public notice thereof, accept for at least 30 days applications for the same facility.[21]

These are a few of the areas where Congress and the Federal Communications Commission, by working together instead of at odds or, as is often the case, each without an understanding of the other, could contribute greatly to effective operation in the public interest. Congress regards the independent commission as a government agency which can exercise discretionary authority without increasing the power of the executive branch. Its "experts" are expected to function

---

[21]_Supra_, Chapter IX.

satisfactorily as long as they are free from partisan
influence and presidential domination. But Congress cannot
realistically expect effective regulation to survive without
a clear legislative mandate to provide the necessary guides;
nor can it expect effective regulation to continue when it
has enacted legislative amendments which only serve to further
hamper, complicate and confuse Commission operations. It is
always vital that the rights of the individual entrepreneur
be protected at all times from governmental infringement,
but it is even more important that these rights are not over-
emphasized to a degree where the rights of the public as a
whole are neglected.

APPENDIX

APPENDIX I

STAFF STUDY

FCC Standards or Comparative Criteria as Applied
in 14 Representative Comparative TV Proceedings

The Commission's Rules relative to television stations
contain no provisions comparable to Section 3.24, which pre-
cribes the factors which the Commission will consider in
assing upon applications for construction permits for
tandard broadcast stations.

The standard comparative issue reads as follows:

To determine on a comparative basis which of the
operations proposed in the above-entitled applications
would best serve the public interest, convenience and
necessity in the light of the record made with respect
to the significant differences among the applications
as to:

a) The background and experience of each of the
above-named applicants having a bearing on its ability
to own and operate the proposed television station.

b) The proposals of each of the above-named applicants with respect to the management and operation
of the proposed station.

c) The programming service proposed in each of the
above-entitled applications.

The criteria are as follows:

1. Local ownership (residence)
2. Integration of ownership and management
3. Participation in civic activities
4. Diversification of occupations (backgrounds) of
      principals (persons controlling)
5. Broadcast experience
6. Past broadcast record (past performance)
7. Planning and preparation
8. Program policies
9. Program proposals
10. Studio proposals
11. Equipment proposals
12. Staff proposals
13. Diversification of control of communications media

It is apparent from the 14 cases examined and summarized in the attachment hereto that the FCC decisions are not governed by the rule of <u>stare decisis</u>. In each case it would have been impossible to predict in advance the degree of weight which would be given to each of the foregoing criteria. In some cases the diversification of control of media of mass communication is given decisive weight; in some it is subordinated to other factors. In certain cases past experience of the applicant is made decisive and in others this factor is subordinated to that of local interest considerations.

CHANNEL 10, SACRAMENTO, CALIFORNIA
Commission Decision of September 29, 1954

1. **Applicants:** McClatchy Broadcasting, Co., and Sacramento Telecasters, Inc.

2. **Preferences with Respect to Comparative Factors:** No preferences were found on the comparative factors of program proposals, staffs, facilities and studios. McClatchy was found to be entitled to a slight preference on the comparative factor of broadcast experience. McClatchy's past broadcast record was considered strong enough to more than offset Telecasters' preferences on the comparative factors of local ownership, integration of management with ownership, participation in civic affairs, and diversification of business backgrounds of principals. Telecasters was granted a substantial preference on the comparative factor of diversification of control of mass media.

3. **Decision:** Telecasters was granted the permit on the basis that McClatchy's preferences on comparative factors were outweighed by Telecasters' freedom from ties with other mass media, either in Sacramento or the central valley.

4. **Initial Decision:** McClatchy.

5. **Voting:** Dissents - none
   Not participating - Commissioners Webster and Sterling.

6. **Mass Media Interests of the Applicants:**

   McClatchy: 1 AM station in Sacramento; a construction permit for a TV station in Fresno; 2 daily newspapers in Sacramento; the only daily newspapers in Fresno and Modesto.

   Telecasters: None.

   There are 51 broadcast stations, 28 daily newspapers, 68 weekly newspapers in the overall service-area. There is 1 newspaper, 4 AM stations, 2 FM stations and 2 UHF stations in Sacramento.

CHANNEL 5 BOSTON, MASS.
Commission Decision of April 24, 1957

1. <u>Applicants</u>: WHDH, Inc., Greater Boston Television Corp., Massachusetts Bay Telecasters, Inc., and Allen B. DuMont Laboratories, Inc.

2. <u>Preferences with Respect to Comparative Factors</u>: None of the applicants was preferred over WHDH with respect to the comparative factors of local residence and integration of ownership with management. Massachusetts Bay and Greater Boston were given minor preferences on the comparative factors of civic participation and diversification of business interests of the principals. WHDH received a strong preference over all other applicants, except DuMont, and a minor preference as to DuMont on the comparative factor of broadcast record. WHDH was preferred over all except DuMont, to which it yielded a slight preference on the comparative factor of experience of principals. WHDH was found to be in the least favorable position on the comparative factor of diversification of mass media. Program proposals were equal as to all applicants.

3. <u>Decision</u>: WHDH was granted the permit on the basis that its overall showing on all the comparative factors other than mass media overcame its weak showing on that factor.

4. <u>Initial Decision</u>: Greater Boston

5. <u>Voting</u>: Dissents: Commissioners Hyde and Bartley dissented, without indicating which applicant they preferred; however, Bartley disqualified WHDH because of its advertising "tie-in" policy between its newspaper and its radio station, and its admission that this policy would continue if it were granted a TV license.

6. <u>Mass Media Interests of the Applicants</u>:

<u>Massachusetts Bay</u> - none
Principals - 1 UHF station in Springfield, Mass.

<u>Greater Boston</u> - none
Principals - 1 AM station in Boston.

<u>DuMont</u> - Two TV stations, 1 in New York City, 1 in Washington.
Principals - 1 TV station in Los Angeles.

<u>WHDH</u> - 1 AM-FM station in Boston; 2 Boston newspapers.

There are 8 daily newspapers in Boston; 6 TV stations; 17 AM and 10 FM stations in the service-area.

CHANNEL 3 HARTFORD, CONNECTICUT
Commission Decision of July 18, 1956

1. **Applicants:** The Travelers Broadcasting Service Corp., and Hartford Telecasting Co.

2. **Preferences with Respect to Comparative Factors:** Neither applicant was considered to have a preference with respect to comparative factors of integration of ownership with management, program policies and proposals, staffs, studio and equipment, and preparation for television. Travelers was considered superior on the comparative factors of past record, experience of principals, local residence and civic participation. Hartford was preferred on the comparative factor of diversification of control of mass media of communication.

3. **Decision:** Travelers was awarded the permit on the basis that its superiority on all the comparative factors except diversification of mass media, outweighed Hartford's preference on this factor. Further, the Commission considered the irresponsible charges made by Hartford against the principals of Travelers reflected adversely upon Hartford.

4. **Initial Decision:** Travelers.

5. **Voting:** Dissents: None

    Commissioner Bartley concurring the result; Doerfer voting to grant without condition; Craven abstaining from voting.

6. **Mass Media Interests of the Applicants:**

    Travelers - 1 AM-FM station in Hartford.

    Hartford - none
    Principals - 1 AM and small interest in a TV station in Santa Barbara, Calif.

    In the Hartford, there are 2 newspapers, 6 AM and 2 FM stations; construction permits for 2 TV stations.

## CHANNEL 13 INDIANAPOLIS, INDIANA
### Commission Decision of March 6, 1957

1. **Applicants:** Indianapolis Broadcasting, Inc.; WIBC, Inc.; Mid-West T. V. Corp.; and Crosley Broadcasting Corp.

2. **Preferences with Respect to Comparative Factors:** No preferences were granted on the comparative factors of planning, programming, studios, facilities and staffing. Mid-West was preferred on the comparative factors of local residence, civic participation, diversification of business background of principals, and diversification of control of media of mass communication. WIBC was preferred on the comparative factor of integration of ownership with management. Crosley was preferred on the comparative factors of past broadcast record and broadcasting experience.

3. **Decision:** Crosley was granted the permit on the basis that its past broadcast record and experience gave the greatest assurance that its operation would be an integral part of the community and a satisfactory service. Its more extensive control of mass media was discounted because of the competition in the area.

4. **Initial Decision:** Mid-West.

5. **Voting:** Dissents: Commissioners Hyde, Bartley and Lee. Hyde and Bartley on the basis that the record should be re-opened. Commissioner Craven concurred with the majority, although he had intended to abstain from voting because of a possible conflict of interest. His vote was taken at the request of the Commission in order to break a deadlock.

6. **Mass Media Interests of the Applicants:**

   Mid-West: None

   WIBC: An Indianapolis newspaper. 1 radio station in Indianapolis.

   Indianapolis Broadcasting: 2 newspapers in Indianapolis, 1 in Muncie, Indiana, 1 in Huntington, West Va., 1 in Vincennes, Indiana, and 1 in Phoenix, Arizona; a radio station in Indianapolis.

   Crosley: 4 TV stations (1 in Cincinnati, 1 in Dayton, 1 in Columbus and 1 in Atlanta); radio station in Cincinnati. Crosley owns no TV stations in Indianapolis, but some of its other TV stations overlap into the area to be served by this license.

There are 3 daily newspapers and 5 weekly newspapers, 5 radio stations and 2 TV stations in Indianapolis.

## CHANNEL 11 ST. LOUIS, MISSOURI
### Commission Decision of March 27, 1957

1. **Applicants:** St. Louis Telecast, Inc.; St. Louis Amusement Co.; Columbia Broadcasting System, Inc.; 220 Television, Inc.; and Broadcast House, Inc.

2. **Preferences with Respect to Comparative Factors:** All applicants were preferred over Columbia Broadcasting on the comparative factors of local residence, diversification of business and professional backgrounds of principals, and diversification of control of media of mass communication. No preferences were granted on the comparative factors of civic participation, staffs, studios, and equipment. 220 was preferred on the comparative factor of integration of ownership with management. CBS was preferred on the comparative factors of past record and program proposals.

3. **Decision:** The past operation of station KMOX by CBS establishes an area of identification with community needs and interests that is considered more persuasive than the other factors on which other applicants were preferred in establishing the probability that the licensee would better serve the community. To set aside the superior overall comparative showing of CBS because of its more extensive control of mass media would assign an undue quality and significance to this factor.

4. **Initial Decision:** CBS

5. **Voting:** Dissents: Commissioners Hyde, Lee and Bartley dissented with Bartley writing an opinion favoring 220 Television.

6. **Mass Media Interests of the Applicants:**

   220 Television has no significant ownership.

   Telecast - none

Broadcast House - none
Principals - Newspapers in St. Louis; East St.
Louis, Decatur, Champaign-Urbana, Murphysboro,
Carbondale, Merrin (Illinois); AM & FM stations
in Decatur, Effingham, Illinois; AM stations in
Oak Ridge, Tenn., Lafollette, Tenn. & Bristol,
Conn.; and AM-FM stations in St. Louis.

CBS - AM-FM stations in New York City, Chicago, Los
Angeles, San Francisco and Boston and St. Louis;
VHF television stations in New York City, Chicago
and Los Angeles; UHF stations in Milwaukee and
Hartford, Conn.

St. Louis Amusement Co. - interests not listed due to
its withdrawal.

There are 10 daily and 45 weekly, semi-weekly and tri-
weekly newspapers; 6 full-time radio and 5 part-time
radio stations; 3 VHF and 1 UHF station in the service-
area.

CHANNEL 7 MIAMI, FLORIDA
Commission Decision of January 18, 1956
as modified by Decision of June 20, 1957

1. Applicants: Biscayne Television Corp., East Coast Television Corp., South Florida Television Corp., and Sunbeam Television Corp.

2. Preferences with Respect to Comparative Factors: No preference on the comparative factors of policies, planning,
   programs, studios, equipment, staff, civic activities
   and diversification of business interest of principals
   was granted. Biscayne was granted preferences on the
   comparative factors of past broadcast record, integration of ownership with management and broadcast experience. All were granted a preference over Biscayne on
   the comparative factor of control of media of mass
   communications.

3. Decision (1/18/56): The Commission awarded the grant to
   Biscayne for the following reasons: It was impressed with
   Biscayne's showing on the integration factor, its broadcast experience, civic activities, past broadcast records
   of vital principals. In spite of Biscayne's poor showing
   on the mass media factor, it shows the best aggregate
   qualifications. It is not to be disqualified automatically by failing the mass media test.

Revised Final Decision (6/20/57): The only change made
in the Summation of Conclusions here is the mention of a
demerit accruing to Biscayne due to a consultant contract
between one of its chief principals and NBC. It then
affirmed the original award. The Court of Appeals remanded this case and told the Commission to re-weigh the
factors of broadcast experience and record, since these
arose out of Biscayne's control of mass media, which is
an adverse, not a preferential, factor.

Prior to consideration of the mass media factor, Biscayne
was in a "commanding position" on the balance sheet of
factors. The Commission does not feel that it should
"depreciate" Biscayne's important preferences in broadcast experience and record because they arise largely
out of its control of mass media.

4. Initial Decision: Biscayne

5. Voting: Final Decision (1/18/56): Dissent of Commissioner Hyde: For failure to determine the merits of
petitions for changes in the TV allocation, and
for the failure to give realistic consideration
to the diversification (of mass media control)
principle in accordance with its own precedents.

Dissent of Commissioner Bartley: For failure to
determine the de-intermixture question.

Revised Final Decision (6/20/57): Dissent of
Commissioner Bartley: a) disagreed with the
majority's conclusions regarding the effect to be
given the consultant contract with NBC vis-a-vis
the provisions and purpose of Section 3.658 of
our Rules, and b) disagreed with the weight and
significance given to the important principle of
diversification of control of the media of mass
communications. Further, he questions whether
the record justified the finding of Biscayne's
"substantial superiority" in the areas of past
broadcast record and integration of ownership with
management. A grant to South Florida would best
serve the public interest.

6. Mass Media Interests of the Applicants:

Biscayne owns 1 radio station in Miami. Principals of
Biscayne control the two large daily newspapers in Miami,
which are strongly competitive.

Principals of Biscayne control a radio and a television station and the only newspaper in Atlanta, Georgia;
a radio and TV station in Dayton, Ohio and the only newspaper; as well as the only newspapers in Springfield, Ohio;

a 45% interest in a radio and TV station in Akron,
Ohio; a 42% interest in a radio and TV station in
Chicago and 1 newspaper; and a daily paper in Detroit.

East Coast Television, South Florida Television and
Sunbeam Television have no interests in other media of
mass communication.

There are 3 daily and 1 weekly newspapers; 9 AM and
6 FM radio stations in Miami.

CHANNEL 12 JACKSONVILLE, FLORIDA
Commission Decision of August 29, 1956

1. Applicants: City of Jacksonville, Florida-Georgia
   Television Co., Inc. and Jacksonville Broadcasting Corp.

2. Preferences with Respect to Comparative Factors: There
   are no preferences on the comparative factors of: programming, probable effectuation, staffing, studios and
   equipment, local ownership, civic participation, diversification of media of mass communications. On the comparative factor of diversification of business background of principals, broadcasting experience and integration of ownership with management, Florida-Georgia is
   preferred. On the comparative factor of past record,
   Jacksonville is preferred.

3. Decision: Florida-Georgia is granted the permit on the
   basis that its broadcast experience, integration of ownership with management and degree of diversification of
   business background of principals outweigh Jacksonville's
   preference on past broadcast record.

4. Initial Decision: Jacksonville Broadcasting Corp.

5. Voting: Dissents: Chairman McConnaughey and Commissioner Bartley voting for Jacksonville Broadcasting
   on the basis that the decisive factor is the
   past broadcast record. Commissioner Craven not
   voting.

6. Mass Media Interests of the Applicants:

   Florida-Georgia - none
      Principals - 1 AM station in Jacksonville; 1 TV
      station in Miami

   Jacksonville Broadcasting - 1 AM station in Jacksonville

City of Jacksonville - 1 AM station in Jacksonville

There are no competing media in the area to be served, as far as the decisions indicate.

CHANNEL 8, TAMPA, FLORIDA
Commission Decision of August 4, 1954

1. **Applicants:** The Tribune Co., Pinellas Broadcasting Co., and The Tampa Bay Area Telecasting Corp.

2. **Preferences with Respect to Comparative Factors:** Tampa was preferred on the comparative factors of diversification of the control of the media of mass communications, local residence, civic participation, and integration of ownership with management, however, the latter 3 factors were offset by the past broadcast records of Tribune and Pinellas. Tribune was preferred on the comparative factors of programming, staffs, studio and equipment.

3. **Decision:** The Commission preferred Tribune over Pinellas on the basis that the former's comprehensive local live program proposals are clearly superior to Pinellas. When this comparative factor is coupled with Tribune's outstanding performance in the past, it is clearly entitled to a preference. Tribune is also entitled to a preference over Tampa because of the location of its studio and the superiority of its equipment, and the superiority of its live programming. The Commission concludes, as to Tampa, "Tribune's overall superiority clearly out weighs the comparative advantages enjoyed by Tampa, because of its lack of other newspaper and radio interests in the area."

4. **Initial Decision:** Tribune

5. **Voting:** Dissents: Commissioner Hennock dissented to the grant to Tribune because of its control of mass media. Commissioners Webster and Bartley dissented and voted for Pinellas without writing opinions.

6. **Mass Media Interests of the Applicants:**

   Tampa.- none
   Principals - 1 radio station, Rochester, N. Y.
   Application for a TV station in Rochester, N. Y.

Pinellas - 1 AM-FM station in St. Petersburg, Fla.
Principals - 1 newspaper in St. Petersburg, Fla.

Tribune - 1 newspaper and 1 AM-FM station in Tampa, Fla.
Principals - 2 newspapers, 1 AM-FM station (which
has applied for a TV construction permit in Richmond, Va.) in Richmond, Va.

There are 19 radio stations, 3 VHF TV channels assigned,
6 UHF channels assigned, and 13 newspapers in the service
area.

## CHANNEL 7, DENVER, COLORADO
Commission Decision June 26, 1953

1. **Applicants:** Aladdin Radio and Television, Inc. and
Denver Television Co.

2. **Preferences with Respect to Comparative Factors:**
Aladdin was preferred on the comparative factors of local
residence, civic participation, integration of ownership
with management, programming, staffing and facilities.
Denver was preferred on the comparative factor of diversification of control of the media of mass communications.

3. **Decision:** Aladdin was granted the permit on the basis
that its superiority on all comparative factors except
the mass media factor outweighed this comparative
advantage of Denver.

4. **Initial Decision:** Aladdin.

5. **Voting:** No dissents. Commissioner Doerfer did not
participate.

6. **Mass Media Interests of the Applicants:**

   Denver - None

   Aladdin - one AM station in Denver.
   Principals - 1 radio station each in the following
   cities: Mineral Wells, Texas, Centralia, Wash.,
   San Francisco, Calif., Hilo Honolulu, Hawaii, Yaki-
   ma, Wash., Richland, Wash., Portland, Ore., Palm
   Springs, Calif. Two radio stations in Seattle,
   Wash. The Portland station and one of the Seattle
   stations have applied for TV station licenses.

There is no indication in the decisions of the extent of
competing media in this area.

CHANNEL 7, SEATTLE, WASHINGTON
Commission Decision of July 25, 1957

1. **Applicants:** Queen City Broadcasting Co. (KIRO); KXA; and Puget Sound Broadcasting Co. (KVI).

2. **Preferences with Respect to Comparative Factors:** Queen City made the strongest showing, being equal or superior to the other applicants in all standards except civic activities and ownership of media of mass communications. With respect to these two comparative factors, Queen City was found equal to Puget Sound in civic activities, but inferior to both with respect to ownership of mass media.

3. **Decision:** Queen City was granted the permit on the basis that its superior showing as to past performance in the public interest, in those comparative factors indicating assurance of effectuation of proposals and in its awareness of local needs more than offset its more extensive control of local mass media. All the applicants owned radio stations.

4. **Initial Decision:** Queen City (KIRO).

5. **Voting:** Dissents: Commissioners Doerfer and Lee dissented, and Commissioner Hyde did not take part.

6. **Mass Media Interests of the Applicants:**

   Queen City - 1 AM station in Seattle.

   Puget Sound - 1 AM station in Seattle.

   KXA - 1 AM station in Seattle, 1 AM station in San Francisco.

   There are no competing media as far as the decisions indicate.

CHANNEL 3, MADISON, WISCONSIN
Commission Decision of December 7, 1955

1. **Applicants:** Radio Wisconsin and Badger Television.

2. **Preferences with Respect to Comparative Factors:** There was no preference granted to the applicants on the comparative factors of broadcast record, policies and program proposals, civic participation, staff, studio and equipment. Badger was granted a preference on the comparative factors of local residence and integration of ownership with management. Radio Wisconsin was granted a preference with respect to the comparative factor of control of local mass media.

3. **Decision:** Radio Wisconsin was granted the permit on the basis that the comparative factor of mass media was decisive in this case. This was a case of local versus non-local control of mass media. The award was made to the applicant with less control over local media.

4. **Initial Decision:** Badger.

5. **Voting:** Dissents: Commissioners Hyde and Bartley dissented on the basis that neither applicant should have been awarded a permit until the determination of the de-intermixture question.

6. **Mass Media Interests of the Applicants:**

Radio Wisconsin owns an AM and an FM station in Madison. Principals of Radio Wisconsin own 4 newspapers, 5 AM, 2 FM and 3 TV stations outside Madison.

Badger owns an AM & FM station in Madison. Principals of Badger have interests in the only 2 newspapers of general circulation in Madison, and interests in 3 AM and 1 TV station outside Madison.

There are 4 AM and 4 FM stations, 3 UHF stations, and 2 daily newspapers in Madison.

CHANNEL 10, KNOXVILLE, TENNESSEE
Commission Decision of January 11, 1956

1. Applicants: Scripps-Howard Radio, Inc., Radio Station
   WBIR, Inc., and Tennessee Television, Inc.

2. Preferences with Respect to Comparative Factors: Scripps-
   Howard and WBIR were compared and WBIR was held to be
   superior on all but two comparative factors, past broadcast record and broadcast experience, thus eliminating
   Scripps-Howard. The comparison of WBIR and Tennessee
   showed that neither was entitled to a preference on the
   comparative factors of equipment, studios and staffings,
   and the diversification of business background of
   principals. WBIR was preferred on the comparative factors
   of programming, broadcast record and integration of ownership with management. Tennessee was preferred on the
   factors of local ownership, civic participation and
   diversification of control of the media of mass communications.

3. Decision: WBIR was granted the permit on the basis that
   the comparative factors of local ownership and civic
   participation, on which Tennessee was preferred, are
   assumptions used in forecasting the probable responsive-
   ness of an applicant to community needs, and do not offset an established broadcast record, such as WBIR's.
   Further, Tennessee's superiority on the factor of diversification of control of mass media is outweighed by
   WBIR's marked superiority in most other aspects.

4. Initial Decision: WBIR.

5. Voting: Commissioner Lee concurred in the result;
           Commissioner Mack abstained from voting.

6. Mass Media Interest of the Applicants:

   Tennessee Television - None

   Scripps-Howard - One press service; 21 newspapers;
       4 AM stations and 3 FM stations.

   WBIR - One radio station in Knoxville, Tennessee.

   Principals: 1 newspaper; 4 AM and 4 FM stations.

   There are 7 daily newspapers, 30 weekly newspapers
   located in the service area. There are one VHF and
   2 UHF, 6 AM and 2 FM stations in the area.

CHANNEL 10, NORFOLK, VIRGINIA
Commission Decision on May 29, 1956

1. **Applicants:** Beachview Broadcasting Corp., and Portsmouth Radio Corp.

2. **Preferences with Respect to Comparative Factors:** Portsmouth was preferred on the comparative factors of civic
   participation, past broadcast record, broadcast experience,
   and diversification of business background of principals.
   Beachview was given a minor preference on the factor of
   diversification of control of media of mass communications. Neither was preferred with respect to the comparative factors of local residence, integration of
   ownership with management, programming, staffs, studios
   and equipment.

3. **Decision:** Portsmouth was granted the permit on the basis
   that it was comparatively superior in all factors except
   diversification of mass media. Beachview's contention
   that it should be granted the permit, since a grant to
   Portsmouth would mean that all television licensees
   would be radio operators, was denied.

4. **Initial Decision:** Beachview.

5. **Voting:** Dissents: Chairman McConnaughey and Webster dissented and voted for Beachview. Lee did not
   participate. Mack abstained from voting.

6. **Mass Media Interests of the Applicants:**

   Beachview - none

   Portsmouth - 1 radio station in Portsmouth.

   There are 8 AM, 3 FM and 4 TV stations in the
   Tidewater area.

CHANNEL 4, NEW ORLEANS, LOUISIANA
Commission Decision of July 11, 1956

1. **Applicants**: Loyola University, The Times-Picayune Publishing Co., and James A. Noe & Co. (James A. Noe, Harry Allsman, Raymond F. Hufft and James A. Noe, Jr., doing business as)

2. **Preferences with Respect to Comparative Factors**: No preference was granted on the comparative factors of planning, color television or staffs. The Times-Picayune was preferred as to programming and civic participation of its principals. Loyola was preferred as to past broadcast record and media of mass communications. As to the other comparative factors, there were different combinations of two applicants that were considered equal but superior to the remaining applicant.

3. **Decision**: On the basis of Loyola's good performance in operating Station WWL in New Orleans and its preference in mass media, the grant goes to it.

4. **Initial Decision**: Times-Picayune.

5. **Voting**: Commissioners Hyde and Bartley concurred in the result; Commissioner Craven abstained from voting.

6. **Mass Media Interests of the Applicants**: Loyola owns an AM station in New Orleans. The Times-Picayune owns the only morning newspaper and the principal (one of two) afternoon newspaper in New Orleans; it also owns an AM station in New Orleans. James Noe, Sr., owns a TV station in Monroe, La. and one radio station in Monroe and New Orleans, and a 50% interest in a radio station in Pine Bluff, Arkansas.

There are 8 AM, 4 FM and 3 TV stations and 2 newspaper publishers in New Orleans, the Times-Picayune and Item companies.

## APPENDIX II

### TIME STUDY OF 14 REPRESENTATIVE
### COMPARATIVE TV PROCEEDINGS

### CHANNEL 10, SACRAMENTO, CALIFORNIA

McClatchy Broadcasting Co. (Docket No. 9013) consolidated with Sacramento Telecasters, Inc. (Docket No. 10293).

1. Date When Case Originated: Applications for construction permits were filed on the following dates:

   McClatchy Broadcasting          May 7, 1948
   Sacramento Telecasters          June 30, 1952

2. Date When the Commission Instructed the Opinion Writer:

   April 6, 1954.

3. Vote of Commission on Final Decision ( September 29, 1954): The permit was granted to Sacramento Telecasters. Released October 4, 1954. Commissioners Webster and Sterling did not participate.

4. Court Action: Notice of appeal filed by McClatchy on November 1, 1954, case no. 12470, United States Court of Appeals, District of Columbia. January 27, 1956, Commission's decision affirmed by appellate court.

5. Total Pages of Transcript, Depositions and Exhibits:

   11,445*

   *In this case there were 128 exceptions whose pages are not shown herein. In addition this figure does not include the number of pages in pleadings, motions, briefs and court proceedings.

## CHANNEL 5, BOSTON, MASSACHUSETTS

WHDH, Inc., consolidated with Greater Boston Television, Corp., Massachusetts Bay Telecasters, Inc. and Allen B. DuMont Laboratories, Inc.

1. Date Case Originated: Applications for construction permits were filed on the following dates:

| | |
|---|---|
| WHDH | December 15, 1948 |
| Greater Boston | January 14, 1953 |
| Massachusetts Bay | February 17, 1954 |
| DuMont | March 23, 1954 |

2. Date When the Commission Instructed the Opinion Writer:

December 19, 1956.

3. Vote of Commission on Final Decision (April 24, 1957): The permit was granted to WHDH. Released April 25, 1957. Commissioners Hyde and Bartley dissented and issued statements; Commissioner Craven abstained from voting.

4. Court Action: Appeals by Massachusetts Bay (case no. 13,896) and Greater Boston (case no. 13,899) on May 24, 1957, to the United States Court of Appeals, District of Columbia, both appeals being 402 (b) appeals.

Pending.

5. Total Pages of Transcript, Depositions and Exhibits:

7,743*

*In this case there were 444 exceptions whose pages are not shown herein. In addition this figure does not include the number of pages in pleadings, motions, briefs and court proceedings.

## CHANNEL 3, HARTFORD, CONNECTICUT

Hartford Telecasting Co., Inc. (Docket No. 10699), consolidated with The Travelers' Broadcasting Service Corp. (Docket No. 8621).

1. Date When Case Originated: Applications for construction permits were filed on the following dates:

   Hartford Telecasting          June 30, 1952
   Travelers Broadcasting       September 10, 1947

2. Date When the Commission Instructed the Opinion Writer:

   March 28, 1956.

3. Vote of Commission on Final Decision (July 18, 1956): The permit was granted to Travelers Broadcasting. Released July 25, 1956. Commissioner Bartley concurred in the result; Doerfer voting to grant the permit without condition #2; Craven abstained from voting.
   February 27, 1957 - Order of the Commission amending the ordering clause of the Final Decision by deleting the language relating to those conditions which were predicated upon the proceeding in Docket No. 11748.

4. Court Action: Appeal by Hartford on July 22, 1957, case no. 14038 to the United States Court of Appeals, District of Columbia. Pending.

5. Total Pages of Transcript and Exhibits:

   8,737*


*In this case there were 198 exceptions whose pages are not shown herein. In addition this figure does not include the number of pages in pleadings, motions, briefs and court proceedings.

## CHANNEL 13, INDIANAPOLIS, INDIANA

Indianapolis Broadcasting Co., Inc., (Docket No. 8906) con-
solidated with WBIC, INC. (Docket No. 8908), Mid-West TV
Corp. (Docket No. 10947) and Crosley Broadcasting Corp.
(Docket No. 10948).

1. Date When Case Originated: Applications for construction permits were filed on the following dates:

   | | |
   |---|---|
   | Indianapolis Broadcasting Co., Inc. | January 23, 1948 |
   | WBIC | February 18, 1948 |
   | Mid-West TV Corp. | June 23, 1952 |
   | Crosley Broadcasting Corp. | December 1, 1953 |

2. Date When the Commission Instructed the Opinion Writer:

   December 5, 1956.

3. Vote of Commission on Final Decision (March 6, 1957):
   The grant was made to Crosley Broadcasting Corp. Com-
   missioners Hyde and Bartley dissenting and issuing
   statements; Commissioner Lee dissenting; Commissioner
   Craven concurring, issuing statement. Released
   March 8, 1957.

4. Court Action: WBIC filed Notice of Appeal with the
   Commission on July 19, 1957, Case No. 14035, United
   States Court of Appeals, District of Columbia. On
   July 22, 1957, Indianapolis and Mid-West filed Notices of
   Appeals to the same court, Case Nos. 14037 and 14039.

   These cases are still pending in the appellate court.

5. Total Pages of Transcript and Exhibits:

   5,295*

   *In this case there were 286 exceptions whose pages are
   not shown herein. In addition this figure does not
   include the number of pages in pleadings, motions,
   briefs and court proceedings.

## CHANNEL 11, ST. LOUIS, MISSOURI

220 Television, Inc. (Docket No. 10790) consolidated with Broadcast House, Inc. (Docket No. 10917), St. Louis Amusement Co. (Docket No. 10788), Columbia Broadcasting System, Inc. (Docket No. 10789) and St. Louis Telecast, Inc. (Docket No. 8809).

1. Date When Case Originated: Applications for construction permits were filed on the following dates:

   | | |
   |---|---|
   | 220 Television | October 12, 1953 |
   | Broadcast House | November 3, 1953 |
   | St. Louis Amusement | July 25, 1951 |
   | CBS | October 16, 1952 |
   | St. Louis Telecast | January 29, 1948 |

2. Date When the Commission Instructed the Opinion Writer:

   January 16, 1957.

3. Vote of Commission on Final Decision (March 27, 1957): The Commission granted the permit to CBS. Commissioners Hyde and Lee dissented; Bartley dissented and issued a statement. Released March 29, 1957.

4. Court Action: Appeal by Broadcast House on April 25, 1957, 220 Television on April 26, 1957, and St. Louis Telecast on April 26, 1957, case nos. 13839, 13844 and 13845, United States Court of Appeals, District of Columbia.

   Pending.

5. Total Pages of Transcript, Depositions and Exhibits:

   8,154*


*In this case there were 384 exceptions whose pages are not shown herein. In addition this figure does not include the number of pages in pleadings, motions, briefs and court proceedings.

## CHANNEL 7, MIAMI, FLORIDA

South Florida Television Corp. (Docket No. 10857), consolidated with Sunbeam Television Corp. (Docket No. 10858), Biscayne Television (Docket No. 10854) and East Coast Television Corp. (Docket No. 10856).

1. **Date When Case Originated:** Applications for construction permits were filed on the following dates:

   | | |
   |---|---|
   | South Florida Television | November 19, 1953 |
   | Sunbeam Television | December 14, 1953 |
   | Biscayne Television | December 8, 1952 |
   | East Coast Television | December 22, 1952 |

2. **Date When the Commission Instructed the Opinion Writer:**

   July 20, 1955.

3. **Vote of Commission on Final Decision** (January 18, 1956): Initial decision granting permit to Biscayne Television adopted by the Commission. See attached statements of Commissioners Hyde and Bartley; Hyde dissenting; Bartley dissenting and issuing a statement; Craven abstaining from voting.

   June 20, 1957 - decision adopted directing that the decision of January 18, 1956, be revised as set forth therein and that no further revision is made therein. Commissioner Hyde dissenting; Bartley dissenting and issuing statement; Craven abstaining. Released June 21, 1957.

4. **Court Action:** February 3, 1956: Notice of Appeal filed by Gerico Investment Co., case no. 13154 in the United States Court of Appeals, District of Columbia.

   February 21, 1956: Notice of Appeal by South Florida, Sunbeam and East Coast, case nos. 13180-183.

   July 22, 1957: Notice of Appeal by Sunbeam from decision of June 20, 1957, United States Court of Appeals, District of Columbia, case no. 14041.

   All appeals pending.

5. **Total Pages of Transcript and Exhibits:**

   3,709*

   *In this case there were 379 exceptions whose pages are not shown herein. In addition this figure does not include the number of pages in pleadings, motions, briefs and court proceedings.

## CHANNEL 12, JACKSONVILLE, FLORIDA

City of Jacksonville (Docket No. 10833), consolidated with
Florida-Georgia Television Co., Inc. (Docket No. 10834), and
Jacksonville Broadcasting Corp. (Docket No. 10835).

1. Date When Case Originated: Applications for construction permits were filed on the following dates:

   City of Jacksonville          August 2, 1951
   Jacksonville Broadcasting      June 30, 1952
   Florida-Georgia               August 15, 1952

2. Date When the Commission Instructed the Opinion Writer:

   February 6, 1956
   July 5, 1956

3. Vote of Commission on Final Decision (August 31, 1956):
   The grant was made to Florida-Georgia. Commissioners
   Hyde, Doerfer, Lee and Mack voted with the majority.
   Dissenting were Chairman McConnaughey, who voted for
   Jacksonville Broadcasting, and Commissioner Bartley, who
   issued a separate statement. Commissioner Craven
   abstained.

4. Court Action: An appeal was taken by City of Jacksonville, September 18, 1956, to the United States Court of
   Appeals, District of Columbia, where it is still pending.

5. Total Pages of Transcript and Exhibits:

   11,130*


   *In this case there were 437 exceptions whose pages are
   not shown herein. In addition this figure does not
   include the number of pages in pleadings, motions,
   briefs and court proceedings.

## CHANNEL 8, TAMPA, FLORIDA

The Tribune Co. (Docket No. 10250), consolidated with
Tampa Bay Area Telecasting Corp. (Docket No. 10252, and
Pinellas Broadcasting Co. (Docket No. 10251).

1. Date When Case Originated: Applications for construction permits were filed on the following dates:

   | | |
   |---|---|
   | Tribune Co. | March 8, 1948 |
   | Tampa Bay Area Telecasting | June 27, 1952 |
   | Pinellas Broadcasting | May 5, 1948 |

2. Date When the Commission Instructed the Opinion Writer:

   November 23, 1953.

3. Vote of Commission on Final Decision (August 4, 1954):
   The permit was granted to The Tribune Co. Released
   August 6, 1954. Commissioners Webster and Bartley dissenting and voting for Pinellas; Hennock dissenting and
   issuing statement.

4. Court Action: Appeal by Pinellas to the United States
   Court of Appeals, District of Columbia, case no. 12545.
   Affirmed by the appellate court.

5. Total Pages of Transcript, Depositions and Exhibits:

   7,138*

   *In this case there were 592 exceptions whose pages are
   not shown herein. In addition this figure does not
   include the number of pages in pleadings, motions,
   briefs and court proceedings.

CHANNEL 7, DENVER, COLORADO

Aladdin Radio & Television, Inc. (Docket No. 9041) consolidated with Denver Television Co. (Docket No. 10240).

1. <u>Date When Case Originated</u>: Applications for construction permits were filed on the following dates:

   Aladdin                          April 19, 1948
   Denver Television                July 2, 1952

2. <u>Date When the Commission Instructed the Opinion Writer</u>:

   April 23, 1953.

3. <u>Vote of Commission on Final Decision</u>: (June 26, 1953): The application was granted to Aladdin. Released June 30, 1953. Commissioner Doerfer took no part. No dissents recorded.

4. <u>Court Action</u>: None.

5. <u>Transcript, Depositions and Exhibits</u>: In Archives - not examined.

## CHANNEL 7, SEATTLE, WASHINGTON

Queen City Broadcasting Co. (Docket No. 9030) consolidated with Puget Sound Broadcasting Co., Inc. (Docket No. 10759) and KXA, Inc. (Docket No. 10758).

1. Dates When Case Originated: Applications for Construction permits were filed on the following dates:

| | |
|---|---|
| Queen City | May 10, 1948 |
| Puget Sound | January 28, 1953 |
| KXA | May 13, 1952 |

2. Date When the Commission Instructed the Opinion Writer:

January 2, 1957.

3. Vote of Commission on Final Decision (July 25, 1957): Application granted to Queen City, but KXA given leave to file a rejoinder, and the motion of Puget Sound to expunge Queen City's brief and proposed findings of facts, granted by the Examiner, is affirmed by the Commission.

Commissioner Doerfer dissented; Hyde took no part and Lee dissented and voted to reopen the record.

September 11, 1957: Petitions for Stay denied and Commission's decision of July 25, 1957, modified by incorporating therein Appendix A of this Memo. Op. & Order. Commissioner Hyde dissented; Lee dissented, voting to grant the Stay and reopen the record; Ford took no part.

This case apparently is still before the Commission. The last entry on the cards is October 31, 1957.

. Total Pages of Transcript, Depositions and Exhibit:

8,910*

*This figure does not include the number of pages in pleadings, motions, briefs and court proceedings.

## CHANNEL 3, MADISON, WISCONSIN

Badger Television Co., Inc. (Docket No. 10641) consolidated
with Radio Wisconsin, Inc. (Docket No. 8959).

1. Date When Case Originated: Applications for construction permits were filed on the following dates:

   Badger Television          December 15, 1952
   Radio Wisconsin            April 7, 1948

2. Date When the Commission Instructed the Opinion Writer:

   March 16, 1955.

3. Vote of Commission on Final Decision: (December 7, 1955):
   Permit granted to Radio Wisconsin. Released
   December 12, 1955. Dissenting statement of Commissioners
   Hyde and Bartley attached.

4. Court Action: Petition for a stay by Badger filed with
   United States Court of Appeals, District of Columbia,
   on January 11, 1956, denied February 14, 1956.

5. Total Pages of Transcript and Exhibits:

   3,150*


*In this case there were 60 exceptions whose pages are
not shown herein. In addition this figure does not
include the number of pages in pleadings, motions,
briefs and court proceedings.

CHANNEL 10, KNOXVILLE, TENNESSEE

Scripps-Howard Radio, Inc. (Docket No. 10512) consolidated
with Tennessee Television, Inc. (Docket No. 10514) and
Radio Station WBIR, Inc. (Docket No. 10513).

1. Date When Case Originated: Application permits were
   filed for construction permits on the following dates:

   | | |
   |---|---|
   | Scripps-Howard | July 25, 1949 |
   | Tennessee Television | June 30, 1952 |
   | WBIR | January 24, 1951 |

2. Date When the Commission Instructed the Opinion Writer:

   July 20, 1955.

3. Vote of Commission on Final Decision (January 11, 1956):
   Permit granted to WBIR. Released January 13, 1956.
   No record of the voting.

4. Court Action: Notice of Appeal filed by Tennessee
   Television on May 27, 1957, case no. 13905, United
   States Court of Appeals, District of Columbia.
   Pending.

5. Total Pages of Transcript and Exhibits:

   5,526*


*In this case there were 334 exceptions whose pages are
not shown herein. In addition this figure does not
include the number of pages in pleadings, motions,
briefs and court proceedings.

CHANNEL 10, NORFOLK, VIRGINIA

Portsmouth Radio Corp. (Docket No. 10801) consolidated with
Beachview Broadcasting Corp. (Docket No. 10800).

1. Date When Case Originated: Applications for construction permits were filed on the following dates:

   Portsmouth                  August 3, 1953
   Beachview                   February 12, 1953

2. Date When the Commission Instructed the Opinion Writer:

   May 2, 1955.

3. Vote of Commission on Final Decision (May 29, 1956):
   Initial Decision of Charles J. Frederick adopted granting the permit to Portsmouth. No votes.

4. Court Action: Appeal by Beachview, October 23, 1956,
   case no. 13,583 to the United States Court of Appeals,
   District of Columbia.
   Pending.

5. Total Pages of Transcript and Exhibits:

   5,316*

*In this case there were 144 exceptions whose pages are
not shown herein. In addition this figure does not
include the number of pages in pleadings, motions,
briefs and court proceedings.

CHANNEL 4, NEW ORLEANS, LOUISIANA

Loyola University (Docket No. 8936) consolidated with
Noe & Co. (a partnership composed of James A. Noe, Harry
Allsman, Raymond F. Hufft and James A. Noe, Jr., doing busi-
ness as Noe & Co.) (Docket No. 10796) and The Times-Picayune
Publishing Co. (Docket No. 10795).

1.  Date When Case Originated: Applications for construc-
    tion permits were filed on the following dates:

    Loyola University                  March 3, 1948
    Times-Picayune Publishing Co.      May 31, 1950
    Noe & Co.                          June 27, 1952

2.  Date When the Commission Instructed the Opinion Writer:

    December 9, 1955.

3.  Vote of Commission on Final Decision (July 11, 1956):
    Permit granted to Loyola University.  The votes were
    not given.  Released July 13, 1956.

    June 27, 1957, the final decision was modified and
    some of the original conclusions were changed (the
    diversification and integration factors), but the final
    result remained unchanged.  Chairman McConnaughey took
    no part and Commissioner Craven abstained from voting.

4.  Court Action:  Noe & Co. and Times-Picayune Publishing
    Co. appealed to the United States Court of Appeals,
    District of Columbia, case nos. 14064 and 14067.

    These cases are still pending.

5.  Total Pages of Transcript, Depositions and Exhibits:

    4,295*

    *In this case there were 326 exceptions whose pages are
    not shown herein.  In addition this figure does not
    include the number of pages in pleadings, motions,
    briefs and court proceedings.

BIBLIOGRAPHY

# BIBLIOGRAPHY

## A. BOOKS

Archer, Gleason L. Big Business and Radio. New York: The American Historical Co., Inc., 1939.

——————————. History of Radio to 1926. New York: American Historical Society, 1938.

Banning, William P. Commercial Broadcasting Pioneer: WEAF. Harvard University Press, 1946.

Bernstein, Marver H. Regulating Business by Independent Commission. Princeton University Press, 1955.

Broadcasting-Telecasting Yearbook, 1958.

Chaffee, Zachariah. Government and Mass Communications. University of Chicago Press, 1947.

Chenery, William L. Freedom of the Press. New York: Harcourt, Brace and Company, 1955.

Commission on Freedom of the Press. A Free and Responsible Press. Chicago: The University of Chicago Press, 1947.

Freedom of the Press, prepared and released by the Newspaper-Radio Committee. New York: 1942.

Hyneman, Charles S. Bureaucracy in a Democracy. New York: Harper Brothers, 1950.

Landis, James M. The Administrative Process. New Haven: The Yale University Press, 1938.

Lessing, Lawrence. Man of High Fidelity, Edwin Howard Armstrong. Philadelphia: Lippencott, 1956.

Robinson, Thomas Porter. Radio Networks and the Federal Government. New York: Columbia University Press, 1943.

Rose, Cornelia B. A National Policy for Radio Broadcasting. New York: Harper Brothers, 1940.

Schmeckebier, Lawrence F. The Federal Radio Commission. Washington: Brookings Institution, 1932.

Seldes, Gilbert. The Great Audience. New York: The Viking Press, 1951.

Seldes, Gilbert. The Public Arts. New York: Simon and Schuster, 1956.

Shurick, E. P. J. First Quarter-Century of American Broadcasting. Midland, 1946.

Schwartz, Bernard. The Professor and the Commissions. New York: A. Knopf, 1959.

Swenson, Rinehart John. Federal Administrative Law. New York: The Ronald Press, 1952.

The National Association of Radio and Television Broadcasters. The Television Code. Washington, D. C., 1952.

Truman, David B. The Governmental Process. New York: Alfred A. Knopf, 1951.

Warner, Harry P. Radio and Television Law. Bender, 1953 (rev. ed.).

White, Llewellyn. The American Radio. Chicago: University of Chicago Press, 1947.

## B. CASES

1923

*Hoover v. Intercity Radio, 286 F. (2d) 1003 (1923).

1926

*United States v. Zenith Radio Corporation, 12 F. (2d) 616, 617 (1926).

1928

Great Lakes Broadcasting Assoc., Federal Radio Commission Docket 4900 (1928).

1931

*Duncan v. United States, 48 F. (2d) 128, C. C. A. 9th (1931).

*KFKB Broadcasting Association v. Federal Radio Commission, 47 F. (2d) 670 App. D. C. (1931).

1932

Sorenson v. Wood. 123 Nebr. 348, 243 N. W. 82 (1932).

*Trinity Methodist Church South v. Federal Radio Commission.
62 F. (2) 850, App. D. C. (1932).

1936

In the matter of WRBL Radio Station, Inc., 2 FCC 687 (1936).

1938

In the matter of Metropolitan Broadcasting Corp., 5 FCC 501
(1938).

1939

*Saunders Brothers Radio Station v. Federal Communications
Commission. 106 F. (2d) 321 (1939).

1940

Federal Communications Commission v. Saunders Brothers.
309 U. S. 470 (1940).

1941

*National Broadcasting Company v. The Federal Communications
Commission. 319 U. S. 190 (1941).

1942

Josephson v. Knickerbocker Broadcasting Co., 38 N. Y. S.
(92d) 985 (1942).

*National Broadcasting Company, Inc., et al. v. United
States. 47 Fed. Supp. 940 (1942).

1943

*National Broadcasting Company v. Federal Communications
Commission. 319 U. S. 190 (1943).

1945

In the matter of Powell Crosby, Jr., Transferor and the
Aviation Corporation, Transferee. 11 FCC 108 (1945).

1948

In re application of Johnson Broadcasting Co., et al. 12 FCC
970 (1948).

*Johnson Broadcasting Co. v. Federal Communications
Commission. 175 F. (2d) 395 (1948).

In re application of Port Huron Broadcasting Co., 12 FCC
1069 (1948).

*Simmons v. Federal Communications Commission. 169 F. (2d)
670 (1948).

1949

*Johnson Broadcasting Company v. Federal Communications
Commission. 85 U. S. App. D. C. 40, 175 F. (2d) 351
(1949).

*Mansfield Journal Co. v. The Federal Communications
Commission. 173 F. (2d) 646 (1949).

*Simmons v. Federal Communications Commission. 335 U. S.
846 (1949).

1950

*United States v. Morton Salt Company. 338 U. S. 632, 644
(1950).

1951

In re application of WDSU Broadcasting Corp. 7 RR 769 (1951).

1952

In re application of Kansas City Broadcasting Company, Inc.
5 RR 1057, (1952).

1953

In re application of Aladdin Radio and Television, Inc.
9 RR 1 (1953).

In re application of Aladdin Radio and Television, Inc., et al.
9 RR 38 (1953).

*American Broadcasting Company, Inc. v. Federal Communications
Commission. 110 F. Supp. 374 (1953).

In re application of Broadcast House, Inc., et al. 10 RR 11
(1953).

In re application of McClatchy Broadcasting Co. 9 RR 1190
(1953).

In re application of Radio Fort Wayne, Inc., et al. 9 RR
1221 (1953).

In re application of Tampa Times Co., et al. 10 RR 77
(1953).

<u>In re</u> application of the Tribune Co., et al. 10 RR 77 (1953).

1954

<u>In re</u> application of Cowles Broadcasting Co., et al. 10 RR
1289 (1954).

<u>In re</u> application of Evansville Television, Inc., et al.
11 RR 411 (1954).

*<u>Federal</u> Communications Commission v. American Broadcasting
Corporation. 347 U. S. 284 (1954).

<u>In the</u> matter of Odessa Television Co., et al. 11 RR 775
(1954).

<u>In re</u> application of Radio Fort Wayne, Inc. 9 RR 1221
(1954).

<u>In re</u> application of Sangamon Valley Television Corporation,
et al. 11 RR 783 (1954).

<u>In re</u> Southern Newspapers, Inc. 10 RR 59 (1954).

<u>In re</u> application of WKRG-TV, Inc., et al. 10 RR 225 (1954).

<u>In re</u> application of WKRG-TV, Inc., et al. 10 RR 258 (1954).

<u>In re</u> application of WKRG-TV, Inc., et al. 10 RR 261 (1954).

<u>In re</u> application of WREC Broadcasting Service, et al.
10 RR 1347 (1954).

<u>In re</u> application of WSAU, Inc., et al. 10 RR 402 (1954).

<u>In re</u> application of WSAU, Inc., et al. 10 RR 407 (1954).

1955

<u>In re</u> application of Biscayne Television Corporation, et al.
11 RR 1113 (1955).

<u>In re</u> application of City of Jacksonville, et al. 12 RR 125
(1955).

<u>In re</u> application of Petersburg Tile Corporation, et al.
10 RR 567 (1955).

<u>In the</u> matter of Queen City Broadcasting Corporation.
12 RR 260 (1955).

<u>In the</u> matter of Radio Station KFH, et al. 11 RR 116a (1955).

In re application of Radio Wisconsin, et al. 10 RR 1224
(1955).

In re application of Scripps-Howard Radio, Inc., et al.
11 RR 985 (1955).

In re application of Southland Television Co., et al. 10 RR
733 (1955).

*Storer Broadcasting Co. v. United States. 220 F. (2d)
204 (1955).

In re application of Superior Television, Inc., et al.
11 RR 1173 (1955).

In the matter of Westinghouse Radio Stations, Inc.
10 RR 934 (1955).

1956

In re application of Loyola University Inc., et al.
12 RR 1017 (1956).

1957

*Caples Co. v. United States, U. S. App. D. C. 15 RR
2005 (1957).

In re Indianapolis Broadcasting Inc., et al. 12 RR 883

In re application of St. Louis Telecast Inc., et al.
22 FCC 625, 12 RR 1289 (1957).

1958

*Beachview Broadcasting Corporation v. FCC. App. D. C.
October 22, 1958.

*St. Louis Amusement Company v. FCC appellee, CBS, KWK, Inc.,
220 Television, Inc., Broadcast House Inc., intervenors.
D. C. App. August 28, 1958.

*United States v. Radio Corporation of America and the
National Broadcasting Company. U. S. Dis. Court E. D. Pa.
January 10, 1958. (16 RR 2020).

*WIBC, Inc. v. FCC, appellee, and Crosley Broadcasting
Corporation, intervenor. App. D. C. September 25, 1958.


*Federal Cases

## C. ARTICLES

Edelman, Murray. "The Licensing of Radio Services in the United States," University of Illinois Studies in Social Science, Vol. 31, No. 4 (1950).

Friedrich, Carl J. and Sternberg, Evelyn. "Congress and the Control of Radio Broadcasting," The American Political Science Review, 37 (October, 1943), 797.

## D. LAW ARTICLES

"Administrative Enforcement of the Lottery Broadcast Provisions," Yale Law Review, 58 (June, 1949), 1093.

Barber, Owen G. "Competition, Free Speech, and the FCC Network Regulations," George Washington Law Review, 12 (November, 1943), 51.

Bernard, J. T. "Administrative Procedure in the Federal Communications Commission," Rocky Mountain Law Review, 24 (December, 1951).

Corrad, Edwin. "Economic Aspects of Radio Regulation," Virginia Law Review, 34 (April, 1948), 299.

Davis, Kenneth Culp. "Administrative Powers of Supervision, Prosecuting, Advising, and Adjudicating," Harvard Law Review, 63 (December, 1949), 195.

"Diversification and the Public Interest: Administrative Responsibility of the FCC," Yale Law Journal, 66 (January, 1957).

"FCC, Administrator Extraordinary and Licensor Plenipotentiary," Virginia Law Review, 36 (March, 1950).

"Federal Communications Commission Comparative Hearings," Harvard Law Review, 64 (April, 1951), 948.

"Federal Regulation of Radio, Procedural Aspects," Southwestern Law Journal, 5 (Spring, 1951).

Hugin, Adolph C. "Radio Broadcasting Under Government Regulation," Notre Dame Lawyer, 4 (November, 1951), 417.

"Import of the Federal Communications Commission's Chain Broadcasting Rules," Yale Law Journal, 60 (January, 1952), 70.

Jansky, Maurice. "Analysis of the Standards of Public Interest, Convenience and Necessity as Defined by the Federal Communications Commission," George Washington Law Review, 6 (November, 1937), 21.

McManus, Martin J. "Federal Legislation Regulating Radio," Southern California Law Review, 20 (February, 1947), 141.

Miller, Neville. "Legal Aspects of Chain Broadcast Regulations," Air Law Review, 12 (July, 1941), 293.

Neal, John S., Jr. "The Federal Communications Commission and Its Licensing Function in the Public Interest," Temple Law Quarterly, 21 (October, 1947), 135.

"Old Standards in New Context, Comparative Analysis of FCC Regulation," University of Chicago Law Review, 18 (Autumn, 1950).

Penstone, Giles H. "Meaning of the Term Public Interest, Convenience, and Necessity Under the Communications Act of 1934, as Applied to Licenses to Construct New Broadcast Stations," George Washington Law Review, 9 (June, 1941), 873.

Schwartz, Bernard. "The Administrative Procedure Act in Operation," New York University Law Review, 29 (1954).

Wall, Thomas H. "Program Evaluation by the Federal Communications Commission: an Unconstitutional Abridgement of Free Speech?" Georgetown Law Review, 40 (November, 1951), 1.

Warner, Harry P. "The Administrative Process of the Federal Communications Commission," Southern California Law Review, 19 (May, 1946), 229.


E. MAGAZINE ARTICLES


Bendiner, Robert. "The FCC, Who Will Regulate the Regulators?" The Reporter, September 19, 1957.

Fly, James Lawrence. "Regulation of Radio Broadcasting in the Public Interest," The Annals, 213 (January, 1941), 102.

Jaffe, Louis 7 "The Scandal in TV Licensing," Harper's magazine, September, 1957.

## PUBLIC DOCUMENTS

### F. CONGRESSIONAL HEARINGS

U. S. Congress, House. Committee on Merchant Marine and Fisheries. A Bill to Regulate Radio Communication. (H. R. 7357) 68th Cong., 1st sess. Washington: Government Printing Office, 1924.

U. S. Congress, House. Committee on Merchant Marine and Fisheries. A Bill to Regulate Radio Communication. (H. R. 5589) 69th Cong., 1st sess. Washington: Government Printing Office, 1926.

U. S. Congress, House. Committee on Interstate and Foreign Commerce. Amend Section 309 (c) of the Communications Act. (Protest Procedure, H. R. 5614) 84th Cong., 1st sess. Washington: Government Printing Office, 1955.

U. S. Congress, House. Committee on Interstate and Foreign Commerce. Amending the Communications Act of 1934. (S. 658) 82d Cong., 1st sess. Washington: Government Printing Office, 1951.

U. S. Congress, Senate. Committee on Interstate and Foreign Commerce. Amendments to the Communications Act of 1934. (S. 1973) 81st Cong., 1st sess. Washington: Government Printing Office, 1949.

U. S. Congress, House. Committee on Merchant Marine and Fisheries. Bill to Amend Act to Regulate Radio Communications Approved August 13, 1912, and for Other Purposes. (H. R. 11964) 67th Cong., 4th sess. Washington: Government Printing Office, 1923.

U. S. Congress, House. Committee on Interstate and Foreign Commerce. Color Television. 83rd Cong., 1st sess. Washington: Government Printing Office, 1953.

U. S. Congress, Senate. Committee on Interstate and Foreign Commerce. FCC Policy on Television Freeze and Other Communications Matters. 82d Cong., 1st sess. Washington: Government Printing Office, 1951.

U. S. Congress, Senate. Committee on Interstate and Foreign Commerce. For Regulation of Interstate and Foreign Commerce by Wire or Radio. (S. 2910) 73rd Cong., 2d sess. Washington: Government Printing Office, 1934.

U. S. Congress, House. Committee on Interstate and Foreign
Commerce. For the Regulation of Interstate and Foreign
Commerce by Wire or Radio. (H. R. 8301) 73rd Cong.,
2d sess. Washington: Government Printing Office, 1934.

U. S. Congress, Senate. Committee on Interstate and Foreign
Commerce. Hearings on Confirmation of Commissioners.
70th Cong., 1st sess. Washington: Government Printing
Office, 1928.

U. S. Congress, House. Subcommittee of the Committee on
Appropriations. Independent Offices Appropriations
1940-1955. 76th Cong.-84th Cong. Washington: Government Printing Office, 1939-1955.

U. S. Congress, Senate. Subcommittee of the Committee on
Appropriations. Independent Offices Appropriations
1940-1955. 76th Cong.-84th Cong. Washington: Government Printing Office, 1939-1955.

U. S. Congress, House. Subcommittee of the Committee on
Interstate and Foreign Commerce. Investigation of
Radio and Television Programs. 82d Cong., 2d sess.
Washington: Government Printing Office, 1952.

U. S. Congress, House. Select Committee of the House.
Investigation of the Federal Communications Commission.
80th Cong., 2d sess. Washington: Government Printing
Office, 1948.

U. S. Congress, Senate. Committee on Interstate and Foreign
Commerce. Nomination of Thad H. Brown on Reappointment
as Federal Communications Commissioner. 76th Cong.,
3rd sess. Washington: Government Printing Office, 1940.

U.S. Congress, Senate. Committee on Interstate and Foreign
Commerce. Nomination of Wayn Cox and George E. Sterling
to the Federal Communications Commission. 80th Cong.,
2d sess. Washington: Government Printing Office, 1948.

U. S. Congress, Senate. Subcommittee of the Committee on
Interstate and Foreign Commerce. Nomination of Robert F.
Jones to the Federal Communications Commission. 80th
Cong., 1st sess. Washington: Government Printing Office,
1947.

U. S. Congress, Senate. Committee on Interstate and Foreign
Commerce. Nomination of Robert E. Lee to be a Member
of the Federal Communications Commission. 83rd Cong.,
2d sess. Washington: Government Printing Office, 1954.

U. S. Congress, Senate. Committee on Interstate and Foreign Commerce. Nomination of E. M. Webster to the Federal Communications Commission. 81st Cong., 1st sess. Washington: Government Printing Office, 1949.

U. S. Congress, House. Committee on Interstate and Foreign Commerce. Proposed Changes in the Communications Act of 1934. (H. R. 5497) 77th Cong., 2d sess. Washington: Government Printing Office, 1942.

U. S. Congress, Senate. Committee on Interstate and Foreign Commerce. Reaffirming the Use of the Ether for Radio Communication. (S. 1 and S. 1754) 69th Cong., 1st sess. Washington: Government Printing Office, 1926.

U. S. Congress, House. Special Subcommittee on Legislative Oversight. Pursuant to H. Res. 99 Pertaining to the Independent Regulatory Commissions. 85th Cong., 2d sess. Washington: Government Printing Office, 1959.

U. S. Congress, Senate. Committee on Interstate and Foreign Commerce. Status of UHF and Multiple Ownership of TV Stations. 83rd Cong., 2d sess. Washington: Government Printing Office, 1954.

U. S. Congress, House. Select Committee of the House. Study and Investigation of the Federal Communications Commission. (H. Res. 21) 78th Cong., 1st sess. Washington: Government Printing Office, Part 1, Feb. 1943, Part 2, May, 1944, Pt. 3, Nov. 1944, Pt. 4, Dec. 1944, Pt. 5, Feb. 1945.

U. S. Congress, House. Committee on Merchant Marine, Radio, and Fisheries. To Amend the Act for the Regulation of Radio Communication. (H. R. 8825) 70th Cong., 1st sess. Washington: Government Printing Office, 1928.

U. S. Congress, Senate. Committee on Interstate and Foreign Commerce. To Amend the Communications Act of 1934. (S. 814) 78th Cong., 1st sess. Washington: Government Printing Office, 1944.

U. S. Congress, Senate. Committee on Interstate and Foreign Commerce. To Amend the Communications Act of 1934. (S. 1333) 80th Cong., 1st sess. Washington: Government Printing Office, 1947.

U. S. Congress, House. Committee on Merchant Marine, Radio, and Fisheries. To Amend the Radio Act of 1927. (H. R. 7716) 72d Cong., 2d sess. Washington: Government Printing Office, 1933.

U. S. Congress, Senate. Committee on Interstate and Foreign Commerce. To Amend the Radio Act of 1927. (H. R. 7716) 72d Cong., 1st sess. Washington: Government Printing Office, 1932.

U. S. Congress, Senate. Committee on Interstate and Foreign Commerce. To Authorize a Study of the Radio and Television Rules and Regulations of the Federal Communications Commission. (Sen. Res. 113) 77th Cong., 1st sess. Washington: Government Printing Office, 1941.

U. S. Congress, House. Committee on Merchant Marine, Radio, and Fisheries. To Continue (until March 16, 1930) the Federal Radio Commission. (H. R. 15430) 70th Cong., 2d sess. Washington: Government Printing Office, 1929.

U. S. Congress, Senate. Committee on Interstate and Foreign Commerce. To Continue (until March 16, 1930) the Powers of the Federal Radio Commission. (S. 9937) 70th Cong., 2d sess. Washington: Government Printing Office, 1929.

U. S. Congress, Senate. Committee on Interstate and Foreign Commerce. To Investigate the Actions of the Federal Communications Commission in Connection with the Development of Television. (Sen. Res. 251) 76th Cong., 3rd sess. Washington: Government Printing Office, 1940.

U. S. Congress, Senate. Committee on Interstate and Foreign Commerce. To Prohibit the Advertising of Alcoholic Beverages by Radio. (S. 517) 76th Cong., 1st sess. Washington: Government Printing Office, 1939.

U. S. Congress, Senate. Committee on Interstate and Foreign Commerce. Workload of the Federal Communications Commission. 83rd Cong., 1st sess. Washington: Government Printing Office, 1953.

## G. CONGRESSIONAL REPORTS

U. S. Congress, House. Committee on Merchant Marine and Fisheries. A Bill to Regulate Radio Communication. House Report 404, 69th Cong., 1st sess. Washington: Government Printing Office, 1926.

U. S. Congress, House. Committee on Merchant Marine and Fisheries. Act for the Regulation of Radio Transmission. House Report 464, 69th Cong., 1st sess. Washington: Government Printing Office, 1926.

U. S. Congress, House. Committee on Merchant Marine and
Fisheries. Act for the Regulation of Radio Transmission.
Conference Report to accompany H. R. 9971. House
Report 1886, 69th Cong., 2d sess. Washington: Govern-
ment Printing Office, 1926.

U. S. Congress, Senate. Committee on Interstate and Foreign
Commerce. Act for the Regulation of Radio Transmission.
Senate Report 772, 69th Cong., 1st sess. Washington:
Government Printing Office, 1926.

U. S. Congress, Senate. Committee on Interstate and Foreign
Commerce. Amendments to the Communications Act of 1934.
Senate Report 741, 81st Cong., 1st sess. Washington:
Government Printing Office, 1949.

U. S. Congress, House. Committee on Merchant Marine and
Fisheries. Bill to Amend Act to Regulate Radio Com-
munications Approved August 13, 1912, and for Other
Purposes. House Report 1416, 67th Cong., 4th sess.
Washington: Government Printing Office, 1923.

U. S. Congress, House. Committee on Interstate and Foreign
Commerce. Communications Act Amendments, 1952. Conference Report to Accompany S. 658. House Report 2426,
82d Cong., 2d sess. Washington: Government Printing
Office, 1952.

U. S. Congress, Senate. Committee on Interstate and Foreign
Commerce. Communications Act Amendments, 1951. Senate
Report 44, 82d Cong., 1st sess. Washington: Government
Printing Office, 1951.

U. S. Congress, Senate. Committee on Interstate and Foreign
Commerce. Communications Study. Senate Report 49,
81st Cong., 1st sess. Washington: Government Printing
Office, 1949.

U. S. Congress, House. Committee on Interstate and Foreign
Commerce. Conference Report to Accompany S. 3285.
House Report 1918, 73rd Cong., 2d sess. Washington:
Government Printing Office, 1934.

U. S. Congress, House. Committee on Interstate and Foreign
Commerce. For the Regulation of Interstate and Foreign
Commerce by Wire or Radio. House Report 1850, 73rd Cong.,
2d sess. Washington: Government Printing Office, 1934.

U. S. Congress, Senate. Committee on Interstate and Foreign
Commerce. For the Regulation of Interstate and Foreign
Commerce by Wire or Radio. Senate Report 781, 73rd Cong.,
2d sess. Washington: Government Printing Office, 1934.

U. S. Congress, House. Subcommittee of the Committee on
Interstate and Foreign Commerce. Investigation of Radio
and Television Programs. House Report 2509, 82d Cong.,
2d sess. Washington: Government Printing Office, 1952.

U. S. Congress, House. Select Committee of the House.
Investigation of the Federal Communications Commission.
House Report 2095, 78th Cong., 2d sess. Washington:
Government Printing Office, 1945.

U. S. Congress, House. Select Committee of the House.
Investigation of the Federal Communications Commission.
House Report 2479, 80th Cong., 2d sess. Washington:
Government Printing Office, 1949.

U. S. Congress, House. Select Committee of the House.
Investigation of the Port Huron Decision and the Scott
Decision. House Report 2461, 80th Cong., 2d sess.
Washington: Government Printing Office, 1948.

U. S. Congress, House. Committee on Interstate and Foreign
Commerce. Network Broadcasting. House Report 1297,
85th Cong., 2d sess. Washington: Government Printing
Office, 1958.

U. S. Congress, Senate. Report of the Ad Hoc Advisory
Committee on Allocations to the Committee on Interstate
and Foreign Commerce. 85th Cong., 2d sess. Washington:
Government Printing House, 1958.

U. S. Congress, Senate. Committee on Interstate and Foreign
Commerce. Resolution Authorizing Air Investigation and
Study of the Broadcasting Industry, of Broadcasting in
the United States, and of Interstate and Foreign Commerce
by Radio. Senate Report 1203, 75th Cong., 1st sess.
Washington: Government Printing House, 1937.

U. S. Congress, House. Special Subcommittee on Legislative
Oversight. Independent Regulatory Commissions. House
Report 2711, 85th Cong., 2d sess. Washington: Govern-
ment Printing Office, 1959.

U. S. Congress, House. Committee on Interstate and Foreign
Commerce. Suspension of Certain Provisions of the Communications Act during War. House Report 2597, 77th
Cong., 2d sess. Washington: Government Printing Office,
1942.

U. S. Congress, Senate. Committee on Interstate and Foreign
Commerce. Television Network Regulations and the UHF
Problem. Memorandum by Harry M. Plotkin. Washington:
Government Printing Office, 1955.

U. S. Congress, Senate. Committee on Interstate and Foreign
Commerce. To Amend the Communications Act of 1934.
Senate Report 1567, 80th Cong., 1st sess. Washington:
Government Printing Office, 1948.

U. S. Congress, House. Committee on Merchant Marine, Radio,
and Fisheries. To Amend the Radio Act of 1927. House
Report 1336, 71st Cong., 2d sess. Washington: Government
Printing Office, 1931.

U. S. Congress, Senate. Committee on Interstate and Foreign
Commerce. To Amend the Radio Act of 1927. Senate
Report 1578, 71st Congress, 3rd sess. Washington:
Government Printing Office, 1931.

U. S. Congress, House. Committee on Merchant Marine, Radio,
and Fisheries. To Amend the Radio Act of 1927. House
Report 221, 72d Cong., 1st sess. Washington: Government
Printing Office, 1932.

U. S. Congress, Senate. Committee on Interstate and Foreign
Commerce. To Amend the Radio Act of 1927. Senate
Report 564, 72d Cong., 1st sess. Washington: Government
Printing Office, 1932.

U. S. Congress, Senate. Committee on Interstate and Foreign
Commerce. To Amend the Radio Act of 1927. Senate
Report 1045, 72d Cong., 2d sess. Washington: Government
Printing Office, 1933.

U. S. Congress, House. Committee on Merchant Marine, Radio,
and Fisheries. To Amend the Radio Act of 1927 so as to
Make Only Citizens of the United States Eligible for
Licenses. House Report 1116, 72d Cong., 1st sess.
Washington: Government Printing House, 1932.

U. S. Congress, Senate. Committee on Interstate and Foreign
Commerce. To Continue the Federal Radio Commission.
Senate Report 56, 71st Cong., 2d sess. Washington:
Government Printing Office, 1929.

U. S. Congress, House. Committee on Merchant Marine, Radio,
and Fisheries. To Continue (Until March 16, 1930) the
Powers of the Federal Radio Commission. House Report
396, 70th Cong., 2d sess. Washington: Government
Printing Office, 1929.

U. S. Congress, House. Committee on Merchant Marine, Radio,
and Fisheries. To Continue Until Otherwise Provided by
Law the Powers and Authority of the Federal Radio Commission. House Report 35, 71st Cong., 2d sess.
Washington: Government Printing Office, 1929.

U. S. Congress, Senate. Committee on Interstate and Foreign
Commerce. To Prohibit the Advertising of Alcoholic
Beverages by Radio. Senate Report 338, 76th Cong.,
1st sess. Washington: Government Printing Office, 1939.

### H. CONGRESSIONAL RECORD

U. S. Congress, House. Congressional Record. 61st Cong.-
85th Cong. Washington: Government Printing Office,
1909-1958.

U. S. Congress, Senate. Congressional Record. 61st Cong.-
85th Cong. Washington: Government Printing Office,
1909-1958.

### I. COMMERCE DEPARTMENT DOCUMENTS

Commerce Department. Division of Radio Communications.
Proceedings of the Fourth National Radio Convention and
Recommendations for Regulation of Radio. Washington:
Government Printing Office, 1926.

------------------. Division of Radio Communications.
Recommendations for the Regulation of Radio Adopted by
the Third National Radio Convention. Washington:
Government Printing Office, 1924.

### J. FEDERAL COMMUNICATIONS COMMISSION

### DOCUMENTS

Federal Communications Commission. An Economic Study of
Standard Broadcasting. Washington: Government Printing
Office, 1947.

----------------------------. First-Nineteenth Annual
Reports, 1934-1953. Washington: Government Printing
Office, 1935-1954.

----------------------------. Public Service Responsibilities of Broadcast Licensees. Washington: Government Printing Office, 1946.

----------------------------. Report on Chain Broadcasting. Washington: Government Printing Office, 1941.

K.  FEDERAL RADIO COMMISSION DOCUMENTS

Federal Radio Commission. First-Sixth Annual Reports,
    1928-1933. Washington: Government Printing Office,
    1928-1933.

L.  MISCELLANEOUS PUBLIC DOCUMENTS

Censorship Office. Code of Wartime Practices for American
    Broadcasters. Washington: Government Printing Office,
    1942, 43, 45.

Federal Trade Commission. Report Number 1686.

Opinions of the Attorney General. (1912) p. 579.

Opinions of the Attorney General. (1926) pp. 126-32.

"Report of the Commission on Organization of the Executive
    Branch of the Government, Committee on Independent
    Regulatory Commissions, Staff Report on FCC." Prepared
    by William W. Tolub, Mimeograph, 1948. Copies in
    National Archives.

Radio Laws of the United States, 1953 edition, Compiled
    by Elmer A. Lewis. Washington: Government Printing
    Office, 1953.

Radio Service Bulletin. September 1, 1922.

United States of America before the Federal Trade Commission.
    In the matter of the General Electric Company, The
    American Telephone and Telegraph Co., The Western
    Electric Co., Westinghouse Electric and Manufacturing Co.,
    the International Radio Telegraph Co., The United Fruit
    Co., Wireless Specialty Apparatus Co., and Radio Cor-
    poration of America. Docket No. 1115 (1924).

M.  NEWSPAPERS

New York Times. February 28, 1922.

New York Times. March 13, 1926.

New York Times. June 15, 1947.

## N. TRADE JOURNALS

Broadcasting Magazine, Broadcasting-Telecasting, 1932-1958.

Variety, May 22, 1934.

## O. UNPUBLISHED DOCUMENTS

Hottman, Henry. "Some Problems of Federal Regulation of
the Broadcast Industry." Unpublished Ph.D. dissertation.
University of Colorado (1947).

Olson, Paul R. "Regulation of Broadcasting in the United
States." Unpublished Ph.D. dissertation. University of
Iowa, 1931.

Fowler, Paul Clifton. "The Formulation of Public Policy
for Commercial Broadcasting by the Federal Communications
Commission." Unpublished Ph.D. dissertation. Indiana
University, 1956.

## AUTOBIOGRAPHY

I, Robert Sears McMahon, was born in Columbus, Ohio, June 19, 1927. I received my secondary education in the parochial schools of Columbus, Ohio, and my undergraduate training at Fordham University, which granted me the Bachelor of Arts degree in 1949. From Ohio State University, I received the Master of Arts degree in 1951, after which I became a member of the faculty of Purdue University. In 1956, I returned to Ohio State University to fulfill my residence requirements for the Degree of Doctor of Philosophy. While a Doctor of Philosophy candidate, I was one of six journalists to be awarded a Congressional Fellowship from the Political Science Association for study and work in Washington, D. C. While there, I began my investigations for the Subcommittee on Legislative Oversight (House of Representatives, 85th Congress) and became a staff member in 1958, during which time I wrote the study, "Regulation of Broadcasting - Half a Century of Government Regulation of Broadcasting and the Need for Further Legislative Action" (U. S. Printing Office, 1958, 174 pp.).

# DISSERTATIONS IN BROADCASTING

*An Arno Press Collection*

Bailey Robert Lee. **An Examination of Prime Time Network Television Special Programs, 1948 to 1966.** *(Doctoral Thesis, University of Wisconsin, 1967)* 1979

Burke, John Edward. **An Historical-Analytical Study of the Legislative and Political Origins of the Public Broadcasting Act of 1967.** *(Doctoral Dissertation, The Ohio State University, 1971)* 1979

Foley, K. Sue. **The Political Blacklist in the Broadcast Industry:** The Decade of the 1950s. *(Doctoral Dissertation, The Ohio State University, 1972)* 1979

Hess, Gary Newton. **An Historical Study of the Du Mont Television Network.** *(Doctoral Dissertation, Northwestern University, 1960)* 1979

Howard, Herbert H. **Multiple Ownership in Television Broadcasting:** Historical Development and Selected Case Studies. *(Doctoral Dissertation, Ohio University, 1973)* 1979

Jameson, Kay Charles. **The Influence of the United States Court of Appeals for the District of Columbia on Federal Policy in Broadcast Regulation, 1929-1971.** *(Doctoral Dissertation, University of Southern California, 1972)* 1979

Kirkley, Donald Howe, Jr. **A Descriptive Study of the Network Television Western During the Seasons 1955-56 to 1962-63.** *(Doctoral Dissertation, Ohio University, 1967)* 1979

Kittross, John Michael. **Television Frequency Allocation Policy in the United States.** *(Doctoral Dissertation, University of Illinois, 1960)* 1979

Larka, Robert. **Television's Private Eye:** An Examination of Twenty Years Programming of a Particular Genre, 1949 to 1969. *(Doctoral Dissertation, Ohio University, 1973)* 1979

Long, Stewart Louis. **The Development of the Television Network Oligopoly.** *(Doctoral Thesis, University of Illinois at Urbana-Champaign, 1974)* 1979

MacFarland, David T. **The Development of the Top 40 Radio Format.** *(Doctoral Thesis, University of Wisconsin, 1972)* 1979

McMahon, Robert Sears. **Federal Regulation of the Radio and Television Broadcast Industry in the United States, 1927-1959:** With Special Reference to the Establishment and Operation of Workable Administrative Standards. *(Doctoral Dissertation, The Ohio State University, 1959)* 1979

Muth, Thomas A. **State Interest in Cable Communications.** *(Doctoral Dissertation, The Ohio State University, 1973)* 1979

Pearce, Alan. **NBC News Division:** A Study of the Costs, the Revenues, and the Benefits of Broadcast News and **The Economics of Prime Time Access.** *(Doctoral Dissertation, Indiana University, 1972)* 1979

Pepper, Robert M. **The Formation of the Public Broadcasting Service.** *(Doctoral Dissertation, University of Wisconsin, 1975)* 1979

Pirsein, Robert William. **The Voice of America:** A History of the International Broadcasting Activities of the United States Government, 1940-1962. *(Doctoral Dissertation, Northwestern University, 1970)* 1979

Ripley, Joseph Marion, Jr. **The Practices and Policies Regarding Broadcasts of Opinions about Controversial Issues by Radio and Television Stations in the United States.** *(Doctoral Dissertation, The Ohio State University, 1961)* 1979

Robinson, Thomas Porter. **Radio Networks and the Federal Government.** 1943

Sadowski, Robert Paul. **An Analysis of Statutory Laws Governing Commercial and Educational Broadcasting in the Fifty States.** *(Doctoral Thesis, The University of Iowa, 1973)* 1979

Schwarzlose, Richard Allen. **The American Wire Services:** A Study of Their Development as a Social Institution. *(Doctoral Thesis, University of Illinois at Urbana-Champaign, 1965)* 1979

Smith, Ralph Lewis. **A Study of the Professional Criticism of Broadcasting in the United States. 1920-1955.** *(Doctoral Thesis, University of Wisconsin, 1959)* 1979

Stamps, Charles Henry. **The Concept of the Mass Audience in American Broadcasting:** An Historical-Descriptive Study. *(Doctoral Dissertation, Northwestern University, 1956)* 1979

Steiner, Peter O. **Workable Competition in the Radio Broadcasting Industry.** *(Doctoral Thesis, Harvard University, 1949)* 1979

Stern, Robert H. **The Federal Communications Commission and Television:** The Regulatory Process in an Environment of Rapid Technical Innovation. *(Doctoral Thesis, Harvard University, 1950)* 1979

Tomlinson, John D. **International Control of Radiocommunications.** 1945

Ulloth, Dana Royal. **The Supreme Court:** A Judicial Review of the Federal Communications Commission. *(Doctoral Dissertation, University of Missouri-Columbia, 1971)* 1979